SHELTON STATE COMMUNITY
COLLEGE
JUNIOR COLLEGE DIVISION
LIBRARY

DISCARDED

SO-BSR-151

DS
779.26
.H77
1990

Hsü, Immanuel
Chung-yueh, 1923-

China without Mao

DATE DUE

CHINA WITHOUT MAO

CHINA WITHOUT MAO

The Search for a New Order
Second Edition

Immanuel C. Y. Hsü

New York   Oxford

OXFORD UNIVERSITY PRESS

1990

Oxford University Press

Oxford   New York   Toronto
Delhi   Bombay   Calcutta   Madras   Karachi
Petaling Jaya   Singapore   Hong Kong   Tokyo
Nairobi   Dar es Salaam   Cape Town
Melbourne   Auckland

and associated companies in
Berlin   Ibadan

Copyright © 1990 by Oxford University Press, Inc.

Published by Oxford University Press, Inc.,
200 Madison Avenue, New York, New York   10016

Oxford is a registered trademark of Oxford University Press

All rights reserved. No part of this publication may be reproduced,
stored in a retrieval system, or transmitted, in any form or by any means,
electronic, mechanical, photocopying, recording, or otherwise,
without the prior permission of Oxford University Press.

Library of Congress Cataloging-in-Publication Data
Hsü, Immanuel Chung-yueh, 1923–
China without Mao : the search for a new order /
Immanuel C. Y. Hsü.—2nd ed.
p.   cm.   Bibliography: p.   Includes index.
ISBN 0-19-506055-5
ISBN 0-19-506056-3 (paper)
1. China—Politics and government—1976–   I. Title.
DS779.26.H77   1990   951.05′7—dc20   89–33100   CIP

Since this page cannot accommodate illustration credits, the page that
follows constitutes an extension of the copyright page.

Printing 9 8 7 6 5 4 3 2 1

Printed in the United States of America
on acid-free paper

For
K. C. Liu

Preface to the Second Edition

Is China going capitalist? This is an intriguing question that has sparked much interest. China today is indeed very different from the way it was just ten years ago. Ever since the party conference of December 1978 (Third Plenum, Eleventh Central Committee), the country has been moving in the direction of accelerated economic development and greater openness to the outside world. The pace of life has become more relaxed, social attitudes have changed, and brighter, more colorful clothes have replaced the somber and conformist attire of the previous generation. In the major cities there has been a growing trend toward a capitalistic life-style. Rock music, disco dancing, and foreign films and plays have all found their way into the urban culture of contemporary China. Along with these have also come the music of Mozart, Beethoven, and Brahms, as well as exhibitions of works of art by Picasso, the French Impressionists, and the American Abstract Expressionists. Even fashion designs and modeling exhibitions inspired by Pierre Cardin and Yves Saint Laurent are in vogue.

Institutionally, China has witnessed significant changes in

agriculture and industry. The commune, once the kingpin of the Maoist rural economic structure, has been dismantled, and in its stead individual farm households have been assigned plots of land to cultivate for a contracted period of time. The land contracts are inheritable, as is the house on the land. Since 1984 the right to this land utilization has been made transferable, and since October 1987 these contracts have even been made salable. It is not inconceivable, then, that one household could acquire the right to cultivate the contracted land of several of its neighbors, thus enhancing its chances for prosperity with each new acquisition. Some claim that this raises the specter of incipient capitalism, but the government emphatically denies this since the land technically remains public. Today the farmers in Sichuan and coastal areas lead an ownerlike life, with many earning in excess of 10,000 yuan a year (*wanyuan hu*).

Almost everywhere one can see the free market in action, with such markets numbering some 40,000 in rural areas and 3,000 in urban centers by 1985. In addition, there has been a burgeoning growth of private enterprises that employ eight or more persons—some 225,000 by June 1988, according to government figures—and a concomitant appearance of new millionaires. Although this may seem an incongruity in a Communist society, the party nonetheless encourages some individuals to get rich first so as to exert a ripple effect on the rest of the nation.

Culturally, ever since the opening in 1979, Chinese consciousness has been bombarded with foreign news, films, plays, political ideas, theories, literature, and popular culture. Suddenly, a new vista has opened for the once-isolated Chinese as to the nature of the modern world and the international trend toward democratization. In response, Chinese students and intellectuals demand greater personal and political liberty as well as advancement in basic human rights, and some even question the ability of the Communist leadership to guide China effectively into the 21st century. The influence of Western "bourgeois liberalism" is undeniable.

The Chinese leadership believes that as long as the state

owns the means of production and all the basic economic structures and as long as it continues to maintain the socialist principle of distribution, there is no cause for alarm over a capitalistic revival. The paramount leader, Deng Xiaoping, accepts economic reforms and the open-door policy as necessary means by which to borrow foreign technology, capital, and managerial skills for China's modernization. To him they are but tools with which to strengthen the Communist rule but never ways by which to move the country toward capitalism or a Western-style democracy. Clearly, Deng wants economic progress and all its benefits but not political liberalization, lest the Communist rule over state and society be compromised. However, he is willing to accept a flexible theory that would make the introduction of market mechanisms in economic reforms look neither capitalistic nor un-Marxist. To that end, Chinese social scientists have advanced the argument that "market mechanism" and "central planning" are but "neutral means and methods that do not determine the basic economic system of a society."

In October 1987 the Thirteenth Party Congress formally proclaimed China to be in a "Primary Stage of Socialism" lasting a hundred years, from 1950 to the middle of the next century. During this period, adoption of capitalist techniques and managerial skills and a mixed economy characterized by a multi-ownership system are all permissible. The saying goes: "Whatever promotes economic development is good; whatever hinders it is not good." Such a view almost sounds like American pragmatism. Ingeniously, the Chinese have invented a theory to fit reality, not vice versa.

Thus, private enterprises are encouraged by the state as conducive to the development of productive forces. Newspapers proudly print stories of successful entrepreneurs: one farmer in Shenyang, Liaoning Province, who organized a local transport team earned one million yuan in 1987. A "king" of the wood-carving trade who employed 3,000 workers and organized a vast network of distribution, netted some $20 million. Even so, Chinese theorists rationalize that since the productive value of all the individual enterprises in 1988 amounted to less than 1 percent of the national industrial output value, any fear of a capitalistic revival is unwarranted.

Nevertheless, the spirit of enterprise is gripping the nation. Everybody is seeking ways to make money. Knowledgeable persons are concerned that the country is rapidly becoming commercialized (*quanmin jieshang*). In this atmosphere, a party theorist remarked, "Who knows what Marxism is anyway? Today we live in a technological world beyond the imagination of Marx." One party official perhaps unwittingly mirrors the leadership's view when he says that capitalism is acceptable as long as it is controlled by socialism.

From this author's own observations during a trip in June 1988—his fifth in recent years—it seems that China has indeed made certain accommodations with aspects of capitalism, but only in a superficial manner. Beneath the veneer the substance remains the same. The psychology and mind-set of the Chinese Communist leadership, as well as the mode of conducting the affairs of state, are basically unaltered.

In the short run, China's flirtation with capitalism has caused ideological confusion, leadership crises, student unrest, and widespread corruption and chaotic management at nearly every level of government and state enterprise. With rising inflation, falling ethics, and ideological ambiguity, the country is in danger of losing a sense of direction. If there were such a thing as a "misery index" to measure the quality of life in 1988, it would have registered the highest since the end of the Cultural Revolution.

Three pressing issues need to be tackled head-on: corruption, special privileges for the few, and rampant inflation. The first two are political in nature; and the third, economic. The party's credibility is at stake in addressing these critical problems. Suspension of price reform for two years may postpone the onset of runaway inflation but not eliminate it. Any delay in rectifying the other two deep-rooted political problems will deepen the party's already serious "triple crisis" involving the loss of the "confidence, trust, and faith" of the people (*sanxin weiji*). To regain self-respect and popular support, the party must quickly rid itself of corruption and special privileges for the few and move in the mainstream of society by introducing political liberalization. The future seems fraught with tension and uncertainties. Great wisdom will be needed to chart a course successfully through this difficult period.

Santa Barbara, Calif.
New Year's Day, 1989

While the manuscript for this edition was in press, the Chinese government launched a violent crackdown against the pro-democracy demonstrators at Tian-an-men Square in Beijing on June 3–4, 1989. A record of the events surrounding this tragedy has been added as a postscript to this book. A fuller account must wait until a proper historical perspective has evolved.

September 15, 1989   I. C. Y. H.

Preface

After Mao, the deluge?

To many, Mao was the personification of Chinese communism, and China without Mao seemed inconceivable. Yet there has been no "deluge," no chaos, but rather the gradual emergence of a pragmatic new order with a different approach to socialist transformation. This new order grew out of a critical reassessment of China's new historical mission and represents a rejection of the Maoist methods.

During the last decade of his life, Mao Zedong attempted to reach the peak of revolution through the gigantic social and political upheaval of the Cultural Revolution. He sought ideological purity through intensified class struggle and the purge of high party and government leaders and intellectuals. Though in appearance an endeavor of noble idealism, the Cultural Revolution ushered in a decade of destruction and disorder. The party was decimated. Industry, agriculture, and science suffered severe losses. Disruption in education left a generation untrained, and scholars were denied years of teaching and research, resulting in an incalculable loss of human resources. Ironically, the Cultural Revolution turned out to be anticultural.

It is significant that the purge of senior party members made way for the rise of Mao's wife, Jiang Qing, who catapulted to the position of first vice-chairman of the Central Cultural Revolutionary Committee in 1966. She built up a radical following which together with the military under Lin Biao became the chief beneficiary of the Cultural Revolution. When Lin was killed following an abortive coup in September 1971, Jiang Qing rose further in national politics. At the Tenth Party Congress in 1973, she and three senior associates—Wang Hongwen, Zhang Chunqiao, and Yao Wenyuan—won leadership positions. With Premier Zhou Enlai and Chairman Mao both in ill health, Jiang Qing's group prepared themselves for succession. Mao patronized them but also warned them not to become a "Gang of Four." With the support of Kang Sheng's secret police, they tyrannized the country. Perceptive leaders were appalled at this state of affairs yet dared not speak out for fear of reprisal.

The death of Mao marked an epochal turning point in Chinese politics. The struggle for succession that ensued led to the smashing of the Gang and the emergence of Hua Guofeng, Mao's "anointed successor," as party chairman and state premier. But Hua was soon challenged by surviving victims of the Cultural Revolution under the leadership of Deng Xiaoping, the deposed former vice-premier. Termed pragmatists, the new leaders question the value of the Cultural Revolution and of Mao's policies of continuous class struggle and uninterrupted revolution. They doubt the efficacy of Mao's economic adventurism, which during his twenty-seven-year rule failed to lift China from poverty and backwardness.

These pragmatists vow that the Cultural Revolution must never be allowed to recur. They advocate unity, stability, discipline, and greater domestic liberty and international cooperation. Most important, they have launched a program of modernization under a younger leadership and tried to stimulate enthusiasm for work through material incentives. Deng's "Economics in Command" has replaced Mao's "Politics in Command." The adoption of the principle, "From each according to his ability, to each according to his work," reflects the new emphasis on expertise. Foreign-trained intellectuals, despised in the past, are now cherished as patriots. With these new policies, the pragmatists hope to render their nation a powerful, prosperous, highly cultured, and advanced socialist state by the year 2000.

The pragmatists gained power at the expense of Hua and the Maoists. Their crowning victory came in June 1981 when the Sixth Plenary Session of the Eleventh Central Committee officially affirmed socialist economic development as the central task of the party and government under the new collective leadership of party Chairman Hu Yaobang, Vice-Chairman Deng Xiaoping, and Premier Zhao Ziyang. The Cultural Revolution was completely repudiated, and Mao was held chiefly responsible for its excesses, while the party assessed itself a fair share of guilt for not having prevented his mistakes.

Public reaction to the new policies is overwhelmingly positive. Long stifled under the strict regimentation of Mao, the people yearned for civil and economic liberalization, and they have gradually come alive to the new order. For all their respect for the Great Helmsman, his passing was in many ways a relief, slowly lifting the heavy burden of omnipresent politics from their shoulders. They welcome the changes.

However, despite public support of the new leadership, the pragmatists' victory remains incomplete. Of its 38 million members, about half joined the party and rose to positions of responsibility during the Cultural Revolutionary decade. This large group's indifferent attitude toward the new policies has prompted the expression "The two ends are hot, but the middle is cold." Unless this pivotal group is won over or reformed, progress toward modernization will be compromised.

Recent changes in China must not lead to mistaken assumptions about a radical transformation in the nature of the Chinese state. Rather, they signify a shift of approach within the framework of the Chinese Communist system. China remains committed to the four basic principles of the socialist line, the proletarian dictatorship, the leadership of the Communist party, and Marxism-Leninism and the Thought of Mao. Still, with the Sixth Plenary Session's rejection of Maoist class struggle and Mao's adventurous economic policies, and with the adoption of a more realistic modernization program, a new order has emerged, and the Maoist era is ended.

Writing contemporary history one lacks the benefit of hindsight and perspective that the study of earlier history affords. The importance of the time dimension in historical judgments is obvious; short-term assessments are perforce tentative. To offset the tendency to subjectivity, the author conducted field research in China in 1979, 1980, and 1981. He lectured at the Beijing, Fudan, and Nanjing Universities and held discussions with many persons in various walks of life. He gained the distinct feeling that China is making progress as the effects of the New Order begin to manifest themselves. However, modernizations will continue to be slow and labored, and it would be unrealistic to expect more than moderate progress in the next decade or two.

A word about the methods of romanizing Chinese characters seems in order. I follow the principle of using the system generally accepted in the geopolitical region of reference. Thus, in reference to mainland China the Pinyin phonetic system is used, and in reference to Taiwan, the Wade-Giles system. Though this requires familiarity with more than one system, it should cause the least confusion in identification of people, places, and literary works (see the guide provided in the back of the book).

In preparing this book I have received valuable help from my research assistants, Cathleen Costa and Eugene Y. C. Lau. To them and to my typist Alice Kladnik, I wish to extend my deep appreciation. I am also indebted to Professors K. C. Liu, Stephen and Eloise Hay, and Charles Litzinger for various comments and suggestions. Responsibility for the final content, however, rests solely with the author.

Santa Barbara, Calif.   I. C. Y. H.
December 4, 1981

Contents

CHINA WITHOUT MAO

PEOPLE'S REPUBLIC
OF CHINA, 1990

▨ Autonomous Regions

━┼━ Main railways (in China and Russia)

1

The Smashing of the Gang of Four

Nineteen seventy-six was a year of agony for China. Deep bereavement was felt in every corner of the land over the loss of three of its great leaders: Premier Zhou Enlai in January, Marshal Zhu De in July, and Chairman Mao Zedong in September. Added to human grief was a series of natural disasters; in July a major earthquake demolished the industrial city of Tangshan, 105 miles southeast of Beijing (Peking), and during the next two months the Yellow River flooded seven times. Compounding the human misery and political instability was the succession crisis precipitated by Mao's wife Jiang Qing and her associates, later dubbed the Gang of Four. Indeed, the tumultuous year was marked by what the Chinese call "natural disaster and human misfortune" (*tianzai renhuo*). It was a time of sorrow, yet like darkness before dawn, also a time of hope. Out of disorder a new order was struggling to be born, and with it was the promise of greater stability, progress, and a better life for the people.

THE DEATHS OF NATIONAL LEADERS

Zhou Enlai (1898–1976)

The death of Zhou Enlai on January 8, 1976, was an irreparable loss. A pillar of strength in both party and government, he was the moderating influence through numerous political storms. Zhou had saved the country from the utter chaos during the upheaval of the Cultural Revolution and had helped thwart the Gang of Four's grasp for supreme power.

Born to a gentry family of Shaoxing toward the end of the Qing dynasty, Zhou attended the Nankai University Middle School before going to Japan for further studies. In 1920 he went to France as a worker-study student and spent the next four years in Europe, where he, along with fellow-student Deng Xiaoping, joined the Chinese Communist Youth Corps and later the Chinese Communist Party. He became a loyal supporter of Mao after the Zunyi Conference of January 1935. As premier from 1949 until his death, Zhou submitted to Mao's oracular leadership, running the machinery of government unobtrusively while quietly moderating certain of Mao's excesses.

Zhou exuded a disarming charm and an urbane sophistication. His savvy manner and vast knowledge of world affairs struck all foreign visitors. Dag Hammarskjold, the late United Nations secretary-general, considered him "the superior brain I have so far met in the field of foreign politics." President Nixon said: "Only a handful of men in the twentieth century will ever match Premier Zhou's impact on world history. . . . None surpass him in keen intellect, philosophical breadth and the experienced wisdom which made him a great leader."[1]

Afflicted with cancer as early as 1972, Zhou appears to have engineered the rehabilitation of Deng Xiaoping in 1973 as vice-premier and groomed him for succession. In response, the radicals launched the Anti-Lin Biao Anti-Confucius Campaign to harass Zhou by allusion. Zhou continued to work even following his hospitalization in the summer of 1974, administering state affairs from his sickbed, receiving visitors, and

Zhou Enlai in one of his last official portraits.

making occasional public appearances. He attended the celebration of the twenty-fifth anniversary of the founding of the People's Republic and delivered the keynote speech at the Fourth National People's Congress in January 1975. This speech laid the groundwork for what has since become known as the Four Modernizations: a comprehensive modernization of agriculture, industry, national defense, and science and technology that would put China in the front ranks of the world by the end of the century.

Dead at seventy-eight, Zhou was mourned by his 900 million countrymen as a beloved elder-protector, hero both in the struggle of revolution and in the management of the affairs of state. He must be credited for long years of invaluable service to the state, especially during the "decade of catastrophe" otherwise known as the Cultural Revolution.

The Emergence of Hua Guofeng

Zhou had carefully groomed Deng Xiaoping to be his successor. In the last year of Zhou's hospitalization, Deng had amassed considerable power and was the de facto premier directing the day-to-day work of the State Council and receiving foreign leaders. Yet, shortly after eulogizing Zhou at the memorial service on January 15, 1976, Deng dropped out of sight without explanation, and on February 6 the *Renmin Ribao* [People's Daily] carried a front-page article attacking the "unrepentent" powerholders who took the "capitalist road." The Cultural Revolutionary group under Jiang Qing were promoting Zhang Chunqiao, second vice-premier, for the premiership, but Zhang was unacceptable to many party seniors and military leaders. On February 7 the Chinese government announced the startling appointment of Hua Guofeng, the sixth-ranking vice-premier and minister of public security, as acting premier. This choice pleased neither the radicals nor the moderates but was not challenged due to Mao's enormous prestige.

In the waning months of his life, Mao, under pressure from his wife, had wanted to favor the Cultural Revolutionary Group but hesitated to offend the senior cadres and military leaders. In this dilemma, Mao appears to have selected Hua, a faithful follower who was ideologically safe and who would adequately serve the state until Jiang Qing's group could assume power. The choice of Hua, a former party first secretary in Mao's home province of Hunan and an agricultural expert, was clearly a compromise as he had close ties with neither the pragmatists nor the radicals. At the same time, in naming Hua, Mao masterfully blocked Zhou's scheme to place Deng in line for succession.

Hua had no power base of his own. In domestic politics he moved cautiously, creating friendships with senior cadres and military leaders and avoiding making enemies in the Politburo. This calculated stance won the approbation of Mao but the enmity of Jiang Qing and Zhang Chunqiao. A member of their writing team, using the nom de plume Liang Xiao (meaning two schools, i.e. Beijing and Qinghua universities) wrote a historical allegory, "A Second Evaluation of Confucius," to attack the one "who assumed the position of Acting Prime Minister in the capacity of grand duke."[2]

Shortly after Hua's appointment, a momentous event took place during the Qingming Festival, when the Chinese traditionally visit the ancestral tombs. Between March 29 and April 4, an increasing number of people went daily to Tian An Men Square to pay tribute to the late Premier Zhou and to lay

Tomb of the Unknown Soldier in Tian An Men Square, Beijing.

wreaths at the Monument to the Martyrs of the Revolution, which had become the symbolic tomb of Zhou. When the wreaths were removed by police and security guards, people were enraged. On April 5, 100,000 gathered at Tian An Men Square in a protest demonstration chanting "the era of Qin Shih Huang is gone," hoisting signs in support of Deng, and singing the praises of Zhou and Deng while criticizing Mao by allusion.[3] Emotion soon reached a feverish pitch, and the demonstration got out of control. Frenzied demonstrators set fire to four motorcars and smashed the windows of a military barrack before they were dispersed by police, security guards, and militiamen.

Mayor Wu De of Beijing linked the violent outburst with the opponents of the "Antirightist Deviationist Campaign." Deng was openly accused of being a ringleader, a capitalist roader, and "the general behind-the-scene promoter of the Rightist Deviationist attempt to reverse correct verdicts." Two days later (April 7) on Mao's recommendation, the Central Committee ordered Deng, "whose problem has turned into one of antagonistic contradictions," dismissed from all party and government posts, but allowed him to "keep his party membership so as to see how he will behave himself in the future."

Meanwhile, the appointment of Hua as premier and first vice-chairman of the party was announced.[4] On April 8, 100,000 people paraded in Tian An Men Square in a counterdemonstration to support the new leadership. Hua emerged as the dark horse winner in the succession struggle for the premiership.

On April 30 Mao gave Hua three crucial handwritten instructions: (1) "Carry out the work slowly, not in haste"; (2) "Act according to past principles"; and (3) "With you in charge, I am at ease."[5] Viewing the instructions as implying Mao's intention to designate him his heir, Hua forwarded the first two to the Politburo in the presence of an infuriated Gang of Four, who now considered him no longer a possible ally but a new enemy. Zhang Chunqiao, who coveted the premiership, indicated through the writer Liang Xiao that the chairman's messages might have been fabricated. Hua remained throughout unperturbed, keeping secret the third instruction and reserving it for future use.

The Tangshan Earthquake

As if the deaths of national leaders and the political confusion of the succession struggle were not enough punishment for the country, a gigantic earthquake measuring 8.2 on the Richter scale occurred on July 28, 1976, in Tangshan, a mining center of 1.6 million inhabitants. It leveled the entire city and caused considerable damage to the nearby metropolis of Tianjin, China's third largest city with a population of 4.3 million. Even Beijing felt the tremors and suffered minor damage. Tangshan itself was reduced to a desert of rubble. A confidential government report listed 655,237 dead and 779,000 injured, although later figures given by the Chinese Seismology Society were considerably lower.[6] Premier Hua remarked that the destruction and loss of lives were on a scale "rarely seen in history." Following tradition the Chinese people viewed such massive natural disasters as portents of social and political upheaval: what more could the people and state survive?

Mao Zedong (1893–1976)

For years Mao had been afflicted with Parkinson's disease, a slowly degenerative sickness causing muscular rigidity and tremors. His health failed rapidly in the last two or three years of his life due to a stroke which affected the left side of his body impairing his speech. Each day moments of clarity and well-being alternated with lapse into a less lucid state, hence the strange meeting times and abrupt notices given to foreign dignitaries who awaited audiences with him.

When President Gerald Ford visited China in early December 1975, he was summoned to Mao's residence with only minutes' notice. The chairman walked with some difficulty but carried on the interview for an hour and fifty minutes, having some trouble with his speech but able to express himself in writing. Although the picture of Mao and Ford released by the Chinese government showed the chairman in remarkably good shape, four weeks later, on December 31, when another American[7] saw him at midnight and on instant notice, Mao looked tired, worn, old, and lonely.

The deterioration of Mao's health accelerated after the New Year, and by June 1976 he could no longer receive foreign visitors. Everybody knew that the end was drawing near, but when death actually came on September 9 it shook the world—not because it was unexpected, but rather because it was so final, so momentous—the man whom the Chinese called their "sun" had fallen. Eulogies came from all over the world. British Prime Minister James Callaghan said: "He will be remembered as a man of great vision and as a thinker with a profound sense of history. China's position in the world of today is a memorial to his unique achievement." President Ford said: "It is tragic that a man of this great remarkable ability, skill, vision, and foresight has passed away."[8] The world had lost a towering figure, and 900 million Chinese, the hero of their revolution.

A full assessment of Mao must wait until history has had time to digest his impact on China and the world; for now, only preliminary remarks are in order. For China, Mao was Lenin and Stalin combined. He was a great revolutionary, the most successful of the mid-twentieth century. His greatest achievement was the seizure of power through the creative adaptation of Marxist-Leninist theory to the realities of the situation in China. Influenced by Li Dazhao, he came to believe in the liberation of the peasant as the prelude to the liberation of China. He evolved the strategy of organizing the peasantry to encircle the cities and created a successful model of revolution for the Third World. He envisioned the ultimate application of this strategy to the international scene, urging the Third World to unite, engulf, and effect the eventual downfall of the Western bourgeois societies.

Throughout his life, Mao was motivated by a perpetual restlessness. He rebelled against his father, against landlord and capitalist, against Nationalist rule, against Soviet domination and revisionism, and finally against his own party establishment and senior associates. Impatient for change, he wanted

Official portrait of Mao Zedong.

to transform the state, the society, and human nature in one stroke—"Ten thousand years are too long; seize the day, seize the hour!" A purist at heart, he kept up the momentum of revolution by creating incessant upheaval, exhausting both country and people. Much national energy was spent on mass movement and internecine strife, which impeded national progress. His twenty-seven-year rule brought little improvement in people's living standard.

It thus appears that after the success of revolution in 1949, the genius that was in Mao was largely spent. The ingredients that led him to the seizure of power could not lead him to successfully administer the sprawling state. After the first years of liberation, Mao's leadership faltered. The Antirightist-Campaign (1957) did irreparable damage to the intellectuals whose knowledge and skills China sorely needed. The rush to commune was too hasty; the Great Leap Forward went backward; the fight with Peng Dehuai was ill-conceived; and the decimation of the party during the Cultural Revolution was an unmitigated disaster. The fostering of Jiang Qing as a national leader and possible successor worked against the wishes of the people and Mao's senior associates. In his last years Mao spun himself farther and farther into a cocoon of his own making, insensitive to the feelings of the masses he had always claimed to represent. He died a lonely and unhappy man, his dream of transforming human nature and turning China into a powerful modern state unfulfilled. Historical perspective will in due time allow a full assessment of Mao's achievements and mistakes. For now, my own view of his life might be summed up in the following words:

As a revolutionary,   革命有餘
   Mao had few peers.   建國不足
As a nation-builder,
   He was unequal to the task.

THE GANG OF FOUR

The Plot of the Gang

The absence of a constitutional mechanism for the peaceful transfer of power led to a succession crisis when the incumbent leader died. The intense power struggle that erupted following Mao's death was led by his wife, Jiang Qing, who aspired to succeed him as chairman, to make Wang Hongwen chairman of the Standing Committee of the National People's Congress, and to install Zhang Chunqiao premier of the State Council. Yao Wenyuan, already in charge of the party's propaganda department, was probably to be designated a "cultural tsar" with added titles. These four, the hard core of the Cultural Revolutionary Group, conspired to seize power, but their major obstacle was Hua Guofeng. As the first vice-chairman of the party, premier of the State Council, and the object of Mao's instruction ("With you in charge, I am at ease"), Hua had a firm claim to succession. Hua also had the support of Wang Dongxing, Mao's chief bodyguard and head of the 20,000-man 8341 special unit.

Jiang Qing's trump card, Mao, was gone. Still in her deck were control of the media and of the urban militia in key places such as Shanghai, Beijing, Tianjin, Shenyang, and Guangzhou.[9] Before Mao's death the Four had schemed to distribute weapons and ammunition to the Shanghai militia, establishing a sort of National General Militia Headquarters to rival the Military Commission in Beijing. The day after Mao's death, six million rounds of ammunition were issued to the Shanghai militia.[10]

Jiang Qing received additional military support from Mao's nephew, Mao Yuanxin, political commissar of the Shenyang Military Region. He organized a 10,000-man task force in preparation for a march on Beijing to support Jiang Qing's planned coup. He was also seen in Baoding trying to bring about the disaffection of the 38th regiment and in Tangshan attempting to enlist support from army units sent there for earthquake relief work.[11]

In spite of this support, the Jiang Qing faction remained weak militarily due to the militia's lack of firepower and good commanders. To compensate, Jiang Qing tried to recruit two militarily powerful Politburo members—General Chen Xilian (commander of the Beijing Military Region) and Su Zhenhua (political commissar of the navy). Both men informed Hua of these approaches.[12] The Four had tried earlier to elicit support from Marshal Zhu De, only to be rejected and ridiculed.[13] Thus, while the Gang of Four dominated media and education, they were unable to increase substantially their military power.

The senior party cadres and military leaders, who loathed Jiang Qing and her cohorts but had been powerless against them as long as Mao lived, decided secretly after the Tian An Men Square Incident that only a countercoup could stop the Four from seizing power. They entrusted to Ye Jianying, minister of defense, the delicate task of cultivating friendship with Hua and of promising him their support as Mao's successor.[14] Hua knew only too well the Gang's record and ambitions.

Another anti-Jiang Qing force was also in secret operation. Deng Xiaoping, dismissed in April and hunted by the Gang, had fled to Canton under the protection of Ye Jianying and Xu Shiyou. These three, in a secret meeting also attended by several others including Zhao Ziyang (later general secretary) decided to fight the Four by forming an alliance with the Fuzhou and Nanjing Military Regions, with headquarters in Guangzhou. Should Jiang Qing gain power, they would establish a rival provisional Central Committee to contest her. After Mao's death Deng secretly returned to Beijing to await developments.[15]

The Gang meanwhile were plotting to assassinate Politburo members, with Hua, Ye, and several others as the main targets. Facing a common threat, the two became close allies and made the necessary preparations for a coup, which included the winning over of Wang Dongxing. A three-way coalition thus formed, with Ye as the mastermind, Hua laying out the plan of action, and Wang implementing it. Shanghai would be secured first; and for this purpose the help of General Xu Shiyou of the Guangzhou Military Region, who had extensive connections in the Shanghai-Nanjing area, was enlisted to obtain the cooperation of the Shanghai garrison commander and win control of the key city *before* the urban militia could act.[16] In Beijing, Hua had the firm support of Commander Chen Xilian, Mayor Wu De, and the cooperation of the garrison forces, the army, and special unit 8341.

The "Deathbed Adjuration"

During the mourning period, Jiang Qing appeared more preoccupied with succession than grief. Soon after Mao's death she went to the General Office of the Central Committee (under Wang Dongxing) and obliged the secretary on duty to hand over a batch of Mao's documents. Only after Hua's personal intercession did she reluctantly return them, and then only after two of the documents had been tampered with. Hua ordered all of Mao's paper sealed. The two altered pieces were:[17]

1. A June 3, 1976, document of Mao's meeting with Politburo members including Hua, Ye, Wang Hongwen, and Zhang Chunqiao, at which time Mao allegedly told them: "From now on you should help Jiang Qing carry the Red Banner. Don't let it fall. You should alert her against committing the errors she has committed." That such a meeting had taken place was not in question, but the date was; Hua had been in Chengdu, Sichuan, on June 3.

2. In the second of the three instructions Mao gave Hua (April 30), Jiang Qing substituted "Act according to the principles laid down" for "Act according to past principles." The significance of this change was obvious: if Mao had asked Politburo to help his wife carry on the Red Banner, then this was the principle laid down, and Jiang Qing was the intended successor.

The news media, under Jiang's control, played up the chairman's "deathbed adjuration"; and on September 16 the *Renmin Ribao* [People's Daily], *Hongqi* [Red Flag], and the *Liberation Army Daily* jointly editorialized, "Chairman Mao Will Live Forever in Our Hearts," stressing Mao's behest to "act according to the principles laid down." Hua was enraged, taking note of the three Chinese characters that had been altered from the original version. Hua believed the succession should be decided according to past principles; the first vice-chairman of the party should logically succeed the deceased chairman until the next plenary session of the Central Committee elected a new chairman.

At the memorial service on September 18, Hua retaliated in a masterly veiled speech in which he quoted Mao's famous dictum, "Political power grows out of the barrel of a gun," implying that he had the support of the military. Hua also quoted Mao's command, the "Three do's and don't's": (1) "Practice Marxism and not revisionism"; (2) "Unite, don't split"; and (3) "Be open and aboveboard, and don't intrigue and conspire."[18] The significance of this quotation could not be lost, for on the occasion of the original command, Mao had warned his wife and her cohorts "not to function as a gang of four." Hua still made no mention of the third instruction Mao gave him.

While Hua's speech could possibly have revealed too much of his intentions for his own good, in the confusion of the moment his opponents appeared to have taken no particular notice. To prevent any suspicion he allowed the Gang to continue to play important roles in state affairs.[19] The Gang continued to believe that it was both safe and strong.

The October 6 Coup

Several stormy Politburo meetings took place toward the end of September. On or about the 29th Hua pointed out the "wrong propaganda policy" of emphasizing the deathbed adjuration and neglecting the "Three do's and don't's." Jiang Qing responded that Hua was incompetent to lead the party and demanded that she be made chairman of the Central Committee. Hua retorted that he was not only competent but knew how to "solve problems"—in retrospect an ominous reference to his intention to remove the Four. The meeting ended inconclusively. On September 30 another meeting was called to discuss the National Day Ceremonies on October 1. On that occasion Hua led the procession of the Politburo members for picture taking. The photos (under Yao's direction) showed Hua at the far left and Jiang in the center of the picture to extol her importance. Little did she know that this was to be her last public appearance.

The struggle escalated in the early days of October. The

"deathbed adjuration" appeared forty-two times in the *Renmin Ribao* [People's Daily] and the *Guangming Daily*, compared with eleven times for the "Three do's and don't's." The Gang, still oblivious to the impending doom, was preparing to celebrate their ultimate victory. Jiang Qing and Wang Hongwen had numerous portraits taken in anticipation of the "top happy news."[20]

The Gang secretly set October 6 as the date of their coup. On October 2 they asked Mao Yuanxin to dispatch an armored division from Mukden (Shenyang) to Beijing, and the deputy chief-of-staff to transfer the 21st regiment from Baozhe, Shaanxi, to the capital. The Gang planned to set up a headquarters with Wang Dongxing and his 8341 special unit as the chief instrument of their coup, but the plan underwent a last-minute change as the Gang developed doubts about Wang's loyalty. They decided instead to rely on the 38th regiment stationed in Beijing.

October 4 was a momentous day. A bold article by Liang Xiao in the *Guangming Daily* stated that Mao's adjuration would "forever be the guide for continuous advance and the guarantee of victory to the members of the Chinese Communist Party. . . . All chieftains of the revisionist line who attempt to tamper with this principle laid down necessarily have to tamper with Marxist-Leninist-Mao Zedong Thought." "Past chieftains" were specifically named: Liu Shaoqi, Lin Biao, Chen Boda, and Deng Xiaoping. It warned that no revisionist chieftain would dare to challenge Mao's adjuration, meaning, of course, Hua. The anti-Gang forces regarded this article as a "mobilization order" and were ready to strike.[21]

In the early morning of October 5, a secret meeting was held in the headquarters of the commander of the People's Liberation Army, with five participants: Hua, Ye, Wang, Beijing Garrison Commander Chen Xilian, and Vice-Premier Li Xiannian (an ally of Deng Xiaoping). They decided to act decisively and quickly before the Gang could stage their coup by arresting all four leaders in a single swoop. Hua and Ye assumed overall direction with Chen Xilian assigned the duty of safeguarding Beijing and Wang Dongxing, the job of arresting the Four. Hua dispatched soldiers to guard the Great Wall against possible attack from Mukden and transferred another regiment to Beijing to watch over the 38th regiment. Meanwhile, the Guangzhou Military Region was alerted to ready two divisions for airlift to Beijing on instant notice.

Hua next invited the Four to attend an emergency Politiburo meeting at midnight, October 5, at the party headquarters in Zhongnanhai. Wang Hongwen arrived first. He resisted arrest and killed two guards but was himself wounded and subdued. Then came Zhang Chunqiao and Yao Wenyuan; both fell into the trap. Jiang Qing was in bed when her captors arrived. She shouted: "How dare you to rebel when the Chairman's body is not yet cold!"[22] Others arrested included Mao Yuanxin, Minister of Culture Yu Huiyong, and Nanjing Military Region Commander Ding Sheng. In the small hours of October 6, the Gang was felled in one clean sweep. The Four were placed in solitary confinement in separate locations in Beijing.

On October 7 Hua Guofeng and Wang Dongxing each delivered two reports and Ye Jianying, one, to the Politburo. These reports, containing detailed charges against the Four, must have been prepared in extreme secrecy some time prior to the arrest. The Gang had been so smoothly and resolutely smashed that no question of civil strife arose; the success must be credited to the three protagonists who had long years of experience in security and military matters. The grateful Politburo named Hua chairman of the party Central Committee and concurrently chairman of the Military Commission, and put him in charge of editing the fifth volume of the *Selected Works of Mao Zedong.*[23]

Strictly speaking, the process of the selection of Hua as Mao's successor was of dubious legality. Article 9 of the party constitution stipulated that the party chairman must be elected in a plenary session of the Central Committee, and the Third Plenary Session of the Tenth Central Committee had not yet met. But the party and the country were willing to overlook the legal formality and make Hua the new leader at once.

Hua Guofeng, immediate successor to Mao as party chairman (and premier).

Much publicity was now given to Mao's message to Hua, "With you in charge, I am at ease," to create the image that Hua was the "anointed" successor.

On October 24 a million soldiers and civilians held a victory rally at Tian An Men Square to celebrate the smashing of the Gang of Four. A smiling Hua appeared, accompanied by top military leaders indicating the key role the military had played in the "palace revolution" and its continued support of Hua. Hua was hailed as a "worthy leader" of the party, a "worthy helmsman" to succeed Mao, and a brilliant chief who most nearly possessed the merits of Mao and Zhou.[24] The following day, the *Renmin Ribao* [People's Daily], *Hongqi* [Red Flag], and the *Liberation Army Daily,* under new management, jointly editorialized a "Great Historic Victory." Later, the Third Plenary Session of the Tenth Central Committee (July 1977) described the smashing of the Gang of Four as the eleventh major struggle in the history of the party, of almost equal importance with the Zunyi Conference (1935) and credited Hua with saving the revolution and the party.[25]

Several factors accounted for Hua's success. As first vice-chairman of the party and premier of the State Council, he had all the advantages of an incumbent leader. He enjoyed the support of the military and party leaders, and had won the cooperation of Wang Dongxing and the 8341 unit. He had taken the pulse of the country and knew the people's hatred of Jiang Qing and the Gang; in smashing them he was expressing the "common aspiration" of the people. And finally, having been a member of the committee investigating the Lin Biao affair, he knew that indecision was the chief cause of Lin's downfall and therefore acted decisively and swiftly to surprise and overwhelm the conspirators.

On the other hand, the Gang's failure must be traced first and foremost to the death of Mao. Under Mao's patronage the Four issued orders in his name and rode roughshod over the uncooperative. They mistreated thousands of respected elders and leaders, and used terrorists and secret agents to browbeat unsympathetic intellectuals and the people. In addition, the Gang led decadent, privileged, bourgeois private lives. Jiang Qing, for example, kept a "silver" jet for her own use, enjoyed the most expensive of German photographic equipment, wore silk blouses, and received guests in lavish settings.[26] While these excesses alienated the masses and mocked the ideals of proletarian revolution, Mao's patronage of the Gang effectively stilled criticism.

The second major source of the Gang's weakness was the imbalance between military strength and media control. The Gang did not control the army but only the militia, which lacked organization and firepower, so they relied heavily on their control of the media and cultural scene to mold public opinion and to give an exaggerated image of power. Perhaps the loud support and broad coverage they received lured them into believing that they were stronger than they actually were. Moreover, Jiang Qing was overly confident that as Mao's wife, nobody would dare oppose her. But the fact was, the minute she became his widow, her fate was sealed.

Charges Against the Gang

On December 10, 1976, the Central Committee issued a 118-page document in four parts, *Zhongfa* 24, entitled "Evidence of Crime of the Anti-Party Clique of Wang Hongwen, Zhang Chungiao, Jiang Qing and Yao Wenyuan." Part I deals with the Gang's attempted "usurpation of the Party and seizure of power." Evidence includes the report of a secret visit by Wang to Mao in October 1974 accusing the hospitalized Zhou of conspiring with Deng, Ye, and others. Wang hoped to arouse Mao's suspicion and have Zhou dismissed. Another piece of evidence was the testimony of Mao's niece Wang Hairong that Jiang Qing aspired to be chairman, with Wang Hongwen and Zhang Chunqiao in top government positions.

Part II deals with the Gang's crime of adulterating the line laid down by Mao. In a February article, "On the Correct Handling of Contradictions Among the People," Mao pointed out that revisionism and rightist opportunism were more dangerous than dogmatism, and during his tour of the country in 1971 Mao announced the basic principles which became the "Three do's and don't's." The Gang did not follow Mao's line but overtly adulterated it by stressing empiricism as the most immediate danger.

Part III deals with alleged crimes against Hua Guofeng after he became acting premier (February 7, 1976) and premier-first-vice-chairman (April 7). The Gang was charged with adulterating Mao's instructions to Hua ("Act according to past principles") by prompting Liang Xiao to disseminate a fabricated version to news media and by opposing the Central Committee headed by Hua. Part IV concerns the Gang's attack on the party during Mao's illness and after his death.[27]

The Four were permanently expelled from the party, removed from all official posts, and branded as conspirators, ultrarightists, counterrevolutionaries, and representatives of Kuomintang.

From the Western standpoint, neither political machination nor aspiration to the highest offices in a country is a crime, but to conspire to overthrow the goverment is. The evidence against the Gang may be insufficient to substantiate the charges. What was clearly criminal was the Gang's unauthorized issuance of orders in the name of Mao, their killing of hundreds of thousands through their agents, their intimidation of people through terrorism and torture, and their disruption of education and industrial production, setting the country back by decades. Yet does not the ultimate responsibility for all this rest with Mao?

MAO AND THE GANG

There is no way to dissociate Mao from the Gang. Without him there could have been no Gang, for without his wife they would have had no safely protected leader. Jiang Qing, a former left-wing movie actress, came to Yenan after the Long March and became Mao's secretary. They fell in love and Mao asked for her hand, much to the consternation of Mao's third wife who protested violently and refused to divorce him. Senior cadres also disapproved of the marriage, but nonetheless the two were married in 1939. Reportedly, before the marriage senior officials exacted a promise from Mao that his wife not be active in politics for life or at least twenty years.[28]

It was only after the establishment of the People's Republic that Jiang received a minor appointment from Premier Zhou as a member of the Film Steering Committee in 1950. She was a delegate to the Third National People's Congress in 1954. Apart from these minor involvements, she lived a quiet life in poor health until 1958.

However, as her health improved in the early 1960s, the twenty-year waiting period had come to an end, and she became more active. In 1962 she reviewed for Mao the Peking Opera's repertoire and recommended that many works be banned. At this time she was introduced to Zhang Chunqiao, chief of the propaganda department in Shanghai, and writer Yao Weyuan. With their help Jiang Qing carried out the reform of the Peking opera and offered several model revolutionary plays including *The Red Lantern* and *Taking Tiger*

Mountain by Strategy. This won Mao's approval, and Jiang Qing gradually became his spokesman in art, literature, and culture. In 1965 Mao and Jiang directed Yao to write the essay entitled "Comment on the New Historical Play *Hai Rui Dismissed from Office*," which became the opening shot of the Cultural Revolution. In 1966, a Central Cultural Revolutionary Committee was formed with Chen Boda (Mao's secretary) as chairman, and Jiang Qing as first vice-chairman, a position of national prominence. The original Cultural Revolutionary Group thus consisted of Mao, Jiang Qing, Zhang Chunqiao Yao Wenyuan, and Chen Boda.

Mao had said: "Revolution hinges on the barrel of the gun and on the pen." In his struggle with Liu Shaoqi, Mao relied on the pens of the Jiang Qing group to dominate the propaganda machine, and the guns of Lin Biao to provide security and military support. Lin became a close ally of Mao and to ingratiate himself with Jiang Qing, asked her to preside over the army's Literary and Art Work Forum and appointed her advisor to the army's Cultural Revolutionary Group. Thus in the second stage of the development of the Cultural Revolutionary Group, Lin was an ally of Jiang Qing.

After the successive fiascoes of naming first Liu and then Lin as his successors, Mao seemed frustrated and discouraged at the thought of naming yet another. He felt he could trust no one except his own assertive wife to carry on his ideas of revolution. So step by step he arranged for her to advance to the forefront of national politics. In his 1973 New Year Message, Mao declared: "The trade unions, the Communist Youth League, the Red Guard, the Little Red Soldiers, poor and lower-middle peasants and women's organizations should be consolidated step by step." Thus in one stroke the Cultural Revolutionary Group gained control of mass organizations, especially the trade union federations.

Next, Mao's plan involved increasing the Group's prominence at the Tenth Party Congress in August 1973. The Group now included Wang Hongwen, the fiery Shanghai cotton-mill worker who organized workers and masses to topple the Shanghai mayor and party secretary. Wang was catapulted to a vice-chairmanship of the party, with Zhang Chunqiao on the Standing Committee of the Politburo, and Jiang Qing and Yao Wenyuan both Politburo members. In all, the Cultural Revolutionaries accounted for three of the five vice-chairmen of the party, four of the nine members of the Politburo Standing Committee, and eleven of the twenty-one members of the Politburo. They were clearly placed in strategic positions poised for the ultimate assumption of supreme power.

Mao's third strategy was to create large-scale militia units to rival the People's Liberation Army, with Wang Hongwen in charge of the model Shanghai militia. Wang was also made a vice-chairman of the influential Military Commission, while Zhang Chunqiao became director of the General Political Department of the People's Liberation Army, infiltrating the regular military establishment.

Jiang Qing's position received a further boost during Premier Zhou's illness when she received foreign visitors in her capacity as a state leader. Between May and October, 1974, she had received Archbishop Makarios, President Gnassingbe Eyadema of Togo, the head of the Nigerian Federal Military Government, and others, although by November she stopped receiving state visitors, perhaps due to the criticism of party seniors. Meanwhile party writers circulated inspiring stories about Empress Lü (187–179 B.C.) and Empress Wu Zetian (A.D. 684–705), implying that Jiang Qing, too, could be a good ruler.

As Zhou's condition worsened, it appeared that Deng Xiaoping would assume control of the State Council as premier. But in the fall of 1975 Mao launched an "Antirightist Deviationist" Campaign against Deng, and after Zhou's death, Deng disappeared from public view. Mao then chose Hua Guofeng to be acting premier and later premier and first vice-chairman of the party in April 1976 primarily to stop Deng from returning to power. It is likely Mao hoped that Hua, who had gained prominence during the Cultural Revolution, would be a transitional figure who would assist Jiang Qing to power. But, as the old Chinese saying goes, "A wise man may calculate a thousand times, but inevitably there will be a miss!"

Mao realized his wife's "wide ambitions" to become chairman, and he also knew of the countless number of people she had wronged, harmed, arrested, or killed during the decade of the Cultural Revolution. On July 17, 1974, Mao had warned the Gang: "You'd better be careful; don't let yourselves become a small faction of four." In May 1975 he admonished them with the "Three do's and don't's," ending with, "Don't function as a gang of four; don't do it anymore."[29] Mao was thus aware of the Gang's excesses and could have restrained their leader by a simple order. That this was not done reflected his failings as party chairman and the Great Helmsman.

When the American playwright Arthur Miller visited China in 1978, he met with Chinese writers, artists, movie directors, and stage managers. He learned that many of the country's leading artists and intellectuals had been killed or imprisoned and tortured. To Miller it was inconceivable that Jiang Qing could have committed such injustices without the support of Mao. Quoting Mao, "People are no chives; their heads do not grow back when they are cut off," Miller concluded: "It has become impossible to believe that a 'faction' could have swung the People's Republic around its head without the consent of the Great Helmsman."[30] For Miller, Mao's lack of leadership could not be blamed on his physical infirmity, for people were jailed and killed in the 1960s when he was still strong enough to swim six and one-half kilometers in the Yangtze River. Miller's final judgment: the Gang of Four was "merely a screen for the still-sacrosanct name of Mao."[31]

Although deified before 900 million people, Mao in private life was an aged and doddering husband. As he increasingly submitted to Jiang Qing's pressures, he lost all sense of proportion in state affairs. A communism tainted with familial favoritism smacks of "socialist feudalism." Yet from the dramatic events of 1976 and the defeat of radicalism, there came a promise of greater stability, better life, and a new drive for modernization.

NOTES

1. *The New York Times,* Jan. 9, 1976, pp. 11–12.
2. Ch'en Yung-sheng, "The 'October 6th Coup' and Hua Kuo-feng's Rise to Power," *Issues & Studies,* XV:10:81–82 (Oct. 1979).
3. Mao had likened himself to this first emperor of the Qin dynasty who unified China in 221 B.C.
4. Text of Central Committee announcement in English carried by *The New York Times,* April 8, 1976, p. 16.
5. *Peking Review,* Dec. 24, 1976, p. 8. See also Richard C. Thornton, "The Political Succession to Mao Tse-tung," *Issues & Studies,* XIV:6:35 (June 1978).
6. There were 240,000 dead and 164,000 injured. *Los Angeles Times,* June 11, 1977.
7. Julie Nixon Eisenhower.
8. *The Times,* London, Sept. 10, 1976, p. 7; *International Herald Tribune,* Paris, Sept. 10, 1976, pp. 1, 3.
9. Chien T'ieh, "The Chiang Ch'ing Faction and People's Military Forces," *Issues & Studies,* XII:1:23 (Jan. 1976).
10. *Peking Review,* Feb. 4, 1977, pp. 5–10; Andres D. Onate, "Hua Kuo-feng and the Arrest of the 'Gang of Four'," *The China Quarterly,* 75:555–56 (Sept. 1978).
11. Onate, p. 555.
12. *Ibid.,* pp. 558–89.
13. Zhu De (1886–1976) died in July 1976 of undisclosed causes, and his son-in-law, General Pi Dingzhun, was killed in a mysterious airplane crash en route to Zhu's funeral.
14. Ch'en Yung-sheng, p. 78.
15. Testimony by Zhang Binghua, former director of the Propaganda Department of the CCP Central Committee, quoted in Ch'en Yung-sheng, pp. 85–86.
16. Onate, p. 556.
17. *Ibid.,* p. 549.
18. Complete text of the speech in *Peking Review,* Sept. 24, 1976, pp. 12–16.
19. On September 26, 1976, Zhang Chunqiao signed an international trade and economic agreement with Jamaica, and on September 30 the Gang of Four joined other leaders in a forum atop the Tian An Men.
20. *People's Daily,* Dec. 17, 1976; Onate, pp. 552–53.
21. *People's Daily,* Dec. 17, 1976.
22. Reported in *Central Daily News,* Taipei, Sept. 23, 1980.
23. The selection of Hua, although supposedly made on October 7,

was possibly made later. In the initial Politburo announcement of October 7, there was no mention of Hua's appointment. The October 29, 1976, issue of *Peking Review* carried an article, "Great Historic Victory" (p. 14) which belatedly stated: "In accordance with the arrangements Chairman Mao had made before he passed away, the October 7, 1976 resolution of the Central Committee of the Communist Party appointed Comrade Hua Guofeng chairman of the Central Committee of the Communist Party of China and Chairman of the Military Commission of the C.P.C. Central Committee."

24. "Comrade Hua Kuo-feng Is Our Party's Worthy Leader" and "Great Historic Victory," both in *Peking Review*, No. 44, Oct. 29, 1976, pp. 14–16; No. 45, Nov. 5, 1976, pp. 5–6.
25. *Peking Review*, No. 47, Nov. 19, 1976.
26. Roxane Witke, *Comrade Chiang Ch'ing* (Boston, 1977), pp. 37–38.
27. Complete text of the charges in *Issues and Studies*, Sept., Oct., 1977.
28. Witke, pp. 148–57, 335.
29. Joint editorials of *Renmin Ribao* [People's Daily], *Hongqi* [Red Flag], and *Liberation Army Daily*, Oct. 25, 1976.
30. Inge Morath and Arthur Miller, *Chinese Encounters* (New York, 1979), pp. 21, 40.
31. *Ibid.*, p. 7.

FURTHER READING

Bonavia, David, *Verdict in Peking: The Trial of the Gang of Four* (New York, 1984).

Chang, Chen-pang, "Mao Tse-tung and the Gang of Four," *Issues & Studies*, XIII:9:18–33 (Sept. 1977).

Chang, David W., *Zhou Enlai and Deng Xiaoping in the Chinese Leadership Succession Crisis* (Lanham, Md., 1983).

Ch'en, Yung-sheng, "The 'October 6th Coup' and Hua Kuo-feng's Rise to Power," *Issue & Studies*, XV:10:75–86 (Oct. 1979).

Cheng, J. Chester, *Documents of Dissent: Chinese Political Thought Since Mao* (Stanford, 1981).

Chi, Hsin, *The Rise and Fall of the "Gang of Four"* (tr. from *The Seventies Magazine*), (New York, 1977).

Domes, Jürgen, "The Gang of Four and Hua Fuo-feng: An Analysis of Political Events in 1975–76," *The China Quarterly*, 71: 473–97 (Sept. 1977).

Fox, Galen, "Campaigning for Power in China," *Contemporary China*, III:1:80–95 (Spring 1979).

"Great Historic Victory," *Peking Review*, 44:14–16 (Oct. 29, 1976).

"How the 'Gang of Four' Used Shanghai as a Base to Usurp Party and State Power," *Peking Review*, 6:5–10 (Feb. 4, 1977).

Hsü Kai-yu, *The Chinese Literary Scene: A Writer's Visit to the People's Republic* (New York, 1975).

Leng, Shao-chaun, with Hungdah Chiu, *Criminal Justice in Post-Mao China: Analysis and Documents* (Albany, 1985).

Liu, Alan P. L., "The Gang of Four and the Chinese People's Liberation Army," *Asian Survey*, XIX:9:817–37 (Sept. 1979).

"Mao Tse-tung (1893–1976)—the Man Who Changed the Life of China," *International Herald Tribune*, Paris, Sept. 10, 1976.

"Mao Tse-tung," *The Times*, London, Sept. 10, 1976.

Morath, Inge, and Arthur Miller, *Chinese Encounters* (New York, 1979).

Nee, Victor, and James Peck (eds.), *China's Uninterrupted Revolution* (New York, 1975).

Oksenberg, Michel, and Sai-cheung Yeung, "Hua Kuo-feng's Pre-Cultural Revolution Human Years, 1946–66: The Making of a Political Generalist," *The China Quarterly*, 69:3–53 (March 1977).

Oksenberg, Michel, "Evaluating the Chinese Political System," *Contemporary China*, III:2:102–111 (Summer 1979).

Onate, Andres D., "Hua Kuo-feng and the Arrest of the 'Gang of Four,'" *The China Quarterly*, 75:540–65 (Sept. 1978).

Roots, John McCook, *An Informal Biography of China's Legendary Chou En-lai* (New York, 1978).

Schram, Stuart R., *Mao Zedong: A Preliminary Reassessment* (Hong Kong, 1983).

Teiwes, Frederick C., *Leadership, Legitimacy, and Conflict in China: From a Charismatic Mao to the Politics of Succession* (Armonk, N.Y., 1984).

Terrill, Ross, *White-Boned Demon: A Biography of Madame Mao Zedong* (New York, 1984).

"Tough New Man in Peking," *Time* Magazine, Jan. 19, 1976, pp. 24–31.

Tsou, Tang, "Mao Tse-tung Thought, the Last Struggle for Succession, and the Post-Mao Era," *The China Quarterly*, 71:498–527 (Sept. 1977).

Uhalley, Stephen Jr., *Mao Tse-tung: A Critical Biography* (New York, 1975).

Wang, Hsueh-wen, "The 'Gang of Four' Incident: Official Exposé by a CCPCC Document," *Issues & Studies*, XIII:9:46–58 (Sept. 1977).

Wei, Hua, and Tang Hsiao, "A Criticism of Chang Chun-chiao's

'Thoughts on February 3, 1976,' " *Peking Review*, 5:16–18 (Jan. 28, 1977).

Wilson, Dick, *Chou: The Story of Zhou Enlai, 1898–1976* (London, 1984).

——— (ed.), *Mao Tse-tung in the Scales of History: A Preliminary Assessment Organized by the China Quarterly* (Cambridge, Eng., 1977).

Witke, Roxane, *Comrade Chiang Ch'ing* (Boston, 1977).

Wong, Paul, *China's Higher Leadership in the Socialist Transition* (New York, 1976).

2

Deng Xiaoping
and China's New Order

Since the cataclysmic year 1976, the changes wrought by the party, the government, and the people of China had altered the surface as well as the depths of Chinese politics. Beginning with Deng Xiaoping's quick return to power, China's priorities were thoroughly reorganized. In the meetings of party and government councils, in the communications media, and in the actions of the average citizen a cry for change was heard: for normalcy, stability, and most notably, for modernization and the material and cultural benefits it implied. By analyzing the proceedings of the party and government meetings, examining the assertions of the media, and paying special attention to private manipulations as well as to the expressions of the common people, one could draw a reasonably accurate picture of China's "new beginning."

Following the downfall of the Gang of Four, Chairman Hua Guofeng faced three pressing issues: (1) his legitimacy as Mao's successor; (2) the rehabilitation of Deng Xiaoping; and (3) the reordering of economic priorities to promote modernization. Regarding the succession, Mao's instruction to Hua ("With you in charge, I am at ease") was regarded by Ye and

Deng supporters[1] as reflecting Mao's personal view rather than the will of the party, whose constitution has specific provisions governing the election of the party chairman. By implication, Hua's assumption of the chairmanship of the Central Committee and of its Military Commission was deemed unconstitutional; but, if he would agree to the reinstatement of Deng, this question of legitimacy could be negotiated or even withdrawn. Thus, the two issues came into balance. As a result of mediation by Marshal Ye and Vice-Premier Li Xiannian, who desperately desired a smooth transition to the post-Mao era, Hua agreed in principle to rehabilitate Deng, and to revise the five-year economic plan to accelerate the Four Modernizations. In late November 1976 Hua announced that Deng's reinstatement would be discussed at the next Central Committee meetings in July 1977. In return, he received support from Ye, Li, and others for chairmanship of the Central Committee and its Military Commission.

DENG'S REHABILITATION

Deng's many supporters in the party and the army had mounted an extensive campaign demanding his rehabilitation. At the first anniversary of Zhou Enlai's death in January 1977, there were demonstrations and wall posters in Beijing calling for Deng's return to office. The Politburo which met that month cleared Deng of involvement in the Tian An Men Square Incident of April 1976, reclassifying his case from "antagonistic contradiction" to "contradiction among the people," i.e. rectifiable. Hua polled the 200-odd Central Committee members as to their views on the Deng case, and in March the Politburo agreed to restore Deng to all his former positions, provided he admit his past mistakes.

Deng wrote two letters to Hua, Ye, and the Central Committee, and in the second he said: "I firmly welcome Mr. Hua as chairman of our party. I firmly support the crushing of the Gang of Four by the party Central Committee under Chairman Hua. I am well and I ask Chairman Hua to send me to the front line [of work]."[2] Hua replied: "You have made mistakes and you should be criticized. [But] you are not responsible for the Tian An Men Square Incident. Not only will you be sent to the front line, but to the firing line [of work]."[3] In May Deng's two letters were distributed by Hua to cadres at different levels and they won the approval "of all comrades in the party."[4] Meanwhile, in volume five of the *Selected Works of Mao Zedong* edited by Hua and released in April 1977, there appeared no less than nine passages praising Deng's political stance in the 1950s.

While negotiating Deng's rehabilitation, Hua also labored to refine his image as an advocate of modernization and as an expert in economics. He attended a number of conferences on agriculture, finance, banking, and industry including the national conference on agriculture at Dazhai in December 1976 and the industrial conference at Daqing in April and May 1977. At the same time, Hua, Ye, and Deng all intensified their efforts to appoint provincial party secretaries in an attempt to strengthen their respective positions at the next two vital party meetings: the Third Plenum of the Tenth Central Committee and the Eleventh Party Congress in July and August 1977. Their maneuvers resulted in the appointment for four Hua supporters,[5] four Ye supporters,[6] and five Deng supporters[7] in addition to Zhao Ziyang, party first secretary of Sichuan since December 1975.

At the Third Plenum of the Tenth Central Committee meeting, three resolutions were passed to confirm earlier Politburo decisions. First was the approval of Hua as chairman of the party and of the Military Commission; next was the acceptance of Hua's recommendation that Deng be restored to his former posts—Politburo Standing Committee member, vice-chairman of the Central Committee, first deputy premier of the State Council, vice-chairman of the Military Commission, and chief of the General Staff of the Liberation Army—all top positions in the party, the military, and the government. The third resolution condemned the antiparty activities of the Gang of Four and accused them of "conspiring to overthrow Comrade Zhou

Enlai," of "violently attacking and falsely accusing Comrade Deng Xiaoping," of being "extremely hostile and thoroughly opposed to" Mao's choice of Hua, and of "plotting to overthrow the party Central Committee headed by Comrade Hua Guofeng and bring about a counterrevolutionary restoration." The Four were officially expelled from the party for good.[8]

With the Gang of Four and their chief supporters removed, the party began a vast personnel reshuffle. The party approved the appointments of Mao's former bodyguard Wang Dongxing and Vice-Premier Li Xiannian to the Politburo Standing Committee, boosting the membership to nine. At the close of the Tenth Central Committee meetings, Hua's supporters slightly outnumbered Deng's, with Ye's providing a balance between them. It was of note that in the Central Committee itself, 84 percent of the 201 members were veteran party cadres and military leaders, a third of whom had been victims of the Cultural Revolution and now filled the seats vacated by Gang supporters.

The Eleventh Party Congress held between August 12 and 18, 1977, continued the personnel reshuffle. Hua retained the party chairmanship, and four vice-chairmen were appointed: Ye, Deng, Li Xiannian, and Wang Dongxing. These five constituted the Standing Committee of the Politburo. The Politburo itself had ten new faces, and its power structure fell roughly into the following three groups: Hua and Deng each had nine supporters and Ye five.[9] With none of the three in command of a majority, Ye continued to hold the balance. Yet certain changes, such as Hua's relinquishment of the post of minister of public security to a Deng supporter (Zhao Cangbi), indicated Deng's growing power.

In spite of the emerging power struggles, the Congress closed with a call for unity, discipline, stability, and cooperation—a sharp contrast to the continuous upheaval and factional strife that characterized the Mao era. A Disciplinary Committee was established to monitor the conduct of 35 million party members. In many ways the Congress seemed to signal the beginning of the end of the Maoist era.

DENG'S DRIVE FOR POLITICAL DOMINANCE

Personnel changes made in the party meetings discussed above must not be confused with government appointments. Government appointments recommended by the party must be approved by the National People's Congress. Hence, the Fifth People's Congress was scheduled for the spring of 1978, and to prepare for its convocation it was decided that all twenty-nine provincial revolutionary committee leaders had to be re-elected. By February 1978 the re-election process had been completed and the Congress convened accordingly from February 26 to March 5, 1978.

Enlargement of the Power Base

A key issue at the Congress was whether or not the post of the state chairmanship, occupied previously by Mao and Liu Shaoqi, should be resurrected; it was decided in the negative. Ye accepted the chairmanship of the Congress's Standing Committee, a sort of titular headship of state formerly occupied by Zhu De until his death in 1976. There was much talk about Deng's advancement to the premiership, but Hua retained the position. Deng consolidated his power as first deputy premier in charge of the Four Modernizations. Fang Yi, a protégé of both Ye and Deng, was made responsible for the development of science and technology, the basis of the other modernizations (agriculture, industry, and national defense). Another important post, the chairmanship of the State Planning Commission, went to Yu Qiuli, a veteran economic planner and Deng supporter. Such appointments demonstrated the give-and-take among the leaders in hopes of achieving some semblance of equilibrium.

At the close of the Congress, Hua called for unity, modernization, better international relations, a 10 percent industrial growth, and a 4 to 5 percent annual increase in agricultural expansion. These targets seemed overly ambitious, in some cases more than doubling recent average increases. However,

Military statesman Marshal Ye Jianying.

in the euphoric atmosphere of the post-Gang period, ambition and progress were the order of the day; nothing seemed impossible, however unrealistic to the critical eye.

At the same time, in spite of the unity represented by the three-way coalition of Hua, Ye, and Deng, tension continued to mount. On the surface, Hua and Deng maintained a working relationship; Hua treated Deng with due respect as a party senior of the Long March generation, while Deng treated Hua with the courteous condescension that an elder Chinese family member exhibits toward a younger one. Yet Deng's strategy for political domination put him in conflict with Hua. Deng's growing power as well as his strategy were obvious enough, but Hua lacked the organization to halt it.

Deng was intent upon enlarging his power base by rehabilitating men who had suffered under Mao and the Gang in the name of "righting the wrong" (*pingfan*). He took a strong stand against leaders associated with the Cultural Revolution and the Gang of Four, especially those who had criticized him and blocked his succession to Zhou Enlai. These included Hua (who rose under Mao's patronage), Wang Dongxing (head of Mao's bodyguard), Wu De (mayor of Beijing), and Ji Dengkui (a doctrinaire Politburo member). Deng attacked not Hua but his associates, chiselling away at his political periphery so that the center would be rendered hollow. Meanwhile, Deng also cultivated able, younger followers, placing them in key positions so that they could perpetuate his economic policies.

Deng, however, did not limit himself to attacks on individuals or the appointments of "young blood"; he simultaneously eroded the ideological power base of his former adversaries by combatting the embedded supremacy of "Mao Thought." To this he announced in May and June of 1978 two clever guiding principles: "Practice is the sole criterion of truth" and "Seek truth from facts." By implication Mao Zedong's thought was no longer the standard by which a policy or an action must be judged; in fact, the thought itself must be subject to the scrutiny of facts, practice, and truth. The problem of Mao's leadership and his responsibility for the Cultural Revolution and China's ills became a major concern of the post-Gang government.

The Fifth National People's Congress met again from June 18 to July 1, 1979, to deliberate and ratify earlier decisions reached by the party Central Committee in December 1978. The ratifications involved: (1) establishing the primacy of agriculture and of speeding its development; (2) shifting the focus of state and party work to socialist construction while revising overly ambitious targets for the Four Modernizations; (3) enacting a legal system for the protection and enhancement of democracy; and (4) approving key personnel changes in government.

The parliamentlike Congress had a presidium chaired by the elder statesman Ye with the help of Secretary General Ulanfu, an ethnic minority leader and Deng supporter. The Dengists clearly dominated the day. Peng Zhen, former mayor of Beijing, disgraced during the Cultural Revolution, headed the Committee on Legal Code; Hu Yaobang, a Politburo mem-

The Democracy Wall in Bejing, 1979.

ber and head of party propaganda, directed the Committee on Qualifications of New Congress Delegates. Three new vice-premiers were appointed, all formerly victims of the Cultural Revolution: Chen Yun, Bo Ibo (both veteran economic planners), and Yao Yilin (formerly minister of commerce). The presidency of the Chinese Academy of Sciences went to Fang Yi. Deng was said to have declined the premiership, preferring the less assuming title of first deputy premier while exercising the de facto power of premier. Clearly, titles mean little in contemporary China; it is the exercise of power and the ability to control decisions that count.

Hua and Deng had apparently reached a tacit understanding; the former would support Deng's personnel changes and economic policies, while the latter would slow moves toward a critical assessment of Mao's role in the Cultural Revolution, which could prove both embarrassing and injurious to Hua. Nonetheless, the Congress's repeated calls for stability, unity, modernization, a legal system, and democracy were a subtle repudiation of Mao's rule, which had been marked by ceaseless upheaval, factional strife, and poor economic planning.

Hua himself announced that "the root causes of unending political turmoil and splits" had been eliminated and that stability and unity were the desires of the people. He called for an acceleration in the development of agriculture and light industry in the next three years, accompanied by a realistic revision of the timetable for the Four Modernizations. He encouraged a restrained hope for democracy, a legal system, and material incentives when he implied that modernization would not succeed unless the majority of the people believed that a large measure of democracy had been granted.

In establishing realistic goals for modernization, economic reports were delivered which revealed important statistics for the first time in twenty years, suggesting a "return to normalcy." Food production in 1978 was up 7.8 percent from 1977, and the forecast for 1979 was 2.4 percent higher. Crude oil production rose 11.1 percent over 1977, and the growth in 1979 was estimated at 1.9 percent. The 1979 budget totalled Ch$112 billion, of which 18 percent was allocated to the military. Agriculture received a notable increase in investment from 10.7 percent to 14 percent of the budget. To alleviate the hardships of the farmer, whose per capita annual income was only Ch$75 ($48) in 1978 compared with Ch$664 ($430) for the average urban worker, the government raised farm products purchase prices so that farm income would increase by Ch$10 ($6.6) per farmer, a small but not insignificant improvement.[10]

The prospect of an improving economy, more realistic modernization goals, and a better protected democracy generated the Congress's closing spirit of national unity and stability. The sensitive issue of personnel change was resolved by adding new officials without dismissing existing ones and by allowing Chairman Hua to retain his premiership. Hua also scored something of a victory by championing the cause of farmers and by his ardent support of the Four Modernizations.

The Congress, however, signaled a more definite victory for Deng in the development of his economic policy and in the enhancement of his power base. In spite of their political rivalry, the Hua-Deng leadership was, above all, committed to a policy of national reconstruction through economic development and modernization, and to a new stability built on the fruits of this new order. However, the accomplishment of these goals was still predicated upon the four fundamental principles: the dictatorship of the proletariat, party leadership, the socialist line, and Marxism-Leninism and the Thought of Mao. Thus, no one knew how long the new state of greater relaxation and freedom would last.

"Economics in Command": Removal of Opponents and Introduction of "New Blood"

The Fifth Plenum of the Eleventh Central Committee (February 23–29, 1980) marked the end of the transitional period from Mao's death to the meteoric rise of Deng as the most powerful figure in Chinese politics. The party rejected Mao's "politics in command" for Deng's "economics in command" hoping to turn China into an advanced nation by the year 2000. Any activity or person deemed unsympathetic to this course would be curtailed or removed. Thus, though divergent views were allowed to a degree, acts of dissidence such as posters on "Democracy Wall" attacking the government were not tolerated. Wei Jingsheng, leader of the democratic movement, was sentenced to fifteen years' imprisonment, and several of his associates were also severely penalized. The government and the party were fearful that the delicate stability might be disturbed by too large a dosage of unaccustomed freedom, but they were willing to allow some creativity, initiative, and enthusiasm that the new national goals generated. Their compromise resulted in a "restrained democracy" with moderate controls.

The trend toward eliminating dissension was not limited to Democracy Wall. Four Politburo members who were lukewarm or unsympathetic toward Deng and his policy were relieved of their high party and government posts. Three of them were linked to the Cultural Revolution: Wang Dongxing (a party vice-chairman and formerly Mao's chief bodyguard), Wu De (former mayor of Beijing), and Ji Dengkui (vice-premier).

Deng Xiaoping, vice-chairman of the party and main architect of China's new order.

The fourth, General Chen Xilian, was formerly head of the Beijing Military Region.

On the other hand, two more of Deng's dynamic protégés were appointed to the Politburo Standing Committee—Zhao Ziyang, an effective party first secretary in Sichuan, and Hu Yaobang, Deng's right-hand man in party affairs. Hu also became head of the newly re-organized party Secretariat in charge of the party's daily affairs. Four other Deng supporters were appointed to the Secretariat: Fang Yi (vice-premier and Academy of Sciences president), Yu Qiuli (vice-premier and head of the State Planning Commission), Peng Chong (veteran cadre), and Yang Deze (vice-minister of defense and chief of staff of the Armed Forces, a post now vacated by Deng).

Meanwhile, the rehabilitations that so benefited Deng continued. To clear the name of the former Chief of State Liu Shaoqi, who was disgraced and discredited along with Deng during the Cultural Revolution, the party resolved that he be posthumously restored to honor. On May 17, 1980, a national

Hu Yaobang, party general secretary, 1981–86.

memorial service was held, and Liu was praised as a great proletarian fighter. The occasion was viewed as a negation of the values of the Cultural Revolution and a denial of Mao's infallibility.

From the personnel changes it was apparent that the new party line was to introduce "new blood" at the highest level. To this end the party approved Deng's idea of a "collective leadership" capable of carrying on the party line irrespective of the fate of the present leaders.

Hua's Resignation from the Premiership

At the Third Plenum of the Fifth National People's Congress (August 29–September 10, 1980) the Dengists rose to the pinnacle of power. Deng had long urged separating party and government functions as well as ending lifelong appointments to cadres. The Congress approved his reorganization plan, initiating an orderly transfer of power to a collective leadership of relatively young pragmatists committed to modernization regardless of the fates of Deng and other aging leaders.

Hua graciously submitted his resignation as premier and nominated Zhao Ziyang as his successor. Deng and six other vice-premiers resigned for reasons of old age, other important appointments, or "voluntary" withdrawal. In the first category, apart from Deng, were Li Xiannian and Chen Yun, both seventy-five; Defense Minister Xu Xiangqian, seventy-eight; and Wang Zhen, a party military official, seventy-three. The second category included Wang Renzhong, who was also party minister of propaganda; and among those who withdrew "voluntarily" was Chen Yonggui, sixty-five, an illiterate model-peasant hand-picked by Mao and Zhou as the party's "token peasant" vice-premier.

As these resignations had been discussed in advance, their announcement aroused no surprise. What made news was the undiscussed appointment of three new vice-premiers: Foreign Minister Huang Hua, sixty-four; Minister of Nationality Affairs Yang Jingren, seventy-four; and General Zhang Aiping, seventy, the deputy army chief of staff. With these appointments,

Premier Zhao Ziyang, 1981–87.

the total number of vice-premiers dropped from eighteen to fourteen. These new appointees were not particularly young and continued to hold their party positions. Five vice-chairmen of the People's Congress whose ages ranged from seventy-nine to eighty-eight resigned, but Ye, eighty-two, remained chairman of the Standing Committee of the Congress. Thus the principles of Deng's reorganization were not strictly followed. Hua's report on the personnel reshuffle, his last as premier, was warmly applauded by the 3,000 Congress delegates.

It should be noted that the National Congress was only concerned with government appointments. Those who retired or resigned did not lose their party positions. Hua remained chairman of the Central Committee and of its Military Commission; and Deng still held his party vice-chairmanship, and the four former vice-premiers, their seats on the Politburo. With Zhao as premier and Hu as party general secretary, the pragmatists were in firm control of both government and party. For the first time an orderly transfer of power seemed to have been achieved while the incumbents were still healthy, creating a precedent which might avoid the wrenching political turmoil and uncertainty of the past.

Deng believed the new system would perpetuate his policies of modernization while ridding the country of its tendency toward political cultism. In this regard, he had a broader perspective than Mao and seemed to be more anxious to solve the succession problem. Mao's revolutionary romanticism gave way to Deng's pragmatic nation-building in a new political order born of a new historical situation. Hua saw this and gracefully relinquished the premiership and his status as the successor to Mao. Further changes would surely unfold during the next party plenum in mid-1981.

With the emergence of a new order in the post-Mao era, China was to be run by a collective leadership that consisted of a group of pragmatic administrators with proven records of success. As former party first secretary in Sichuan (1975–80), Zhao Ziyang had achieved an economic miracle by lifting Sichuan from chaos to relative prosperity in four years— raising industrial output by 81 percent and grain output by 25 percent, and creating 600,000 new jobs. He encouraged private plots, sideline handicraft work, free markets, pay according to work, and greater autonomy for local industries. Zhao's executive vice-premier, Wan Li, formerly party first secretary in Anhui, had won fame for his farm modernization programs there. Zhao and Wan were expected to put their experience to work on a national scale, combining market forces with the planned economy of socialism. Zhao asserted that so long as the principles of public ownership of the means of production and pay according to work were maintained, any structure, system, policy, or measure that promoted production was acceptable. He said, "We must not bind ourselves as silk-worms do within cocoons. . . . All economic patterns which hold back development of production should be abolished." Such pragmatism reflected the new spirit of the government, anxious to make up for lost time.

THE DEMYSTIFICATION OF MAO

During the last fifteen years of his life, Mao, the Chinese "Lenin and Stalin combined," was sanctified as an all-knowing, all-wise demigod who could do no wrong. Millions waved the "Little Red Book" of quotations from Chairman Mao, chanting its passages like magic formulas that could turn defeat into victory. It was an incredible cult of personality that surpassed even Stalin's. The wonder was not so much that Mao permitted it, but that 900 million believed in it. Perhaps they really didn't, but for a time they surely acted as if they did.

Once Mao was dead and the Gang of Four smashed, Mao's image quickly became tarnished. His responsibility for the rise of the Gang was common knowledge; yet no one dared to debunk him as Khrushchev had Stalin. Leaders gingerly invoked Mao's sayings of the 1950s to refute his later policies, but de-Maoification had to be handled with care because Hua, until the 1977 Party Congress had confirmed his status, derived the legitimacy of his position largely from Mao's patronage. Hua honored Mao's legacy in order to consolidate his own position while reinterpreting Mao to suit his need in the changing times and circumstances.

The foremost question facing the nation was how to deal with the question of Mao's responsibility for China's recent ills. Before any answers could be offered, the party had elevated Zhou Enlai to a position of near-parity with Mao, ending the solitary eminence of the Great Helmsman. Zhou's wife, Deng Yingchao, was appointed to a vice-chairmanship of the National People's Congress. That Mao's wife was in jail and Zhou's in high honor symbolized a national consensus reflecting the demystification of Mao.

The first year after Mao's death witnessed a growing sense of relief and a movement toward a new beginning. The structural references introduced by Mao or the Gang apparently no longer fit the realities of life where stability, unity, discipline, and economic progress were the new order. The revolutionary rhetoric and cultural intolerance which had rendered China an intellectual desert of artistic insipidity gave way to some degree of relaxation and freedom of expression. The cultural straightjacket dictated by the Gang (e.g. that China needed only eight model operas, or "more knowledge means more reactionism") was now condemned as absurd and counterproductive. Beethoven, Mozart, and Shakespeare, once symbols of "bourgeois decadence and running dogs of imperialism," reappeared in mid-1977; so did the works of the great Tang poets Li Bo and Tu Du, "products of the feudal past." In September 1977, colleges and universities which had suffered frequent interruptions during the Cultural Revolution began to admit students through competitive entrance examinations based on academic performance rather than on political "redness," and the mandatory two-year rural apprenticeship was dropped. For the first time in a decade, China had a normal freshman class, which graduated in 1981.

In industry worker participation in management was no longer the first priority; professional personnel were installed wherever possible. To reward productivity, wages of workers were increased and material incentives used to boost work enthusiasm. The principle "from each according to his ability, to each according to his work" was adopted. State Planning Commission Chairman Yu Qiuli said: "We must combat the situation in which no one accepts responsibility. We must struggle against anarchism."[11] It was a direct slap at Mao's cultural revolutionary values.

With the rehabilitation of Deng in July 1977, Mao's desanctification was accelerated. First by indirect and later by open criticism, Mao's pedestal was chipped away. At the Eleventh Party Congress in August, Hua declared an end to the Cultural Revolution in contradiction of Mao's assertion that cultural revolution was a continuing process to be renewed every seven or eight years. Deng emphasized discipline and hard work to advance modernization: "There must be less empty talk and more hard work." The "empty talk" of the Cultural Revolution had offered no concrete improvements, and Deng's "economics in command" triumphed as the new line.

By mid-1978 Mao's demigod status was questioned in public. An article in a historical journal remarked that even the most farsighted and resourceful of historical figures should not be considered gods.[12] The *Renmin Ribao* [People's Daily] chided some for treating Marxism-Leninism and the Thought of Mao as objects of faith rather than as knowledge: "They make this a blind faith and do not allow people to use their brains, much less to discern truth from falsehood. Marxism is a philosophy and not religious dogma."[13] Deng needed to loosen the country from the grip of Maoist strictures in order to launch his own program of rapid modernization, which was a revolution in itself, albeit of a different nature.

On July 1, 1978, the fifty-seventh anniversary of the founding of the Chinese Communist Party, a speech made by Mao in 1962 was reprinted to show that he confessed to mistakes and an ignorance of economic planning, industry, and commerce: "In socialist construction, we are still acting blindly to a very large degree. . . . I myself do not understand many problems in the work of economic construction . . . [or] much about industry and commerce. I understand something about agriculture but only relatively and in a limited way. . . . When it comes to productive forces, I know very little."[14] The underlying message could not have been more clear—Mao was not an omniscient deity, but a fallible human being.

The second anniversary of Mao's death, September 9, 1978, passed without observance. Shortly after, the Red Guard, a symbol of Mao's support of the Cultural Revolution, was dissolved; both the "Little Red Book" and Mao's quotations on newspaper mastheads disappeared. On October 8 the "cult of Mao" was attacked in the *Renmin Ribao* [People's Daily]: "The proletarian leaders are great but their greatness has a commonplace origin and it does not descend from heaven. To describe them as kinds of deities is to render to them the

greatest insult. . . . For many years such superstition circum-
scribed the minds of some people, and they still need to have
their minds emancipated."[15]

Throughout the second half of 1978 wall posters and articles
continued to criticize Mao's mistakes, implying a concerted
effort to demystify him and to erode his image as a god-hero.
Increasingly the editorials of the *Renmin Ribao* [People's
Daily] referred to Mao as comrade rather than chairman, and
criticisms of his role in the Cultural Revolution—now dubbed
"Ten Years of Great Catastrophe"—became more pronounced.
A Tianjin wall poster entitled "Spanking the Tiger's Hips"
accused Mao of killing millions of people, of launching the
Antirightist Movement (1957) which hurt hundreds of thousands of intellectuals, of prematurely creating communes
(1958) thereby causing the starvation of millions, and of supporting the Gang of Four at the expense of senior cadres. A
poster in Hangzhou decried Mao's involvement in the Korean
War which drained scarce national resources, the Great Leap
Forward which caused economic chaos and famine, and the
Cultural Revolution which set the country back in every
sphere.[16]

Deng's two principles, "Practice is the sole criterion of truth"
and "Seek truth from facts," struck at the very heart of the
Thought of Mao. Actually, verification of truth through practice is Marxist theory; and Mao's thought, until successfully
practiced, could only be theory, not truth.[17] Mao himself had
said: "We must believe in science and nothing else, that is to
say, we must not be superstitious. . . . What is right is right
and what is wrong is wrong—otherwise it is superstition."[18]

A poster displayed on November 22 in front of Tian An Men
Square entitled "Five Questions" applied Deng's slogans to
Mao's achievements:

> We do not question the great achievements of Chairman Mao,
> but that does not mean he did not make mistakes. Let's ask:
>   1. Without Mao's support, could Lin Biao have risen?
>   2. Is it possible that Mao did not know Jiang Qing was a
> conspirator?

3. Is it possible that Mao did not know Zhang Chunqiao was a conspirator?

4. Without Mao's support could the Gang of Four have launched the "Antirightist deviationist wind to reverse past verdicts" campaign and dismissed Comrade Deng Xiaoping?

5. Without Mao nodding his head, could the Tian An Men Incident be judged antirevolutionary?

Mao was a human, not a god. We must ascribe to him the status he deserved. Only so can we defend Marxism-Leninism and the Thought of Mao. Without an accurate understanding of Mao, freedom of speech is empty talk. It is time for all Chinese to shake off the shackles on their thoughts and behavior.[19]

In the application of Deng's precepts to Mao's actions and in the invocation of Marx and early Mao to refute later Mao, a clever way of demystifying Mao was discovered, one which also undermined the position of those whose political lives depended upon his status.

Deng told foreign visitors that such wall posters were a "normal thing," a "safety valve for the anger of the masses."[20] The anger was apparent, as in one poster which stated that assessments of those responsible for the Cultural Revolution had to be made; to say that Mao was "correct in 70 percent and incorrect in 30 percent" was to shield him, for his mistakes were much greater than people realized.[21]

Deng conceded that some restraint was needed to insure stability; still it was clear that there was a conscious effort to strip Mao down to human size. One by one his deeds were undone. Yao Wenyuan's article, "Comment on The Dismissal of Hai Rui," whose publication was directed by Mao and his wife and considered the first shot of the Cultural Revolution, was condemned in November 1978. The verdict that the Tian An Men Square Incident was counterrevolutionary was reversed to read revolutionary. Peng Dehuai, the defense minister purged in 1959, and Tao Zhu, party propaganda chief purged during the Cultural Revolution, were posthumously rehabilitated. In January 1979 the widow of Liu Shaoqi[22] reappeared in public after ten years of detention foreshadowing the rehabilitation of her husband. At Liu's memorial service on May 17, 1980, Deng called him a "communist saint"—a far cry from his previous designation as a "communist traitor." The rehabilitations of Peng and Liu were clear negations of the Great Leap Forward and the Cultural Revolution.

In September 1979 the third anniversary of Mao's death passed unnoticed. By spring of the following year, most of Mao's portraits in public places had been removed, as had the billboards bearing his quotations at street intersections. In March 1980 the party posthumously attacked Mao's secret service head, Kang Sheng. By mid-year Mao's treasured models of production, the Dazhai agricultural commune and the Daqing oil field, lost their "paragon model" status—Dazhai was declared a failure and Daqing inefficient and unscientific. Even Yenan, Mao's revolutionary cradle (which the author visited in May 1980), was left in a state of benign neglect. It was preserved as a revolutionary shrine of the past while current attention was being focused on the Four Modernizations and their success in the future.

These acts of de-Maoification were outer manifestations of an intense continuous debate within the party over the quality of Mao's leadership and over the assessment of his responsibility. The party had scrutinized Mao's thought in light of "truth according to facts" and, due to his failure to modernize China during his twenty-seven-year rule, gave him an "abstract affirmation but a concrete negation." On the other hand, the "Whateverists"—those who obeyed whatever Mao ordered—still carried Mao's banner and wanted to place revolution in command of modernization. To them, "truth according to facts" was just another of Deng's clever slogans intended to cut down Mao's banner.

Yet the Maoist method was widely viewed as inadequate to meet current challenges. The Deng line, as expressed by the president of the Chinese Academy of Social Sciences, called for the blending of socialist and capitalist ways:

> Only when we merge the superiority of the socialist system with the advanced science and technology of the developed

capitalist countries and their advanced managerial experience, only when we combine what is useful in foreign experience with our own specific conditions and successful experience can we . . . speed up the tempo of the Four Modernizations.[23]

While disagreement over Mao's waning reputation continued, the speech delivered by Marshal Ye on the thirtieth anniversary of the People's Republic on October 1, 1979, was a measured indictment of Mao's leadership and misgovernment:

Of course, the Mao Zedong Thought is not the product of Mao's personal wisdom alone; it is also the product of the wisdom of his comrades-in-arms, the party, and the revolutionary people. Mao himself had said: "It is the product of the collective struggle of the party and the people."

Surveying the history of the past thirty years, Ye made clear the mistakes committed by the party under Mao's guidance:

Amidst the immense victories we became imprudent. In 1957, while it was necessary to counterattack a small group of bourgeois rightists, we made the mistake of enlarging the scope [of attack]. In 1958, we violated the principle of carrying out an in-depth investigation, study, and examination of all innovations before giving arbitrary direction, being boastful, and stirring up a "communist storm." In 1959, we improperly carried out the struggle against the so-called right opportunism within the party.

Ye charged that the Cultural Revolution was "the most severe reversal of our socialist cause since the establishment [of the People's Republic] in 1949." Then, pointedly, Ye announced:

Leaders are not gods. It is impossible for them to be free from mistakes or shortcomings. They should definitely not be deified. We should not play down the role of the collectives and the masses; nor should we indiscriminately exaggerate the role of individual leaders.[24]

In this way the party renounced the personality cult of Mao and moved him from the lofty status of demigod to the humble one of human. Still, an important issue remained unresolved: how far the criticism of Mao should go. In February 1980 Ye made an impassionate plea against a complete repudiation of Mao:

> We can pass resolutions to admit our party's mistakes. We can clear the name of Liu Shaoqi and give him a very high and positive assessment. But we should not reject Mao and dig too deeply into our own cornerstones. . . . The Soviets removed Stalin's tomb, and we whip the corpse of Mao. Wouldn't that prompt people to ask, what is right with socialism and what is good about communism? We can occasionally slap our own faces, but we cannot, nor do we have time to, start from scratch. Those who opposed Mao were not necessarily all wrong, just as those who supported him were not necessarily all right. His opponents and his supporters were all his followers. Was it right or wrong to follow him? Who elevated Mao to such heights and who gave him so much power? Was it the people of the entire country? It was given by the party, the party center, and the army under the leadership of the party. . . . If we want to trace the responsibility to the end, we will find that it lies not with Mao alone. It lies with all of us.[25]

Some took exception to Ye's reasoning, insisting that there was no reason for the party or the people to assume the responsibility of mistakes committed by a single leader. At a time when the country was seeking truth from facts and studying the principle "Practice is the sole criterion of truth," a candid assessment of Mao seemed imperative.[26] Yet Ye's sentiments of moderation were shared by a large segment of party members, especially those in rural areas and those who had joined the party during or after the Cultural Revolution who accounted for half of the 38 million members. They were opposed to harsh criticisms of Mao; he was, after all, human and not a god. Complete repudiation of him would risk negating the party itself.

The central leadership appeared ready to assess Mao's career, but the provinces were more hesitant. To many grass roots party members it was inconceivable to reject the late chairman when a gentle critique would suffice. However, party General Secretary Hu Yaobang made it clear in June 1980 that Mao's thought and economic principles were incompatible with the new historical situation in China.

Certainly, the party would neither deny Mao's contributions nor hide his mistakes, especially his part in the Cultural Revolution, the "decade of great catastrophe." An official assessment of Mao was to be made at the party meetings in mid-1981. Meanwhile, volume five of Mao's *Selected Works,* edited by Hua, was to be revised, implying dissatisfaction with the editor and with his selections. Thus, not only the position of Mao but also that of his anointed successor Hua hung in suspense. The true issues of the post-Mao era appeared to be the three mutually supportive and, indeed, inseparable ones which dominated the period: China's new line, the ascendence of Deng Xiaoping, and the demystification of Mao Zedong.

The de-Maoification of politics was bound to continue as the influence of the thrice-resurrected Deng and his policies for China's modernization began to be felt in more aspects of Chinese life. Deng's leadership in directing the Four Modernizations would be critical in determining China's future successes.

NOTES

1. Such as General Xu Shiyou and Wei Guoqing, both Politburo members; Xu was also commander of the Guangzhou Military Region, and Wei, party first secretary in Guangtong.
2. *Renmin Ribao* [People's Daily], March 19 and 30, 1977. The two letters dated October 10, 1976, and April 10, 1977. For contents, see Richard C. Thornton, "The Political Succession to Mao Tse-tung," *Issues & Studies,* XIV:6:47 (June 1978).
3. Thornton, p. 47.
4. "Communiqué of the Third Plenary Session of the Tenth CCPCC," *Hongqi* [Red Flag], No. 8, 1977, p. 6.
5. Hua supporters: Ma Li in Guizhou, Xu Jiadong in Jiangsu, Mao Zhiyong in Hunan, and Song Ping in Gansu.
6. Ye supporters: Su Zhenhua in Shanghai, Tie Ying in Zhejiang, Wang Enmao in Jilin, and Liu Guangtao in Heilongjiang.
7. Deng supporters: Wan Li in Anhui, Huo Shilian in Ninghsia,

Jiao Xiaoguang in Guangxi, An Pingsheng in Yunnan, and Tan Qilong in Qinghai.
8. Thornton, pp. 47–49; *Hongqi* [Red Flag], No. 8, 1977, pp. 7–8.
9. The breakdown of the three groups was approximately as follows:

The Hua Group	*The Ye Group*	*The Deng Group*
Hua Guofeng	Ye Jianying	Deng Xiaoping
Wang Dongxing	Li Xiannian	Xu Shiyou
Chen Xilian	Xu Xianggian	Wei Guoqing
Wu De	Nie Rongzhen	Peng Chong
Ji Dengkui	Su Zhenhua	Liu Bocheng (old, sick)
Li Desheng		Ulanfu
Chen Yonggui		Geng Biao
Ni Zhifu		Yu Qiuli
Zhang Tingfa		Fang Yi
TOTAL 9	5	9

10. Official Beijing figures quoted in *Central Daily News,* June 30, 1979.
11. Quoted in *The New York Times,* June 19, 1977.
12. *The Christian Science Monitor,* April 27, 1978.
13. Quoted in *The New York Times,* May 17, 1978.
14. *Renmin Ribao* [People's Daily], July 1, 1978, p. 3. Tr. mine.
15. "Science and Superstition," *People's Daily,* Oct. 2, 1978. Tr. mine.
16. Quoted in *Central Daily News,* Aug. 5 and 8, 1978.
17. Marx said in his "Theses on Feuerbach": "The question whether objective truth can be attained by human thinking is not a question of theory but is a practical question. It is in practice that man must prove the truth, that is, the reality and power, the temporal nature of his thinking. The dispute over the reality or unreality of thinking which is isolated from practice is a purely scholastic question." See the article, "Practice is the Sole Criterion of Truth," *People's Daily,* May 12, 1978.
18. "Science and Superstition," *Renmin Ribao* [People's Daily], Oct. 2, 1978.
19. Reprinted in *Central Daily News,* Jan. 3, 1979. Tr. mine.
20. *Los Angeles Times,* Dec. 2, 1978.
21. *Central Daily News,* Jan 3, 1979.
22. Wang Guangmei.
23. Hu Qiaomu, "Observe Economic Laws, Speed Up the Four Modernizations," *Peking Review,* No. 45, Nov. 10, 1978, p. 11; see also No. 46, Nov. 17, 1978; No. 47, Nov. 24, 1978.
24. Ye Jianying, "Speech Celebrating the 30th Anniversary of the Founding of the People's Republic of China," *Renmin Ribao* [People's Daily], Sept. 30, 1979. Tr. mine.

25. Reprinted in *Central Daily News*, April 30, 1980. Tr. mine.
26. Statement of Liao Hansheng, political commissar of the Shenyang Military Region.

FURTHER READING

Burns, John P., and Stanley Rosen (eds.), *Policy Conflicts in Post-Mao China* (Armonk, N.Y., 1986).

Bush, Richard C., "Deng Xiaoping: China's Old Man in a Hurry," in Robert B. Oxnam and Richard C. Bush (eds.), *China Briefing, 1980* (Boulder, 1980), pp. 9–24.

Chang, Parris H., "The Rise of Wang Tung-hsing: Head of China's Security Apparatus," *The China Quarterly*, 73:122–137 (March 1978).

Chi, Hsin, *Teng Hsiao-ping: A Political Biography* (Hong Kong, 1978).

Ching, Frank, "The Current Political Scene in China," *The China Quarterly*, 80:691–715 (Dec. 1979).

Ch'iu, Hungdah, "China's New Legal System," *Current History*, 79:458:29–32, 44–45 (Sept. 1980).

Cohen, Jerome Alan, "China's Changing Constitution," *The China Quarterly*, 76:794–841 (Dec. 1978).

Dittmer, Lowell, "Death and Transfiguration: Liu Shaoqi's Rehabilitation and Contemporary Chinese Politics," *The Journal of Asian Studies*, XI:3:455–79 (May 1981).

Goldman, Merle, "The Implications of China's Liberalization," *Current History*, 77:449:74–78, 86 (Sept. 1977).

Hua, Guofeng, "Report on the Work of the Government," *Beijing Review*, 27:5–31 (July 6, 1979).

Jain, Jagdish Prasad, *After Mao What? Army Party Group Rivalries in China* (Boulder, 1976).

Kuo, Warren, "The Political Power Structure in Mainland China," *Issues & Studies*, XIV:6:20–31 (June 1978).

Lampton, David M., "China's Succession in Comparative Perspective," *Contemporary China*, III:1:72–79 (Spring 1979).

————, "Politics in the PRC," in Robert B. Oxnam and Richard C. Bush (eds.), *China Briefing, 1980* (Boulder, 1980), pp. 25–37.

Lee, Leo Ou-fan, "Recent Chinese Literature: A Second Hundred Flowers," in Robert B. Oxnam and Richard C. Bush (eds.), *China Briefing, 1980* (Boulder, 1980), pp. 65–73.

Lieberthal, Kenneth, "Modernization and Succession in China," *Contemporary China*, III:1:53–71 (Spring 1973).

"Man of the Year: Visionary of a New China, Teng Hsiao-p'ing

Opens the Middle Kingdom to the World," *Time* Magazine, Jan. 1, 1979, pp. 13–29.

McDougall, Bonnie S., "Dissent Literature: Official and Nonofficial Literature in and about China in the Seventies," *Contemporary China*, III:4:49–79 (Winter 1979).

McGough, James P., (tr. and ed.), *Fei Hsiao-t'ung: The Dilemma of a Chinese Intellectual* (White Plains, N.Y., 1980).

Montaperto, Ronald N., and Henderson, Jay (eds.), *China's Schools in Flux: Report by the State Education Leaders Delegation, National Committee on United States-China Relations* (White Plains, N.Y., 1980).

Munro, Robin, "Settling Accounts with the Cultural Revolution at Beijing University, 1977–78," *The China Quarterly*, 82:304–333 (June 1980).

National Foreign Assessment Center, *China: A Look at the 11th Central Committee* (Washington, D.C., Oct. 1977).

"On Policy towards Intellectuals," *Beijing Review*, 5:10–15 (Feb. 2, 1979).

Pepper, Suzanne, "An Interview on Changes in Chinese Education After the Gang of Four," *The China Quarterly*, 72:815–824 (Dec. 1977).

——, "Chinese Education After Mao: Two Steps Forward, Two Steps Back and Begin Again," *The China Quarterly*, 81:1–65 (March 1980).

"Premier Hua Reports on the Work of the Government," *Beijing Review*, 25:9–13 (June 22, 1979).

Shambaugh, David L., *The Making of a Premier: Zhao Ziyang's Provincial Career* (Boulder, 1984).

Sullivan, Michael, *The Arts of China*, rev. ed. (Berkeley, 1978).

——, "Painting with a New Brush: Art in Post-Mao China," in Robert B. Oxnam and Richard C. Bush (eds.), *China Briefing, 1980* (Boulder, 1980), pp. 53–63.

Teng Hsiao-ping and the "General Program" (San Francisco, 1977).

"The Communiqué of the Third Plenum of the Tenth Central Committee of the Chinese Communist Party," full text in Chinese in *Hongqi* [Red Flag], 8:5–9, (1977).

Thornton, Richard C., "The Political Succession to Mao Tse-tung," *Issues & Studies*, XIV:6:32–52 (June 1978).

Wakeman, Frederic, Jr., "Historiography in China after Smashing the Gang of Four," *The China Quarterly*, 76:891–911 (Dec. 1978).

3

The Normalization of Relations between China and the United States

Following the Nixon visit to Beijing in 1972, there was a conspicuous lack of progress in Sino-American relations due to unfavorable conditions in both countries. In China the radical Gang of Four, experiencing the heights of their influence, were scheming to seize power in hopes of succeeding Mao; their line was firmly antiforeign and suspicious of any rapprochement with the capitalist Americans. In the United States recognition of China faltered on the Taiwan issue as Beijing insisted on the fulfillment of three conditions: (1) terminate diplomatic relations with the Republic of China on Taiwan, (2) abrogate the United States–Taiwan defense treaty of 1954, and (3) withdraw all American forces from Taiwan. In a global perspective, to accede to these conditions might be perceived as abandoning Taiwan and cast doubt on the credibility of American commitments to other allies. The Taiwan issue had become a mirror of America's international self-image, and thus its resolution took on added significance beyond the problems of normalization.

President Nixon was reportedly prepared to recognize Beijing, but was kept from doing so by the Watergate scandal. His political survival came to depend increasingly on the support of conservatives in Congress who opposed normalization, and the preservation of his presidency seemed far more urgent than the diplomatic recognition of China. He was too deeply mired in the fight for his political life to take action on China.[1]

After Nixon's resignation, interim President Gerald Ford was first immobilized by the debacle of Vietnam's collapse and then by his growing aspirations to seek election in 1976. Though in favor of normalization in principle, Ford, too, realized his need for conservative support and made no moves toward recognizing China. Jimmy Carter, Ford's successor, also favored normalization in principle, but his first year in office was occupied with the Panama Canal Treaties, Strategic Arms Limitation Talks with the Soviets (SALT II), Russian-Cuban activities in Africa, and the Middle East problems. These pressing issues required the support of the conservatives in Congress who often considered themselves "friends of Taiwan."

Indeed, Taiwan became a sensitive issue in American domestic politics standing tenaciously in the way of normalization. American public opinion opposed breaking relations with Taiwan, although it favored the recognition of China.[2] The problem before the United States became one of safeguarding Taiwan if normalization were to occur. Politicians agreed that if arms sales to Taiwan could continue, the United States would not appear to be abandoning a faithful ally, and this would minimize the questions of America's credibility and its commitments to other countries.

An easing of the domestic conditions in both countries was necessary before either would feel ready to move toward normalization. Ultimately, the breakthrough came largely as a result of changes in Chinese policy. These changes came in the form of subtle concessions for which three American presidents had waited for nearly seven years.

THE NORMALIZATION OF DIPLOMATIC RELATIONS

During the three years following Watergate and the resignation of President Nixon, the Chinese had frequently expressed impatience with the lack of progress toward normalization. President Carter saw no urgent reason to accommodate Beijing, especially when he could not seem to find an expedient solution to the Taiwan issue. However, he experienced increasing pressure from his national security advisor, foreign policy staff, and liberal Democrats to jettison formal ties with Taiwan in favor of recognizing China. Biding his time, Carter dispatched Secretary of State Cyrus Vance on an "exploratory mission" to Beijing, in reality a mission of "contact" without substance.

Vance's Visit

Vance was in China from August 21 to 25, 1977. Although he was the first high official of the Carter administration to visit China, the Chinese gave him a lukewarm reception—even the food at the welcoming banquet was unexceptional by Chinese standards, and the occasion was marked by the absence of any Politburo member.[3] Vance did, however, discuss a wide range of subjects with Foreign Minister Huang Hua, Deputy Premier Deng Xiaoping, and Chairman Hua Guofeng. On the issue of Taiwan, Vance suggested the establishment of an American embassy in Beijing and a liaison office in Taipei; but the Chinese rejected the idea, insisting on the fulfillment of the three conditions previously mentioned. The issue of continued American arms sales to Taiwan after normalization was not even discussed.[4] The Chinese would not commit themselves to a nonviolent method of liberating Taiwan, with Hua reaffirming: "Taiwan province is China's sacred province. We are determined to liberate Taiwan. When and how is entirely an internal affair of China, which brooks no foreign interference whatsoever."

To no one's surprise, Vance returned empty-handed. From the American perspective, the mission ventured little and gained little. With the Panama Canal Treaties before Congress for ratification, Washington saw no need for "hasty" action on China. The Chinese, however, considered Vance's visit a step backward in Chinese-American relations.

Brzezinski's Visit

If Vance's reception in China was less than effusive, the visit made by National Security Advisor Zbigniew Brzezinski (May 20–22, 1978) was a study in contrast. As Washington perceived in the Soviet paranoia of a Sino-American axis a powerful weapon for SALT negotiations, concessions to China were suddenly rendered "practical." Brzezinski's mission was to seek upgrading in Chinese-American relations. Before his departure from Washington, D.C., he declared openly that the United States wanted to expand relations with China and make progress toward full normalization. Washington also let it be known that it was ready to accede to the three Chinese demands, while expecting China not to take Taiwan by force and not to object to continued American arms sales to Taiwan after normalization. Thus the Chinese knew in advance of Brzezinski's mission and welcomed him warmly.

In Beijing, Brzezinski announced: "The president of the United States desires friendly relations with a strong China. He is determined to join you in overcoming the remaining obstacles in the way of full normalization of our relations." He remarked that the United States shared China's resolve to "resist the efforts of any nation which seeks to establish global or regional hegemony," adding that "neither of us dispatches international marauders who masquerade as non-aligned to advance big-power ambitions in Africa. Neither of us seeks to enforce the political obedience of our neighbors through military force."[5] The Chinese were delighted with Brzezinski's statements, which clearly maligned both the Russians and the Cubans while intentionally echoing China's own world view. They were all the more pleased because the timing of the visit, May 20, coincided with the inauguration of Chiang Ching-kuo as president of the Nationalist government and was therefore considered a deliberate snub to Taiwan.

Brzezinski returned again and again to the themes of the Soviet threat to world peace and the shared interests of China and the United States in world affairs. Climbing the Great Wall he jested with the accompanying Chinese: "If we get to the top first, you go in and oppose the Russians in Ethiopia. If you get there first, we go in and oppose the Russians in Ethiopia." Having reached the top he joked again: "I was looking but I did not see the polar bear."[6] Such spontaneous but pointed antics were calculated to win the Chinese favor.

Brzezinski briefed the Chinese leaders on the status of SALT II and on the American views of the world situation in order to emphasize that the "long term strategic nature of the United States relationship to China . . . based on certain congruence of fundamental interests" was of an enduring nature. To demonstrate American sincerity, Brzezinski divulged to the Chinese the contents of two secret documents: Presidential Review Memorandum 10 (the U.S. assessment of the world situation), the Presidential Directive 18 (the president's security policy implementation plan). Other American experts consulted with their Chinese counterparts on defense, technology, and bilateral relations.

Although no public announcement was made on normalization, Brzezinski privately informed Hua and Deng that Ambassador Leonard Woodcock would be ready to begin serious negotiations to that end.[7] Satisfied with Brzezinski's visit, the Chinese called it "two steps forward." Later, a member of the Standing Committee of the National People's Congress[8] hinted that if the United States accepted China's three conditions, Beijing would not be likely to attack Taiwan and the normalization could materialize during the Carter administration.[9] Such a statement, though not an official one, seemed an indication of China's willingness to compromise on Taiwan in order to ensure American recognition. In Washington, the ratification of the Panama Canal Treaties cleared the way for President Carter to act more decisively on China.

Toward Normalization

In July 1978 the Carter administration sent an influential scientific and technological mission to China under the leadership of Dr. Frank Press, the president's advisor on science and technology. Dr. Press returned home in mid-July with the report that the Chinese had requested to send students to the United States immediately, rather than waiting for Washington to break relations with Taiwan as they had previously insisted. The Carter administration took this subtle concession as a sign of new flexibility on the part of Beijing.

On September 19 Carter received the new head of the Chinese Liaison Office, Ambassador Chai Zemin, and offered him a proposal for normalization on the basis of three conditions: (1) continued American commercial and cultural ties with Taiwan; (2) the American resolve that the Taiwan-China problem should be peacefully solved; and (3) continued American arms sales to Taiwan after normalization.[10]

In October Carter made his most important decision concerning normalization. Feeling politically secure after his success as a mediator in the Camp David peace talks between Egyptian President Anwar el-Sadat and Israeli Prime Minister Begin, the president decided he could finally afford to break America's commitments to Taiwan and set January 1, 1979, as the deadline for diplomatic recognition of China. It was calculated that by that time the Egyptian-Israeli treaty would have been signed, and in its euphoric wake any criticism of the handling of Taiwan would be defused.[11] On the other hand, if the Middle East agreement failed, a successful normalization with China would serve to assure the American electorate of Carter's statesmanship as a world leader. The president wanted to appear decisive, to use China to speed up the SALT negotiations with the Russians, and to outplay liberal advocates of China's recognition such as Senator Edward Kennedy.[12]

Woodcock, the former president of the United States Automobile Workers, was an experienced and skillful negotiator. In November he presented to the Beijing government the draft of a joint communiqué to which the Chinese responded by asking for certain clarifications. Then, unexpectedly, Deputy Premier Deng announced that he would like to visit the United States— a signal of his willingness to deal. On December 4, the Chinese presented their version of a joint communiqué, and on December 11 Deng was officially invited to the United States.

On December 13 Deng received Woodcock, who said, "Mr. Deputy Premier, I have in my pocket a short communiqué which I'm authorized to show you if you want to see it." Deng had the text translated instantly and responded, "We'll accept that. . . . We cannot accept that. . . . This is nicely put. . . . How about changing this part?"[13] The two met four times in the next two days, and on December 15 Deng said: "We will never agree to your selling arms to Taiwan, but we will set that aside in order to achieve normalization."[14] With this "agreement to disagree," the stage was set for a formal announcement of normalization.[15]

On December 15, 1978, a somber President Carter made a hastily arranged television appearance to announce that the United States and the People's Republic of China had agreed to establish full diplomatic relations on January 1, 1979, including the exchange of ambassadors and the establishment of embassies on the following March 1. The United States would break official relations with Taiwan and abrogate the 1954 Mutual Defense Treaty on January 1, 1980, in accordance with the treaty's termination provision that one year's advance notice was required. The president pledged that Taiwan "won't be sacrificed": the United States would continue to maintain commercial, cultural, and other relations with Taiwan through informal representatives, and the relationship would include arms sales. Then, with obvious exhilaration, he announced that Deputy Premier Deng would visit the United States in January 1979.

In announcing normalization, Carter cited the achievement of Presidents Nixon and Ford showing that normalization had been a bipartisan objective in hopes that conservative criticism would be minimized. Fortunately for him, the "China lobby" had waned so much that it could mount only a feeble protest to normalization. The majority of Americans, while regretting "dumping" the Nationalist government on Taiwan, found it hard to oppose the simple mathematics of the possibility of relations with 900 million people on mainland China compared with the 17 million on Taiwan.[16] In bringing normalization to fruition, Carter projected the image of a determined president and politically he gained more than he lost in popular support.[17]

Simultaneously in Beijing Chairman Hua called an unprecedented news conference for foreign and Chinese journalists to announce the normalization. He specifically pointed out that China did not like the continued American sales of arms to, and maintenance of cultural and commercial links with, Taiwan, but it would not let these issues stand in the way of normalization. "We can absolutely not agree to this. . . . The continued sale of arms to Taiwan by the United States does not conform to the principles of normalization and would be detrimental to the peaceful solution of the issue of Taiwan. . . . Nonetheless, we reached agreement on the joint communiqué."

The salient features of the joint communiqué are as follows:[18]

1. The United States of America and the People's Republic of China have agreed to recognize each other and to establish diplomatic relations as of January 1, 1979.
2. The United States recognizes the government of the People's Republic of China as the sole legal government of China. Within this context, the people of the United States will maintain cultural, commercial, and other unofficial relations with the people of Taiwan.
3. The United States and China reaffirm the principles agreed to by the two sides in the Shanghai Communiqué and emphasize again that:
   a. Both wish to reduce the danger of international military conflict.
   b. Neither should seek hegemony in the Asia-Pacific region or in any other region of the world and each is opposed to efforts by any other country or group of countries to establish such hegemony.
   c. Neither is prepared to negotiate on behalf of any thrid party or to enter into agreements or understandings with the other directed at other states.
   d. The United States acknowledges the Chinese position that there is but one China and Taiwan is part of China.
   e. Both believe that normalization of Sino-American rela-

tions is not only in the interest of the Chinese and American peoples but also contributes to the cause of peace in Asia and the world.
4. The United States and China will exchange Ambassadors and establish Embassies on March 1, 1979.

Separately, the United States issued a statement on Taiwan:[19]

1. On that same date, January 1, 1979, the United States will notify Taiwan that it is terminating diplomatic relations and that the Mutual Defense Treaty between the United States and the Republic of China is being terminated in accordance with the provisions of the Treaty. The United States also states that it will be withdrawing its remaining military personnel from Taiwan within four months.
2. In the future, the American people and the people of Taiwan will maintain commercial, cultural, and other relations without official government representation and without diplomatic relations.
3. The United States is confident that the people of Taiwan face a peaceful and prosperous future. The United States continues to have an interest in the peaceful resolution of the Taiwan issue and expects that the Taiwan issue will be settled peacefully by the Chinese themselves.

Obviously, the initiative for breaking the Taiwan issue came from China with Deng as the chief mover. Normalization would give him the success that had eluded Mao and Zhou, facilitate his visit to the United States, increase trade, and make available to the Chinese American science, technology, capital, and credit. In this light, Taiwan paled into relative insignificance. In any case, China was well aware it lacked the naval capacity to launch an attack on the island and was clearly too absorbed in the Four Modernizations to want a costly, nasty, and prolonged war over Taiwan. Accepting the status quo was expedient because it gave China an American recognition of its title to Taiwan, though not immediate possession of it.[20]

Beijing accepted the new view that China's relations with the United States were more important than Taiwan in the present world setting. The Soviet-Vietnamese treaty of November 1978 with its overtones of military alliance might have prodded the Chinese to seek a closer tie with the United States. Ironically, China's growing preoccupation with its two erstwhile allies may have prompted its rapprochment with its former enemies in the West. It is even possible that China was already contemplating a military confrontation with Vietnam over the worsening situation in Cambodia, and that it was counting on a friendly United States to deter Soviet involvement. At any rate, the Soviet press blasted away at China's motives in seeking American and Western connections.

Meanwhile, in Taiwan, the government had been given barely a few hours' notice of the normalization announcements. President Chiang bitterly vowed that his government would neither negotiate with the communist Chinese government nor compromise with communism. Some 2,000 angry people vented their wrath by besieging the American Embassy and burning the American flag.

In the United States, by contrast, responses were generally favorable. The *Los Angeles Times* editorialized, "No Sinful Sellout"; *The Christian Science Monitor,* "China: It Had To Come"; and *The New York Times,* "The Cost of Stalling on China."[21] The politicians, as usual, were divided: liberal Republicans and Democrats generally supported recognition, while conservatives such as former California Governor Ronald Reagan condemned it as a betrayal; Senator Barry Goldwater called it "one of the most cowardly acts by any president in history." Threatening to sue the president for violating the constitution in abrogating the Taiwan defense treaty, Goldwater insisted that legally the president must consult the Senate to terminate a treaty. Conservative opposition to recognition soon centered on Goldwater's legal action against the president.

Relations with Taiwan

To soften the blow to Taiwan, Carter sent a high-level delegation to Taipei on December 27, 1978, led by Deputy Secretary of State Warren Christopher.[22] He carried the message that despite the termination of formal relations, the United States hoped that trade and cultural ties would continue to expand. The Americans were greeted by 10,000 demonstrators who beat on the sides of the limousines, splashed red paint and hurled eggs, mud, and tomatoes. Other mobs trampled heaps of peanuts under their feet, to show their feelings about Carter by attacking the source of his family business.

President Chiang told the delegation that his government and people were enraged by Washington's failure to consult Taipei in advance of the agreement with Beijing. He insisted that future relations between Taiwan and the United States be conducted on a government-to-government basis, that his government be recognized as the one in actual control of Taiwan, and that it would continue to present itself as the legal government of China. The Americans, however, were only prepared to negotiate a framework for unofficial, nongovernmental contacts. Two days of attempts at talks ended inconclusively, and the delegation returned home with nothing resolved.

American ties with Taiwan were extremely complex. Apart from the defense treaty, the United States maintained fifty-nine lesser treaties and agreements with the government of the Republic of China. These protected the special relationship of the two countries in agricultural commodities, atomic energy, aviation, claims, controlled drugs, economic and technical cooperation, education, investment guarantees, maritime matters, taxation, and trade and commerce.[23]

American investment in Taiwan was considerable. Leading American corporations doing business in Taiwan included such giants as Bank of America, Chase Manhattan Bank, Citicorp, American Express, Ford, RCA, Union Carbide, Zenith, and Corning Glass. In 1978, 220 American corporations had over $500 million invested in Taiwan.[24] Taiwan enjoyed a brisk foreign trade of $23.7 billion in 1978, and a third of it ($7.3 billion) was American. Obviously, American economic ties with Taiwan could not be easily reduced; if anything, they were expected to continue to expand, regardless of withdrawal of diplomatic recognition. Japan's trade with Taiwan had grown 233 percent after it normalized relations with Beijing; Australia's, 370 percent; and Canada's, 539 percent.[25] Similar growth in

America's trade with Taiwan seemed a reasonable expectation. Regarding arms sales to Taiwan, the Pentagon prepared a sixty-page confidential document (Consolidated Guidance 9) which assessed Taiwan's military needs. It recommended that the United States continue military links with Taiwan to protect its armed forces from falling into disarray. Contracts already signed for spare parts and military equipment were to be honored, including a vast array of highly specialized bombs and missiles as well as more conventional equipment. The document called for accelerated arms sales to show Congress that the United States was not totally abandoning Taiwan. The Pentagon considered Taiwan able to repel an enemy attack as long as the United States provided air support, and continued arms and parts sales. With 500,000 men in its regular armed forces and a militia of 2 million, Taiwan's self-defense capabilities were ample though ultimately still dependent on the United States for its key weapons systems.[26]

After an initial spasm of angry outrage, Taiwan's leaders calmed down and weathered the political storm with dignity, dedication, and self-reliance. The sixty-eight-year-old President Chiang told his people on December 24, 1978: "We must undertake careful review, think things out soberly, and design our counter-measures with special calm and prudence to advance and carry out our policy and reach our goal."[27] Taiwan's leaders realized they could not afford to irritate the United States too much, for the American tie, albeit unofficial, was a vital one.

Since the American embassy in Taipei, and the Republic of China embassy in Washington were scheduled to close on March 1, 1979, it was imperative that substitute offices be designated to handle continuing relations. The Nationalist government struggled for some sort of official status, while the American negotiators insisted on unofficial relations. On February 15, 1979, it was finally agreed that there should be an American Institute in Taipei to replace the embassy and a Coordinating Council for North American Affairs in Washington, D.C., to take care of Taiwan's interests, with consulate-like branches in nine major cities. The American Institute would be staffed by "retired" State Department and other government personnel who would work without official titles.

Meanwhile, Congress produced a number of resolutions expressing concerns for the future of Taiwan. One offered by Senators Kennedy and Cranston directed the president to inform Congress of "any danger to the interests, concerns, and expectations of the United States in the peace, prosperity, and welfare of Taiwan," and to meet such danger "in accordance with constitutional processes and procedures established by law." On March 10, 1979, the Senate and the House overwhelmingly supported two slightly different versions of the legislation (the American-Chinese Relations Act, or the Taiwan Relations Act) ratifying the normalization of relations with China and approving the machinery for unofficial relations with Taiwan. The legislation spelled out American determination to maintain extensive relations with the people of Taiwan and "to consider any effort to resolve the Taiwan issue by other than peaceful means a threat to the peace and security of the Western Pacific area and of grave concern to the United States." Passing two versions of the bill necessitated a compromise by a joint conference committee, and the final bill was passed in the Senate (85 to 4) and the House (339 to 50) on March 28.

Beijing protested the language of the bill and charged that it treated Taiwan as if it were a sovereign state, even though all documents would be revised to refer to "the people of Taiwan" rather than the government. By Beijing's definition, "the people" included the "governing authorities on Taiwan." It also asked that the former Nationalist embassy in Washington, which had been turned over to a private organization called The Friends of Free China, and other holdings be designated the legal properties of the People's Republic of China.

In spite of China's dissatisfaction with the tone of the normalization proceedings, they had moved with surprising smoothness. There still remained the lawsuit of Goldwater and twenty-five associates challenging the constitutionality of Carter's termination of the Taiwan defense treaty. They won a favorable ruling from the United States District Court on October

17, 1979, but lost in both the Appeals and Supreme Courts, which ruled that the treaty termination in question was "nonjudicial and political in nature" and dictated by "a traumatic change in international circumstances."[28]

The Vietnamese Invasion of Cambodia

An unacknowledged but possible repercussion of normalization was the Vietnamese invasion of Cambodia under Soviet patronage. Relations between Vietnam and Cambodia had been deteriorating, and in November 1978 Vietnam and Russia had signed what was, in effect, a military alliance. The American announcement of recognition of China was followed ten days later by the Vietnamese invasion of Cambodia. On January 7, 1979, after a chillingly effective blitzkrieg of fifteen days, the Vietnamese forces took the Cambodian capital of Phnom Penh, destroying the Chinese-supported Pol Pot regime. Cambodia appealed to the United Nations Security Council for intervention while Beijing took the invasion as proof of Soviet hegemony in Asia and moved troops toward its border with Vietnam.

While a cause-and-effect relationship between American recognition of China and the Vietnamese invasion of Cambodia was impossible to prove, many secretly opined that normalization had goaded the Soviets and the Vietnamese into action against Cambodia.[29] China faced the difficult decision of how to deal with the aggressors. Deng's visit to the United States would surely help the Chinese assess the American position.

Deng's Visit

China's dynamic, diminutive Deputy Premier Deng Xiaoping flew into Washington, D.C., on January 28, 1979, for a nine-day visit. This being the first visit by a senior official from the People's Republic of China in thirty years, it warranted a more lavish and regal reception than Washington usually provided. Though ranked third on China's official protocol list, Deng was beyond doubt China's most powerful leader. Washington was anxious for him to see the country, to get a sense of its creativity and diversity, and to understand the important role Congress plays in the formulation of national policy. The administration secretly hoped that Deng would speak softly on Taiwan and not make statements irritating to the Soviets.

The first day after his arrival, Deng was officially welcomed on the White House lawn with a nineteen-gun salute and review of the honor guard. Hailing the visit as a "time of reunion and new beginnings" for the two countries, President Carter said; "It is a day of reconciliation when windows too long closed have been reopened." Deng was gracious in his response but would not let the occasion pass without a veiled attack on the Soviet Union: "The world today is far from tranquil. There are not only threats to peace, but the factors causing war are visibly growing." Following the formal welcome, the two leaders and their aides conferred privately for four hours.

At the White House dinner reception attended by hundreds of corporate executives, members of Congress, and other prominent Americans, Carter said: "We have a long-term commitment to a world of diverse and independent nations. We believe that a strong and secure China will play a cooperative part in that community." Deng's reply contained another oblique but unmistakable swipe at the Soviet threat to world peace: "In the joint communiqué on the establishment of diplomatic relations, our two sides solemnly committed ourselves that neither should seek hegemony and each was opposed to efforts by any other country or group of countries to establish such hegemony." Carter, somewhat ill at ease, smiled weakly over his guest's veiled references to Moscow.

After the glittering dinner party, the group moved to the Kennedy Center Opera House for an evening of American music and dance and the basketball wizardry of the Harlem Globetrotters. It was Deng, however, who was the evening's biggest hit. Charming performers and audience alike, he went on stage to shake hands and kiss the foreheads of the children in a choir very much in the style of an American politician running for office. Vice-President Mondale quipped, "It's a good thing you're not an American citizen, because you'd be elected to any office you sought."[30]

In meetings with senators and representatives, Deng took Capitol Hill by storm. On Taiwan he indicated that China no longer used the expression "liberation" but only "unification" with the motherland:

> Until Taiwan is returned and there is only one China, we will fully respect the realities on Taiwan. We will permit the present system on Taiwan and its way of life to remain unchanged. We will allow the local government of Taiwan to maintain people-to-people relations with other people like Japan and the United States. With this policy we believe we can achieve peaceful means of unification. We Chinese have patience. However, China cannot commit herself not to resort to other means.

This was reassuring to legislators like Senator Henry Jackson who would have preferred stronger assurances of nonviolence, but respected Deng's caution in exercising China's options.

As for the Soviet Union, Deng's criticism was stinging. Though not opposed to any strategic arms agreement the United States might reach with the Soviet Union, he stressed, "You can't trust the Russians," bringing nods of agreement from the lawmakers. When alone with newsmen Deng was more forceful in denouncing the Soviets, urging the formation of a common front between the United States, Japan, Western Europe, and China to block Russian expansion the world over. He condemned Soviet support of Vietnam's invasion of Cambodia and suggested that the United States denounce both of them, or at least the Vietnamese, those "Cubans of the Orient," who, Deng insisted, "must be taught some necessary lessons."

With respect to the most-favored-nation status for Chinese trade, Deng noted the Jackson-Vanik amendment, which denied such status to countries that did not permit free emigration, and said with a chuckle: "This is no problem to us. But do you really want 10 million Chinese (to move to the United States)?" This was met with a burst of laughter and perhaps some relief. No one could resist Deng's sense of humor.

Deng played the role of a goodwill ambassador superbly. He struck up a warm friendship with Carter and managed to charm Congress with his quick wit, humor, and controlled self-confidence. His adroit showmanship—shaking hands, hugging, kissing, beaming, laughing, and teasing—endeared him to the American public, persuading them that in a cowboy hat even a Communist was hard to hate. The Chinese people, via television satellite, followed Deng's every movement with pride and delight. The blunt, feisty, irascible man many reporters had portrayed was nowhere to be seen. Deng projected himself as a warm human being rather than as a fiery revolutionary. He made it clear that while China might be poor and backward, it was no international beggar. It needed foreign technology and capital but could also offer a rewarding market for American products. Partly because of Deng's captivating personality and mastery of mass psychology, and partly because of America's taste for the novel and tendency to glamorize new celebrities, Deng's striking success opened the mind and heart of America to the People's Republic of China.

Perhaps an equally constructive, if less tangible, part of the visit was Deng's personal observation of the workings of American democracy and of the operations of a modern economy. The executive branch, though powerful, had its limitations, and Deng witnessed Congress's distinct role in forming national policy. In visits to a Ford assembly plant, the Hughes Tool Company, and the Johnson Space Center, Deng saw the efficiency of American business operations which with space-age technology and hardworking employees could provide the clearly comfortable American standard of living. It is possible that much of what Deng learned could prove useful in shaping China's future.

Deng's key message to the United States—the Soviet threat and the need for a common front against it—received only a polite response. Clearly, the security concerns of the United States did not coincide exactly with those of China. In reality Deng's warnings alerted many Americans to the danger of being drawn inadvertently into undesirable situations. There were renewed calls for balanced relations with both China and the Soviet Union, not allowing either to maneuver the United States into a confrontation with the other.[31]

Deng himself was satisfied with the results of his trip. He and Foreign Minister Huang Hua signed three agreements with Carter and Vance on science and technology, cultural exchanges, and consular relations. The last permitted China to establish consulates in San Francisco and Houston, and the United States to do the same in Guangzhou and Shanghai. In a farewell message to Carter, Deng said that the visit was a "complete success" and expressed the belief that Chinese-American relations "will witness major progress under the new historical conditions." Deng's optimism was surpassed only by the excitement and hopes of the American and Chinese peoples, who could now view one another more freely and with open interest for the first time in thirty years.

The Chinese Invasion of Vietnam

On February 17, 1979, barely a week after Deng's return, a large Chinese invasion force struck into Vietnam. In name the invasion was in retaliation of numerous Vietnamese incursions into China, but in fact it was China's punishment for Vietnam's invasion of Cambodia and for its blatant ingratitude after it had accepted more than twenty-five years of Chinese assistance.

As early as 1950 Mao had offered Ho Chi Minh military, political, and economic aid—the famous battle of Dienbienfu (1954) was fought largely with Chinese weapons and under Chinese direction. During the height of American involvement in Vietnam (1964–71), China dispatched 300,000 technical personnel and troops to Vietnam to help in air defense, engineering work, railway construction, road repairs, and logistics supplies; some 10,000 of them lost their lives. Chinese economic aid to Vietnam between 1950 and 1978 totaled somewhere between $15–20 billion, which represented considerable Chinese sacrifice.[32]

For all these acts of friendship, China had expected Vietnam's gratitude and goodwill but received precious little once

Hanoi gained control over all Vietnam. Perhaps fearful of China's vast influence, Vietnam rejected its dependence on China and turned instead to the Russians for help. Gradually, increasing mistreatment of Chinese residents in Vietnam and of Vietnamese of Chinese descent was followed by a wave of persecution, and 160,000 of them were forced to flee. The crowning insult was Vietnam's conclusion of a Twenty-five-year Friendship and Mutual Defense Treaty with Russia, which served the Soviet purpose of encircling China and represented a stinging Vietnamese rejection of Beijing. China's patience was strained beyond tolerance by Vietnam's invasion of Laos and Cambodia, and the consequent collapse of the Chinese-supported Pol Pot regime.

During his stay in Washington, Deng openly spoke of "teaching the Vietnamese some necessary lessons," but he never specified the type of action China might take. Carter tried to dissuade him from military action but evoked no positive response; Chinese build-up on the Vietnamese border continued. On February 8, 1979, Moscow warned Beijing against "overstepping the forbidden line," and a few days later Vietnam called on "all friendly nations" to stop China from waging war against it.

The Chinese wanted a quick war—a repeat of their invasion into India in 1962—lightning success and rapid retreat before the Russians could decide on a proper response. It was a caluclated risk which Deng thought worth taking. With China's new international connections he anticipated no Soviet miiltary intervention. To calm world public opinion, China declared at the outset of the invasion that it would be a limited operation of short duration, with no design on Vietnamese territory.

The magnitude of the Chinese invasion, involving 250,000 troops and hundreds of tanks, fighter planes, and artillery striking in ten directions along a 450-mile front, suggested a well-prepared military operation. The Chinese forces advanced swiftly and successfully at first, taking four Vietnamese provincial capitals near the border by the end of a week.[33] However, their movement was soon slowed considerably, due largely to the lack of modern weapons. The Chinese had hoped to draw the enemy forces into a major battle and destroy them decisively, but the Vietnamese deliberately avoided a direct confrontation. Of Vietnam's 600,000 troops, about two-thirds were stationed in Cambodia and South Vietnam performing "occupation duties." Rather than risk the security of these areas by removing troops, Vietnam's plan was to employ only regional forces and militia to fight the Chinese, thereby preserving its best troops from annihilation.

As the war dragged on, the prospect for a quick Chinese success faded and the danger of Soviet retaliation increased correspondingly. In an apparent attempt to appease interna-

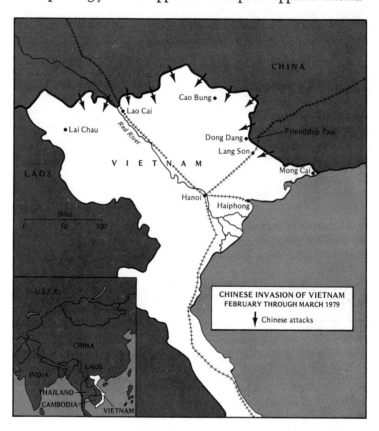

CHINESE INVASION OF VIETNAM
FEBRUARY THROUGH MARCH 1979

↓ Chinese attacks

tional worries about escalation and possible Soviet intervention, Beijing declared that it had no intention of attacking Hanoi. The world community remained concerned, and the United Nations Security Council called for Chinese withdrawal from Vietnam and Vietnamese withdrawal from Cambodia, though the potential of a Soviet or Chinese veto prevented the resolution's passage. The United States "regretted" the outbreak of war but considered its national interests unthreatened. It ruled out any use of force "except under the most extreme, compelling circumstances," meaning Soviet intervention. The Soviets mobilized troops on the Chinese border and Outer Mongolia called up reserve forces to put pressure on China, but there were no signs of imminent intervention.

On March 1 the Chinese proposed peace talks while stepping up their costly assault on Lang Son. There was a general belief, or even hope, that once the Chinese overran Lang Son, they could claim victory and return home. By March 2 the city was in utter ruins, and the Vietnamese abandoned it to take positions in the surrounding hills. The Chinese finally took Lang Son, but the victory was far from resounding. Rather, it was labored, protracted, and unspectacular—a far cry from the lightning blitz that the Chinese had dreamed of. By this time Cuba had offered to send troops to Vietnam, and Russia had warned China to halt its "brazen bandit attack" and evacuate Vietnam immediately. Having taken nearly all the important towns and provincial capitals in northern Vietnam, China declared its objectives fulfilled and called for a ceasefire.

The Vietnamese refused to acknowledge defeat, boasting that their best troops were still intact and capable of defeating any Chinese invasion. Moreover, they claimed that the Chinese had placed themselves in a no-win situation when they announced that the war was to be a short, limited operation. In an amusing but crude way, Hanoi said: "If the Chinese win, they lose. If they lose, they lose. If they withdraw, it is a Vietnamese victory." On March 5 Beijing announced the withdrawal of its troops after seventeen days of fighting, and on the following day Hanoi agreed to hold peace talks. By March 16 the Chinese had completed their withdrawal.

Western military experts wondered why China risked so much, including military confrontation with the Soviets, for so little. They failed to see that China felt both humiliated and betrayed in its rejection by a former supplicant of favors, and that the feeling of betrayal was exacerbated by Vietnam's growing arrogance toward China and other smaller neighbors, as well as by its alignment with Russia. Such open hostility, the Chinese felt, had to be dealt with, or China's credibility would be at stake. As Deng stated, China wanted to teach the Vietnamese that "they could not run about as much as they desired. . . . They controlled Laos, invaded Cambodia, signed a peace treaty with the Soviet Union that was essentially a military alliance, and encroached on Chinese soil as well." Deng also wanted to show the world that China did not fear war or the threat of Soviet intervention. Fortunately, his assessment of the situation turned out to be correct, and China gained some satisfaction in exposing the Soviet Union as a "paper tiger."

If China taught Vietnam a lesson, it also learned one: that China could not fight a modern war effectively without streamlining the military and that the economic consequences of war could be disastrous. In the seventeen-day operation, China sustained 46,000 casualties, lost 400 tanks and armored vehicles, and spent $1.36 billion. Draining the country's scarce resources had an immediate and adverse effect on the Four Modernizations, necessitating a cutback in the 1980 military budget by $1.9 billion. At the same time, the goal of scientific and technological modernization of the military became increasingly imperative.

THE NORMALIZATION OF TRADE
AND OTHER RELATIONS

The diplomatic recognition of China was followed by a series of negotiations for the normalization of commercial, cultural, scientific, and to some extent even military relations. China lacked the most-favored-nation status, making it extremely difficult for Chinese exports to the United States to be competitive. For Washington to grant China this status, it was necessary to settle the question of blocked American assets in China and of frozen Chinese assets in the United States.

Claims Settlement and the Trade Pact

The day after the American liaison office in Beijing became an official embassy on March 1, 1979, Treasury Secretary Michael Blumenthal, who had lived in Shanghai as a youth, initialed an agreement with Chinese Minister of Finance Zhang Jingfu settling the disputes of "frozen assets and blocked claims." The disputes dated back to the early years of the Korean War when in 1950, responding to China's entry into the war, President Truman froze $80.5 million in Chinese assets in the United States. China retaliated by seizing property in China owned by American churches, corporations, schools, and individuals valued at $196.9 million. In reality, the American property in question had been in Chinese hands since the establishment of the People's Republic in October 1949. There were 384 American claims, the largest coming from the Boise Cascade Corporation.

The agreement initialed in Beijing allowed China to retain the American property but pay $80.5 million to settle the total American claims—roughly 41 cents on the dollar. China was to pay $30 million on October 1, 1979, and the rest in installments of $10.1 million each October until 1984. For its part, the United States would "unfreeze" the $80.5 million in Chinese assets, but it was not known how much of it belonged to the Chinese government and how much to banks, corporations, schools, and individuals, both inside and outside of China. A noteworthy point, rarely seen in international settlements, was that the Chinese payment, though equal to the amount of the frozen assets, was not tied to them—American claimants would receive their reimbursements quickly. It appears to be a favorable agreement when compared with other such international settlements, and its compensations were more favorable than the Americans might have hoped for.[34]

The initialed accord had only to be officially signed by representatives of the two governments and was not subject to Congressional ratification. To sign the accord and to negotiate a new trade agreement, Washington sent Secretary of Commerce Juanita Kreps to China. On May 11, 1979, she signed the agreement on "frozen assets-blocked claims" with Chinese Finance Minister Zhang, finally settling the long-standing dispute.

The way was then clear for negotiating a trade pact that would grant each country most-favored-nation status, permitting businessmen to establish offices in each country, providing reciprocal protection for patents, trade marks, and copyrights, as well as enabling regulated banking transactions. Each of these issues required detailed discussion, and it was only on the last day of Kreps' visit that an agreement was reached and initialed.

Two months later the trade agreement was signed, but Congressional approval was delayed due partly to a fear of an influx of Chinese textiles. To soothe Chinese irritation, Carter dispatched Vice-President Walter Mondale to China on a mission of explanation and goodwill.

Mondale in China

Mondale and his family visited China for eight days in August 1979 to reassure the Chinese of American friendship and to explain the delay in approving the trade agreement as due to a "logjam of congressional legislation." Mondale declared at the welcoming banquet: "If we strengthen our bilateral ties, we can both make dramatic economic progress, we can both enrich our cultures. . . . But above all . . . an enduring Sino-American relation will promote the stable international environment we both need to meet our domestic challenge and address problems of global concern."

In a major speech delivered at Beijing University and broadcast by the national Chinese television and radio networks, Mondale warned the Soviets and reassured China: "Any nation which seeks to weaken or isolate you in world affairs assumes a stance counter to American interests." He called for the withdrawal of Vietnamese troops from Cambodia and for an end to Vietnam's expulsion of its citizens as refugees—both declared prerequisites for American recognition of Vietnam.

Predictably pleased by Mondale's tone, what cheered the Chinese most were his assurances that the Carter administration would send the trade agreement to Congress by the end of the year before the Soviets could qualify for most-favored-nation status and that the United States would send experts to help build China's power dams while providing $2 billion in credit over a five-year period.

During the visit, Mondale signed two important agreements: a cultural exchange pact calling for the mutual reception of cinema and art delegations, film festivals, educational and athletic exchanges, as well as a visit to the United States by a Chinese delegation under Cultural Minister Huang Zhen; and an energy pact providing American assistance to China in developing twenty hydroelectric power stations, which required the cooperation of the Department of Energy, the Tennessee Valley Authority, and the United States Army Corps of Engineers.

In all, Mondale's visit was a productive one, and it was to the Americans' credit that they pursued normalization through hard times with the diligence and attention it deserved. Mondale's mission breathed new life into the delicately unfolding relations between the two countries. A few months later, Carter, as promised, submitted the trade agreement for congressional approval. On January 24, 1980, congressional ratification was obtained.

Final Agreements

On September 17, 1980, Chinese vice-premier and veteran economic expert Bo Ibo signed four agreements with President Carter in Washington. They related to the exchange of direct airline service, access to ports, the establishment of new consulate, and limited growth in Chinese textile exports to the United States.

Pan-American Airlines had long desired routes to China, but Beijing would not grant permission until the Chinese Civil Aviation Administration received similar rights in the United States. Until the settlement of the claims dispute, Chinese airplanes ran the risk of detention at American airports because any American claimant could sue and attach Chinese property that entered the United States. Now, with the new agreement, the two countries could formally initiate scheduled airline service for the first time in thirty years. Each country designated an airline to operate two round trips each week on a route including New York, San Francisco, Los Angeles, Honolulu, Tokyo, Shanghai, and Beijing, with a second airline to be added by each in two years.

The marine agreement permitted each nation to call at designated ports (fifty-five American and twenty Chinese) and specified evenly divided cargo ratios: one-third in Chinese ships, one-third in American ships, and one-third in ships of other nationalities. The consular treaty, subject to confirmation by the Senate, allowed China to open three new consulates (New York, Chicago, and Honolulu) and the United States also three more in China. It provided ground rules for the consulates and protection for the citizens of each country.

The textile agreement allowed Chinese exports to the United States to grow (3–4 percent each year for three years) above the unilateral quota set up by the United States in May 1979. It covered six categories of cotton garments and synthetic sweaters but not cloth. The new pact would raise the current level of American textile imports from China (7.2 percent) to one comparable to those of Hong Kong, Taiwan, South Korea, and Japan.

With the signing of these agreements, the long process of normalization which began in December 1978 was finally complete. Official Chinese-American relations reached a state of normalcy close to the pre-1949 level. Renewed diplomacy and trade symbolized American support of a modern, secure, and outward-looking China. Moreover, the United States was prepared to offer for sale to China high technology that had potential military implications.

Brown's Visit

In January 1980 Secretary of Defense Harold Brown went to China for a nine-day visit. Although the trip was arranged before Mondale's mission, it occurred at the time of the Soviet invasion of Afghanistan and hence took on added military significance. In Beijing, Brown seemed more eager than his hosts to develop some kind of security relationship in the face of the Soviet threat. At a banquet on January 6, he openly accused Moscow of overthrowing a friendly government in Afghanistan and executing its president and his family. Brown declared that Sino-American defense cooperation "should remind others that if they threaten the *shared interests* of the United States and China, we can respond with *complementary actions* in the field of defense as well as diplomacy."[35] Brown and Deng got along famously in their mutual mistrust of the Soviets. When Brown suggested that the two countries should coordinate their policies in the face of the Soviet threat, Deng went further proposing a world alliance to block Russian expansion.

As head of the American defense establishment, Brown was expected to offer China some military technology. The United States had stated repeatedly that it would not sell arms to China, but it had indicated a willingness to sell high-technology of dual application (civilian and military)—indeed, all technology at some point has military implications. Brown agreed to furnish China with a receiving station for data transmitted by the Landsat-D satellite, which can gather information about crops, oil, gas, and mineral exploration, and, of course, military information from space. In addition, the United States agreed to provide China with powerful computers for oil exploration. Obviously, the Carter administration had decided to quicken and to expand the transfer of high-technology equipment and skills to China.

To assess China's military capability and the state of its technology, Brown inspected the sixth tank division outside Beijing and watched an air show which featured the famous 38th Air Force Division. Four jets climbed steeply into the sky and then swooped down from a strafing run against dummy targets, showing considerable professional skill but also the limitations of the dated aircraft, copies of the MIG 19.

The Chinese air force reflected the military technology of the 1950s, as did the submarine and shipyard which Brown inspected in Wuhan. But in a few isolated areas Chinese achievements were quite advanced. The highly secret intercontinental missile, CSS-X-4, with a range of 6,000 miles (Beijing to Moscow or the United States' west coast) was not shown to Brown. In May 1980 it was tested successfully with two flights from western China to the Pacific.

China's limited capacity to pay for, as well as to absorb, high technology made for cautious selectivity in buying foreign hardware. Fearful of being overly dependent on one nation, the Chinese spread their purchases among several nations, including Britain, France, and West Germany, as well as the United States.

While military modernization was one of the Four Modernizations, and while the Chinese brass craved a technological revolution in the military, finance limited what could be acquired. The Third Plenum of the Fifth National Peoples' Congress (September 1980) cut the military budget in the larger interests of economic rehabilitation, and only a modest program of acquiring sophisticated weapons and technology could be pursued.

However, if the American "tilt" toward China continued, a closer Sino-American military relationship might be accommodated. Several highly secret "contingency" studies had been made in the United States including the L-32 and Consolidated Guidance No. 8 which projected the emergency stationing of American warplanes in China and the arming of the Chinese at a total cost of $50 billion.[36]

Arms Sales

Sino-American relations took on a new dimension with the Reagan administration's decision to reverse the policy of refusing to sell arms to China. The decision was a result of a critical reassessment of the global strategic position of the United States and a pragmatic recognition that the United States could not stand alone but needed the cooperation of China, Japan, and Europe in order to check the Soviet expansion. In a demonstration of anti-Soviet resolve, President Reagan dispatched Secretary of State Alexander Haig to China in June 1981 to discuss possible military coordination and to offer arms for sale on a case-by-case basis pending Congressional approval and consultation with American allies. The Chinese were gratified to find that Haig shared their perception of the Soviets: attempts at arms control and détente with the USSR were both disagreeable and futile.

The decision on arms sales had greater political than military significance, for it restored the momentum in Sino-American relations and strengthened Washington's anti-Soviet stance. The Chinese were hardly able to purchase large quantities of expensive arms; they seemed to be more interested in acquiring the technology to make the weapons themselves.

A Sino-American military relationship would develop slowly and cautiously at first, but when credits were made available to China later it might progress to something mutually beneficial. China was already performing valuable services by pinning down a quarter of the Soviet forces on the Siberian border and by contributing to a general stability in the Asia-Pacific area. In addition, it seemed that some secret American-Chinese military cooperation had been in motion since the 1980 construction of two spy stations in northwest China. The stations utilized sophisticated American equipment to electronically monitor Soviet missile tests and other military activities, as well as to gather intelligence data. These stations had replaced those the United States lost in Northern Iran after the collapse of the Shah's government. Perhaps more importantly, a closer tie with China gave the United States the psychological security of having one billion people on its side, while China gained a strengthened shield against Soviet attack. As long as Chinese and American interests vis-à-vis the Soviet Union continued to coincide, an improved military relationship appeared to benefit both nations.

It is impossible to sum up the vast benefits of normalization so soon—they continued ad infinitum, depending on one's interests and political persuasion. There were, however, benefits so basic that they were equally appreciated by all. First and foremost, a stable China was in the best interests of the United States and of world peace. In spite of great concern for Taiwan's security, the island after normalization appeared to be in no great danger of a forceful takeover than before the mainland was recognized. China's repeated calls for the unification of Taiwan with the mainland had reduced the frenzied tension many felt. The expansion of cultural ties enabled China to carefully choose the models for and means of modernization while opening wide the vast store of Chinese wisdom, skills, and arts, both traditional and modern, to an interested and appreciative America. Improved accessibility to advancements in Western technology and science would ease China's "New Long March" toward the Four Modernizations, while the expanding, if limited, market for American goods came at a time when the United States needed to increase its exports. And finally, a well-equipped Chinese military might well safeguard what remained of Asian peace, while the Sino-American connection spelled relief for the world from the vacillations of the Soviet-American polarity, with a new, more balanced triangle of power.

NOTES

1. Warren I. Cohen, *America's Response to China: An Interpretative History of Sino-American Relations,* 2nd ed. (New York, 1980), p. 244.
2. *The New York Times,* Dec. 15, 1978, p. 8.
3. *The Wall Street Journal,* Aug. 23, 1977.
4. According to Deputy Premier Deng Xiaoping, *The Christian Science Monitor,* Sept. 8, 1977, p. 3.
5. *The New York Times,* May 21 and 24, 1978.
6. *The Christian Science Monitor,* May 24, 1978.
7. Martin Tolchin, "How China and the U.S. Toppled Barriers to Normalization," *The New York Times,* Dec. 18, 1978, p. A12.
8. Chen Yisong.

9. *The Christian Science Monitor,* May 31, 1978.
10. Tolchin, p. A12.
11. Fox Butterfield, "After Camp David, Carter Set a Date for China Ties," *The New York Times,* Dec. 18, 1978, p. A12.
12. *Ibid.*
13. Takashi Oka, "Leonard Woodcock in China: Listening to the Unspoken," *The Christian Science Monitor,* April 2, 1980, p. B11.
14. *Ibid.*
15. Throughout the secret negotiations only five people in Washington, D.C., knew about them: Carter, Vance, Brzezinski, Defense Secretary Harold Brown, and Hamilton Jordan, the president's de facto chief-of-staff and top political advisor. In the Beijing American Liaison Office, only Woodcock and one other knew about them. The Washington group, however, was supported by Richard Holbrook, Assistant Secretary of State for East Asia and Pacific Affairs, Michel Oksenberg, National Security Specialist in the Far East, and Herbert J. Hansell, a State Department legal advisor.
16. The Gallop poll showed 58 percent approved the President's action and 24 percent disapproved, with 18 percent no opinion. *The New York Times,* Jan. 14, 1979.
17. Stanley D. Bachrack, "The Death Rattle of the China Lobby," *Los Angeles Times,* Dec. 20, 1978.
18. The Department of State, Selected Documents No. 9: *U.S. Policy Toward China, July 15, 1971–January 15, 1979,* Office of Public Communication, Jan. 1979, pp. 45–46.
19. *Ibid.,* p. 48.
20. Linda Mathews, "Is the U.S. About to Take a Dragon by the Tail?" *Los Angeles Times,* Feb. 11, 1979.
21. *Los Angeles Times,* Dec. 26, 1978; *The Christian Science Monitor,* Dec. 18, 1978; *The New York Times,* Dec. 20, 1978.
22. Accompanied by legal advisor Herbert Hansell and Commander-in-Chief of U.S. Forces in the Pacific, Ad. Maurice Weisner.
23. *The New York Times,* Dec. 18, 1978, p. A10.
24. Ross Terrill, *The Future of China* (New York, 1978), p. 201.
25. Department of State News Release, Dec. 1978, "Diplomatic Relations with the People's Republic of China and Future Relations with Taiwan," Office of Public Communication, p. 3.
26. *The New York Times,* Dec. 17, 1978, p. 23.
27. *Los Angeles Times,* Dec. 25, 1978.
28. On October 1, 1979, U.S. District Court Judge Oliver Gasch ruled that President Carter acted unconstitutionally in terminating the pact: He must "receive the approval of two-thirds

of the United States Senate or a majority of both houses of Congress . . . to be effective under our Constitution"; furthermore, the President could recommend treaty termination but the final decision could not be made by him alone. See *Los Angeles Times,* Oct. 20, 1979; *The Christian Science Monitor,* Nov. 14, 1979.

29. CBS radio broadcast by Marvin Kalb, Jan. 9, 1979.
30. *U.S. News & World Report,* Feb. 12, 1979, p. 26.
31. Marvin Stone, " 'No' to a China-U.S. Axis," *U.S. News & World Report,* Feb. 12, 1979, p. 88.
32. *Central Daily News,* Taipei, July 31 and Dec. 7, 1979; Oct. 15, 1981.
33. Lao Cai, Lai Chau, Cao Bang, and Mong Cai.
34. Anthony M. Soloman, "When 41¢ on the dollar is a good deal," *The Christian Science Monitor,* March 28, 1979. Mr. Soloman was Undersecretary for Monetary Affairs, U.S. Treasury. A similar settlement with the USSR was 12 cents on the dollar; with Hungary, 30 cents; with Poland and Rumania, 40 cents.
35. Italics added.
36. Jack Anderson, "U.S. 'Tilt' toward Peking Risks Soviet Reaction," *Santa Barbara News Press,* Sept. 28, 1980.

FURTHER READING

Alexiev, Alex, "Prospects for Accommodation," *Contemporary China,* III:2:36–46 (Summer 1979).

"An Interview with Teng Hsiao-p'ing: Calling for Stronger U.S.-China Ties and a United Front against Moscow," *Time* Magazine, Feb. 5, 1979, pp. 32–33.

Barnett, A. Doak, "Military-Security Relations between China and the United States," *Foreign Affairs,* LV:3:584–597 (April 1977).

Bellows, Thomas J., "Normalization: Process and Prognosis," *Sino-American Relations,* V:3:11–21 (Autumn 1979).

Butterfield, Fox, and William Safire, "China: Unraveling the New Mysteries," *The New York Times Magazine,* June 19, 1977, pp. 32.34, 48–59.

———, "After Camp David, Carter Set a Date for China Ties," *The New York Times,* Dec. 18, 1978, p. A12.

Chang, Jaw-ling Joanne, *United States–China Normalization: An Evaluation of Foreign Policy Decision* (Denver, 1986).

Chay, John (ed.), *The Problems and Prospects of American-East Asian Relations* (Boulder, 1977).

Ch'iu, Hungdah (ed.), *Normalizing Relations with the People's*

Republic of China: Problems, Analysis, and Documents (University of Maryland, School of Law, Occasional Papers, 1978).

Cohen, Jerome Alan, "A China Policy for the Next Administration," *Foreign Affairs*, LV:1:20–37 (Oct. 1976).

Cohen, Warren I., *America's Response to China: An Interpretative History of Sino-American Relations*, 2nd ed. (New York, 1980).

Copper, John Franklin, *China's Global Role* (Stanford, 1981).

Davies, John Paton, "America and East Asia," *Foreign Affairs*, LV:2:365–94 (Jan. 1977).

Department of State, "Diplomatic Relations with the People's Republic of China and Future Relations with Taiwan" (Washington, D.C., Dec. 1978).

————, *U.S. Policy Toward China, July 15, 1971–January 15, 1979*, Selected Documents No. 9, Office of Public Communication (Washington, D.C., 1979).

Folgel, Joshua A., and William T. Rowe (eds.), *Perspectives on a Changing China: Essays in Honor of Professor C. Martin Wilbur* (Boulder, 1979).

Garrett, Banning, "The China Card: To Play or Not to Play," *Contemporary China*, III:1:3–18 (Spring, 1979).

————, "Explosion in U.S. China Trade?" *Contemporary China*, III:1:32–42 (Spring 1979).

Gurtov, Melvin, "China Invades Vietnam: An Assessment of Motives and Objectives," *Contemporary China*, III:4:3–9 (Winter 1979).

Harris, Lillian Craig, "Provocation and Polemic: Sino-Soviet Relations in 1978," *Contemporary China*, III:2:15–24 (Summer 1979).

————, "China and the Northern Tier: Shoring Up the Barrier to Soviet Southward Expansion," *Contemporary China*, III:4: 22–27 (Winter 1979).

Harrison, Selig S., *The Widening Gulf: Asian Nationalism and American Policy* (New York, 1978).

Hsiao, Gene T., and Michael Witunski, *Sino-American Normalization and Its Policy Implications* (New York, 1983).

Johnson, Chalmers, "The New Thrust in China's Foreign Policy," *Foreign Affairs*, LVII:1:125–37 (Fall, 1978).

Karnow, Stanley, "East Asia in 1978: The Great Transformation," *Foreign Affairs*, LVII:3:589–612 (1979).

Kim, Samuel S., *China, the United Nations, and World Order* (Princeton, 1978).

Kim, Se-jin, "American Moral Psyche in Political Perspective," *Sino-American Relations*, VI:1:8–18 (Spring 1980).

Larkin, Bruce D., "China and Asia: The Year of the China-Vietnam War," *Current History*, 77:449:53–56, 83 (Sept. 1979).

Lawson, Eugene K. *Sino-Vietnamese Conflict* (New York, 1984).

Lieberthal, Kenneth, "The Foreign Policy Debate in Peking, as seen through Allegorical Articles, 1973–76," *The China Quarterly,* 71:528–54 (Sept. 1977).

Luttwak, Edward N., "Against the China Card," *Contemporary China,* III:1:19–31 (Spring 1979).

Martin, Edwin W., *Southeast Asia and China: The End of Containment* (Boulder, 1977).

Mendl, Wolf, *Issues in Japan's China Policy* (London, 1978).

Middleton, Drew, *The Duel of the Giants: China and Russia in Asia* (New York, 1978).

Nagorski, Andrew, "East Asia in 1980," *Foreign Affairs,* LIX:3: 667–95 (1980).

Nathan, Andrew J., "Prospects for Sino-American Relations and the Effects on Korea," *Contemporary China,* II:4:14–22 (Winter 1978).

Okita, Saburo, "Japan, China and the United States: Economic Relations & Prospects," *Foreign Affairs,* LVII:5:1090–1110 (Summer 1979).

Oksenberg, Michel, "China Policy for the 1980s," *Foreign Affairs,* LIX:2:304–22 (Winter 1980/81).

———, and Robert B. Oxnam, *Dragon and Eagle: United States-China Relations: Past and Future* (New York, 1978).

Ray, Heman, *China's Vietnam War* (New Delhi, 1983).

Rothenberg, Morris, "The Kremlin Looks at China," *Contemporary China,* III:2:25–35 (Summer 1979).

Scalapino, Robert A., "Asia at the End of the 1970s," *Foreign Affairs,* LVIII:3:693–737 (1979).

———, "Chinese Foreign Policy in 1979," in Robert B. Oxnam and Richard C. Bush (eds.), *China Briefing, 1980* (Boulder, 1980), pp. 75–85.

Segal, Gerald, "China and the Great Power Triangle," *The China Quarterly,* 83:490–509 (Sept. 1980).

Solomon, Richard H., "Thinking Through the China Problem," *Foreign Affairs,* LVI:2:324–56 (Jan. 1978).

Stuart, Douglas T., and William T. Tow (eds.), *China, The Soviet Union, and the West: Strategic and Political Dimensions for the 1980s* (Boulder, 1981).

Sutter, Robert G., *Chinese Foreign Policy after the Cultural Revolution, 1966–1977* (Boulder, 1978).

———, *China-Watch: Towards Sino-American Reconciliation* (New York, 1978).

———, *Chinese Foreign Relations: Development After Mao* (New York, 1986).

Terrill, Ross, "China and the World: Self-Reliance or Independence," *Foreign Affairs*, LV:2:295–305 (Jan. 1977).

———— (ed.), *The China Difference* (New York, 1979).

————, "China in the 1980s," *Foreign Affairs*, LVIII:4:920–35 (Spring 1980).

Tretiak, Daniel, "China's Vietnam War and Its Consequences," *The China Quarterly*, 80:740–67 (Dec. 1979).

Yu, George T. (ed.), *Intra-Asian International Relations* (Boulder, 1978).

4

The Four Modernizations

If there was such a thing as a national consensus in China, it focused on the commitment to the Four Modernizations—of agriculture, industry, science and technology, and national defense. The avowed goal was to turn China into a relatively modern state by the year 2000. The Four Modernizations had been written into the party constitution (Eleventh Congress, August 18, 1977) and the state constitution (Fifth National People's Congress, March 5, 1978); hence the program should not be affected by changes in leadership. Yet, while modernization was the "general mission of a new historical period," an objective shared by Deng, Hua, Ye, and other leaders of both party and state, questions concerning its scope, timetable, and practical implementation were causing much heated debate.[1]

Zhou Enlai was generally credited with initiating the idea of the Four Modernizations in a report to the Fourth National People's Congress in January 1975. Actually, industrialization as the foundation of socialism was a Leninist principle which the Chinese Communists implemented as soon as they achieved power: more than one-half of China's total investment in the 1950s was allocated to industrial development. In 1963 Mao called for the "building of a modernized socialist power"; and it was in response to this call that Zhou proposed, at the Third National People's Congress, December 1964, the socialist construction of a "modernized agriculture, industry, national defense, and science and technology" to be accomplished "within a not too long period of history."[2] However, no concrete action followed due to the onset of the Cultural Revolution.

In January 1975, Zhou renewed his call for an "independent and relatively comprehensive industrial and economic system" by 1980, and an overall modernization of the four sectors before the end of the century. This speech, Zhou's last before a national congress, was generally considered the basis of the current Four Modernizations. Again, little came from it due to the obstruction of the Gang of Four, which condemned modernization as a "road to capitalist restoration." Too sick to fight, Zhou did not risk a confrontation with Mao's wife.

Zhou's chief ally, Deng Xiaoping, was not one to yield easily, however. In the fall of 1975 he drafted three key documents which later served as blueprints for the Four Modernizations.[3] These works were branded by the Gang as "Three Poisonous Weeds," and Deng became the prime target of the "Antirightist Deviationist Wind" Campaign. Deng fought a losing battle as long as the Gang had Mao's support; in his 1976 New Year's Message, Mao warned the nation against overemphasizing material progress.[4] Deng dropped out of sight after delivering Zhou's eulogy on January 15, 1976, and was dismissed from all posts after the Tian An Men Incident in April.

Not until the smashing of the Gang in October were the Four Modernizations revived. Chairman Hua seized the opportunity to promote them in a spirit of revolutionary vigor but without much economic expertise. In the months that followed (as Deng's rehabilitation was being negotiated), acceleration of the Four Modernizations was approved. In May 1977, at the "Learn from Daqing for Industry National Conference," veteran party economist Yu Qiuli declared:

Within the decade (1976–1985) we shall first erect a comparatively complete independent industrial system covering the entire country and accomplish fundamental technical renovation of the national economy. From this foothold we shall establish, step by step, six economic systems of different levels, in the Northeast, Northwest, and Southwest, and in North China, East China, and South Central China. Each shall have its unique features, be capable of independent operations, and exert maximum efforts for the development of agriculture, light industry and heavy industry.[5]

After Deng was formally reinstated, he delivered the closing address at the Eleventh Party Congress in August 1977, stressing the primacy of modernization. As a way to promote the cause, a National Science Conference and a Military Political Work Conference were called in the following spring. At these meetings increasing differences of opinion were revealed between Hua and Deng; the former stressed the use of revolutionary spirit to guide modernization, while the latter emphasized hard work and detailed planning within accepted economic laws.[6] Nonetheless, the two shared a final vision of "electricity in rural areas, industrial automation, a new economic outlook, and greatly enhanced defense strength" by the close of the century.[7]

THE TEN-YEAR PLAN

At the first session of the Fifth National People's Congress in February 1978, Chairman Hua unveiled a grandiose ten-year modernization program for 1976–85; as two years had already passed, it was actually an eight-year plan. It detailed the major goals to be achieved in the four sectors.

The Industrial Sector

Investment for capital construction in industry was to equal or surpass that of the entire previous twenty-eight years, which was estimated at US$400 billion, and the annual rate of industrial growth was set at 10 percent. Hua called for the completion of 120 major projects, including: 10 iron and steel complexes, 10 oil and gas fields, 30 power stations, 8 coal mines, 9 nonferrous metal complexes, 7 major trunk railways, and 5 key harbors. It was hoped that by the end of the century Chinese industrial output in the major sectors would "approach, equal, or outstrip that of the most developed capitalist countries."[8]

Steel. In 1952 steel production (1.35 million tons) had already surpassed the pre-Liberation peak, and it rose to 18.67 million tons by 1960. The Great Leap cut the output back to 8 million tons in 1961, and the Cultural Revolution provided further inhibitions. It was not until 1970 that steel production recovered, reaching 25.5 million tons by 1973. Yet production decreased again under the Gang of Four—in 1976 only 21 million tons were produced. In short, from 1960 to 1976, only small gains were achieved.

The Ten-Year Plan called for increased production to 60 million tons by 1985 and 180 million tons by 1999. To achieve such major increases, a giant steel complex at Jidong (eastern Hebei), capable of producing 10 million tons a year, was planned under contract with German firms at a cost of $14 billion; a six-million-ton complex was to be constructed at Baoshan (a suburb of Shanghai) under contracts with Japanese firms with an estimated initial cost of $2 billion. A number of other sizable plants were to be built elsewhere, and existing plants were to be renovated.

Oil. Before 1957 China's petroleum production was insignificant (1.46 million tons of crude oil per year). Vast advances were made in the 1960s, with new discoveries and the establishment of the Daqing Oil Field in Manchuria, the Shengli Oil Field in Shantong province and the Dakang Oil Field in the Tianjin harbor area. Crude output doubled between 1960 and 1965 and again by 1969. By 1978 it had reached 104 million tons. The Ten-Year Plan called for the construction of ten new oil and gas fields costing $60 billion.[9]

Coal. Coal provided 70 percent of China's primary energy supply, but most of the mines were small and antiquated. The Ten-Year Plan called for eight new mines along with the renovation of existing ones in hopes of doubling production to

900 million tons a year. This meant an annual growth rate of about 7.2 percent compared with 6.3 percent in 1970–77.

Electric Power. Surprisingly, the production of electricity was the weakest link in the modernization plan. In 1978 production totaled 256.6 billion kilowatt hours, ranking China ninth in the world in electricity production, but per capita consumption remained extremely low below both India and Pakistan. The Ten-Year Plan called for the construction of thirty power stations, twenty of them to be hydropower. The largest projects included the 2.7 million kilowatt Gezhouba hydropower station on the Yangtze River near Yichang (Hubei) and the 1.6 million kilowatt Longyang Gorge station on the upper reaches of the Yellow River near Sining (Qinghai). The thirty new plants would increase production by 6 to 8 million kilowatts per year—far short of the 13–14 percent growth rate needed to sustain the goal of a 10 percent annual increase in industry, and leaving nothing with which to increase personal consumption.

The Agricultural Sector

Agriculture was the foundation of the Chinese economy. It supplied 70 percent of the country's industrial raw materials, 60 percent of its total exports, and 80 percent of its domestic consumer goods.[10] Yet, since 1949, agriculture had consistently received less investment than industry and defense. Collectivization and the commune did not materially raise agricultural production. The 1963 movement "In agriculture, learn from Dazhai" was nothing more than a propaganda gimmick, and the Cultural Revolution drove agriculture to the brink of bankruptcy. On August 8, 1977, *Renmin Ribao* [People's Daily] frankly stated that "whenever farms are hit by disastrous natural calamities, drastic reduction in output resulted; in the event of smaller disaster, smaller reduction; even with perfect weather conditions there was not much increase."[11] A Chinese leader admitted that "in 1977, the average amount of grain per capita in the nation was the same as the 1955 level; in other words, the growth of grain production was only about equal to the population growth plus the increase in grain requirements for industrial and other uses."[12] In October 1978 Deng remarked that "only through an all-out effort to restore agriculture to normalcy and increase production quickly can the entire economy be assured of fast development." Agricultural modernization was vital to the success of the Four Modernizations.

When he announced the Ten-Year Plan, Hua called for maximizing farm production through mechanization, electrification, irrigation, and higher utilization of chemical fertilizers. Specifically, the targets included:

1. Increase of gross agricultural products by 4–5 percent annually.
2. Increase of food output to 400 million tons by 1985 (from 285 million tons in 1977, a 4.4 percent annual growth).
3. Mechanization of 85 percent of major farming tasks.
4. Expansion of water works to assure one good *mou* (one-sixth acre) of dependably irrigated land per farming capita totalling 800 million *mou* (121 million acres).
5. Establishment of twelve commodity and food base areas throughout the nation.

Some estimated that the plan's agricultural modernization would require: (1) 12 million 15-horsepower tractors; (2) 4 million powered farm tools; (3) irrigation and pumping facilities totalling 40 million horsepower; (4) 320,000 combines; (5) 400,000 trucks and power machines; (6) 8 billion kilowatt hours of electricity; and (7) 66 million tons of chemical fertilizers.[13]

Such a vast undertaking would cost an estimated $33 billion. It would also require 2 million agricultural engineers and technicians, including 1.2 million mechanics to maintain tractors, combines, power tools and machines; 4 million to man pumping equipment; and 8 million truck drivers and farm products processing personnel. On the other hand, this mechanization of farm operations would release 100 million agricultural laborers to other lines of work. Relocating them and creating new job opportunities would cost $50 billion.[14] William Hinton, an American farm expert, questioned the wisdom of fast mechanization in China in view of the abundance of labor.[15]

To bolster the slow agricultural growth rate of 2 percent annually since 1957, the government laid down several new guidelines. The "production team," hitherto the basic accounting unit responsible for any surplus or deficit, was replaced by the larger "production brigade." Next, the principle "to each according to his work" was adopted to stimulate farm initiative and enthusiasm; hence "more pay for more work and less pay for less work" had become a basic rural economic policy. In addition, encouragement of household "sideline production" should work to supplement the larger economy. Rural families did not own the communally distributed "private" plots but had the right to farm them. They could not rent, sell, or transfer the land, but they did own its products. "Sideline" production made up some 25 percent of total agricultural and subsidiary production. Finally, it was hoped that through intensive development, commune- and brigade-operated enterprises would be able to support large industries and the export trade.

With 800 million people working on farms, it was imperative to resolve the manifold agricultural problems and thus loosen the bottleneck in China's economic development. Only so could the Four Modernizations expect to succeed.

Scientific Modernization

Science and technology were considered basic to successful modernization of the other three sectors. At the National Science Conference in March 1978, a Draft Outline National Plan for the Development of Science and Technology was presented by Vice-Premier Fang Yi, calling for: (1) achieving or approaching the 1970 scientific levels of advanced nations in various scientific and technological fields; (2) increasing professional scientific researchers to 800,000; (3) developing up-to-date centers for scientific experiments; and (4) completing a nationwide system of scientific and technological research. The Outline identified 108 items in twenty-seven fields as key projects for research.[16] It was hoped that by 1985 China would be only ten years behind the most advanced nations, with a solid foundation for catching up to the advanced nations by the end of the century.

To promote science and technology, the National Science and Technology Commission, inactive during the decade of the Cultural Revolution, was reactivated to formulate short-range (three-year), medium-range (eight-year), and long-range (to the year 2000) projects. Hua called for a "March on the Road of Science and Technology," and Deng personally appeared at the National Science Conference to set the tone for the new scientific attitude. Deng brushed aside the Maoist disdain for intellectuals and the "antirightist" bias; expertise was now preferred to "redness," and foreign-trained intellectuals, humiliated in the past, were treated as cherished patriots and as part of the proletariat. A new respect for their knowledge led to their reinstallment in important positions in universities and research organizations, and the younger and talented scientists and engineers were sent abroad for further studies. These intellectuals served as China's bridge with foreign scientific circles.

Military Modernization

China had the largest regular armed force in the world, numbering some 4,325,000. The army alone included 3,250,000 troops, and China's naval and air forces ranked third internationally in terms of numbers.[17] But, except for pockets of intensive development in the strategic sector (e.g. nuclear bombs and ballistic missiles), Chinese military technology remained some twenty to thirty years behind the West. Troops were well trained, highly motivated, and politically indoctrinated but equipped with woefully inadequate weapons. The situation, brought about by a lack of funds and by an underdeveloped technology, worsened with Mao's emphasis on spirit over weapons. His idea of "people's war," employing large numbers of politically motivated, well-trained guerrillas to harass and drive out the invader was primarily a defensive notion, lacking offensive punch. The unspectacular Chinese invasion of Vietnam in 1979 clearly illustrated this. Su Yu, a brilliant strategist and former chief-of-staff, stated that Mao's concepts had "seriously shackled the people's minds and obstructed the development of military ideas."[18]

With extensive Soviet aid in the 1950s, the Chinese built up a nearly self-sufficient defense-manufacturing industry, and some of their products (e.g. the AK-47 rifle) ranked among the world's best.[19] Yet, by and large, Chinese military technology was two or three decades out of date. Truly swift modernization would require massive purchases of foreign weapons and instruments; but that would be prohibitively expensive and also place China at the mercy of foreign suppliers. As the paramount consideration in China's long-term military planning was still the indigenous control of production capabilities, only selective purchases of high-technology systems and weaponry with special contracts for production in China were planned. The purchase of fifty British supersonic Spey jet engines, with plans for the engines to be manufactured in China with the assistance of Rolls-Royce, and the purchase of several thousand HOT antitank missiles from France, with similar production agreements, were examples of this cautious selectivity.[20]

Yet problems still existed—after the purchase of the Spey engine technology, Chinese metallurgical capabilities were found insufficient to produce the alloys needed for the engines.[21] In addition, both the Spey engines and the HOT missiles were prodccts of an already outmoded technology of the 1960s. Even the vertical takeoff *Harrier* purchased from Britain had a short-range, a low-speed, and a high accident rate that reflected the technology of a decade past.[22] While acquiring such equipment might prevent the technological gap from widening, "stop-gap" measures would not ensure the achievement of China's modernization goals.

Chinese experts had visited advanced military establishments in the West to witness the state-of-the-art military technology rather than to purchase it—China's defense needs were so vast and diverse as to defy the country's ability to pay for them. Still, the military sought to prepare the country for a "people's war under modern conditions" requiring "automatic computerized countdown, improved communications and command systems, and rapid, motorized, transportation facilities," with conventional as well as strategic weapons.[23] Under increasing pressure from the brass, Chinese leadership was leaning toward a compromise: "Serious effort should be made to implement the policy of integrating military with non-military enterprises and peacetime production with preparedness against war, and fully tap the potential of the machine-building and national defense industries."[24]

Chinese leaders recognized the urgent need to update obsolete equipment on a massive scale but also saw its astronomical cost. Although China's defense budget was a state secret, Western estimates put it at $32.8 billion in 1976, the third largest globally.[25] A British source put China's 1978 defense spending at 7–10 percent of the GNP, or about $35 billion.[26] The production of new equipment, spare parts, and maintenance accounted for 58 percent of that figure. To modernize fully even a portion of China's military would cost an impossible $300 billion by 1985.[27] Since such an expenditure would require massive infusions of foreign capital and equipment, military modernization occupied a low priority. While modernizing science and technology would eventually benefit the military, it was clear that military modernization would be a highly selective and slow process.

The ultimate irony might be that after straining to acquire current state-of-the-art technology and weaponry, it would take the Chinese five to ten years to integrate such modern equipment into existing structures. It would be imperative to upgrade research and development in laser, metallurgy, optics, communications, and computers; to prepare the scientific-managerial infrastructure for research development, and production; as well as to train military personnel to use, maintain, repair, and refurbish the new equipment. By that time new strides would have been made in the more advanced countries, and China would yet remain behind by ten to fifteen years. While this would represent an improvement over present capabilities, it would have to be seen as falling short of true modernization goals.

MAJOR PROBLEMS OF MODERNIZATION: CAPITAL, MANPOWER, AND PLANNING

The most serious problems in China's modernization were the shortages of investment capital and of qualified personnel. Success of the Four Modernizations was dependent on the resolution of these two basic problems. The Ten-Year Plan would cost somewhere between $350 billion and $630 billion;[28] China's gold and foreign exchange reserve (1978–79) was only $4.5 billion.[29] According to an American estimate, China's GNP in 1978 was $407 billion.[30] Assuming a 5.5 percent annual growth rate, the GNP for 1978–85 would generate $3,956 billion (in 1977 price); if 10 percent of this were allocated for developmental investment, China could conceivably raise $400 billion from domestic savings, still leaving the nation with a shortfall of more than $200 billion.[31]

Past practices might shed light on China's financial stringency. During 1949–59, industrial investment totaled $46.2 billion: $10 billion came from confiscated properties of landlords and capitalists, $3 billion from Soviet credits and loans, and the rest from the difference between the state's low-price purchases of farm products and its high-price sales of industrial products to the farm sector. Of course, the first two sources no longer existed and the third had been severely damaged by the Cultural Revolution and the Gang. Hua reported, "Between 1974 and 1976, the influence of the Gang of Four caused losses worth $63 billion in industrial output and $25 billion in state revenue."[32] The Gang severely crippled the economy, and the consequences had continued to plague the country. In September 1978, an estimated 25 percent of state enterprises were operating in the red.

To raise capital for modernization, China had resorted to clearly un-Maoist methods. First, tourism had been vastly expanded, and the "lure of Cathay" was proving both irresistible to foreigners and highly profitable to China. In 1978, 100,000 foreigners and 600,000 overseas Chinese visited China. Tourism generated $607.2 million in 1980. To attract more foreign visitors, new hotels were being built, increasing the present room capacity of 30,000 to 80,000 by 1985.[33]

Second, China had devised innovative cooperative investment projects with foreign firms. For instance, Konrad Hornschuch AG of West Germany agreed to build two petrochemical plants in China at $21 million, with 50 percent of the first five years' production as payment. The Japanese firm Itoman & Company contracted to provide materials, equipment, and advice to a Shanghai textile plant in exchange for the right to market its line of products.[34]

Third, China had adopted a more flexible attitude toward foreign loans. Formerly, Beijing rejected foreign loans out of fear of foreign control; if a loan was negotiated it was euphemistically referred to as "progress" or "deferred" payments. But on December 6, 1978, China openly concluded a loan agreement with a British consortium of ten banks for $1.2 billion at a 7.25 percent interest rate; by mid-April 1979 some $10 billion in foreign loans and credits had been negotiated.[35] Generally, however, the Chinese remained reluctant to accept large, long-term loans, due to their limited ability to repay and to their historically founded fear of foreign domination.

In spite of these fund-raising devices, China's capital remained very limited, severely constricting the potential for rapid, large-scale importation of foreign equipment and high technology. Indeed, every step in the modernization process raised the problem of insufficient funds.

The shortage of qualified manpower was an equally serious handicap in China's modernization drive limiting the country's capacity to absorb the new technology. Between 1949 and 1966, Chinese higher education produced 1.8 million university graduates of whom at least one-half majored in sciences and engineering.[36] But the twelve-year disruption of the Cultural Revolution caused a loss of 200,000 college graduates per year, a total of 2.4 million or at least 1.2 million scientists and engineers.[37] There was also an extreme shortage of scientific-managerial personnel capable of running large-scale modern industrial plants. Even skilled labor was in short supply. Of the country's 94 million-member work force, only 1.6 percent could be considered technical personnel, and 73 percent of the skilled labor force had received an education of only junior high or lower. This lack of training and education made it difficult for workers to operate and maintain the sophisticated imported equipment and to use work manuals, many of which remained in foreign languages due to a lack of qualified translators. As a result, many expensive foreign machines remained unpacked in their original crates, or were left rusting in the open air.

The integration of Western science and technology into Chinese society was a century-old problem; China's present predicament was clearly the result of the failure to integrate science with the larger society. China's oldest well-educated group, those scientists and intellectuals trained in the West and Japan from 1920 to 1949, were severely attacked during the Anti-rightist movement of 1957 and persecuted beyond human endurance during the Cultural Revolution. They were despised, ridiculed, and derided as the "stinking No. 9's," ranking behind landlords, the rich, counterrevolutionaries, bad elements, rightists, rebels, special agents, and capitalist roaders. Many were plagued and harassed to death, or driven to suicide, others were jailed, tortured, maimed, and crippled. In 1973 an American estimate put qualified Chinese scientific and technological personnel at an incredibly small 65,000, while a leading Chinese scientist and educator[38] gave an even more alarming figure of 60,000 in 1978.[39]

However, with the reopening of the universities and with admissions once again based on a strictly administered national examination, Chinese higher education was recovering and promised to produce a new generation of well-educated intellectuals. The government had designated eighty-eight "key" universities and restored dismissed professors to responsible positions. Academic subjects were receiving new respect, and students studied diligently in hopes of further education abroad. By 1981 more than 5,000 qualified graduate and senior scholars were abroad for advanced research and study, and about 130 delegations visited the United States monthly. The academic atmosphere was improving in the universities; but many intellectuals, recently released from the so-called "cow shed' (*niulan*), understandably felt insecure and were timid, fearful of speaking their minds, and unwilling to commit their views to writing. To arouse their enthusiasm would require a long period of reassurance and trust. Yet most agreed that China's academic institutions had by 1981 become freer than at any time in the past thirty years.

To further cultivate scientifically oriented personnel, the government restored the Chinese Academy of Sciences to a position of power and honor. High-quality basic research was encouraged, and five-sixths of the scientist's time was devoted to scientific work. Scientists and other intellectuals were encouraged by the fact that their work was no longer evaluated by political criteria. In addition to new opportunities to study abroad, famous foreign scholars were being invited to give lectures; and training was available in scientific management, operations research, and systems analysis.

While these undertakings were worthy remedies to past malpractices, it took time to train the personnel necessary to run a modern economy—it was not a process which could be rushed. In 1982, China had 400,000 college-educated scientists and engineers of varying competence, but middle-echelon technical personnel, skilled workers, and local administrators were in desperately short supply.[40] At the same time, it was difficult to work around the party cadres who were entrenched in both central and local scientific and research organizations. Threatened by the new primacy of scientific knowledge and expertise, they banded together to protect their vested interests, inevitably slowing modernization.

Generally, Chinese scientific and technical personnel could be categorized into five groups. The first consisted of those trained before Liberation in 1949, including many educated abroad. Formerly the target for attack, this small group now enjoyed great prestige serving as China's scientific liaison with the outside world. The second group consisted of those trained after Liberation in the Soviet Union (or by Russians in China) during the 1950s, who were now in middle-echelon positions. The third consisted of college graduates of the period before the Cultural Revolution in 1966, now in their late thirties and early forties. Many of them had been sent abroad for further study and might prove a powerful force in the future. The fourth group was made up of students of worker, peasant, or soldier (*gong nong ping*) backgrounds trained during the Cultural Revolution. With the exception of a few, they had been inadequately prepared for the tasks of modernization. The fifth group was comprised of college students admitted to the universities after 1977 and represented in a real sense the future of Chinese scientific manpower. Until this last and growing group was fully trained, China's power to absorb the technology of modernization would remain very limited.

The lack of qualified experts had led to a poor beginning of modernization projects. The most conspicuous case was the Baoshan steel complex near Shanghai. Originally it was to be a $2 billion complex with an annual production capacity of 6 million tons. Modeled after the highly modern and successful Japanese Kimitsu plant, a thousand Japanese experts and technicians came to help with its operation. Unfortunately, the site was ill-chosen, located on swampy land at the edge of the Yangtze River. Hundreds of thousands of steel pilings had to be driven into the ground before the physical structures of the complex could be built. When work began in late 1979, it was quickly discovered that the power supply was insufficient and that the site lacked accessible deep water ports to receive iron ore from Australia and Brazil. The first stage was completed only after confronting countless difficulties and spending $5 billion. The financial burdens were unbearable, and the Chinese government unilaterally halted the second stage of construction by the end of 1980 causing consternation and anger on the part of the Japanese suppliers.

Another giant steel complex, to be built with German aid in Jidong, Hebei (at $14 billion for a production capacity of 10 million tons per year), was located in an earthquake-prone region—its progress had been faltering at best. A third example of poor planning concerned the Wuhan Iron and Steel Company, which purchased West German equipment capable of producing 4 million tons of steel annually. The huge German machines required so much electricity that they drained the electricity supply of the entire province, making other industries inoperable. Furthermore, Wuhan had been unable to supply the six million tons of raw steel required to produce four million tons of finished steel per year. For each day production was delayed, an estimated two million German marks were lost—a deplorable waste in capital-scarce China.

RETRENCHMENT AND REVISED PRIORITIES

The original Ten-Year Plan was more of a political wish than an economic blueprint, and it lacked careful study as to its feasibility. During the first year of the program, some 100,000 construction projects were launched by the government costing $40 billion; with military and scientific procurements the total reached 24 percent of the 1978 national income of $198 billion. Large foreign contracts were also negotiated including the Baoshan steel complex ($2 billion), the Jidong steel complex ($14 billion), and a hotel construction project with the U.S. International Hotel Corporation ($500 million). In addition, regional organizations contracted a large number of sizable agreements with foreign suppliers, which, together with local construction projects, raised the total investment for 1978 to 36 percent of the national income, quite close to the 40 percent rate of the disastrous Great Leap years. Such zealous over-spending was clearly insupportable.[41]

Economic realities soon set in to force a critical reassessment. A debate at the highest level took place regarding the scope and priorities of investment. In July 1978, Hu Qiaomu, president of the Chinese Academy of Social Sciences, called for greater emphasis on agricultural production which reflected the results of the top echelon's reassessments.[42] Similar sentiments were expressed in December 1978 at the meetings of the Eleventh Central Committee (Third Plenum). On February 24, 1979, the *Renmin Ribao* [People's Daily] editorialized against a hasty, impractical approach to modernization: "Judging from our experience . . . China has suffered more from rashness than from conservatism. . . . Many projects were started hurriedly without the preparatory work that should have been done, thus failing to proceed from realities. . . . A frightful waste of manpower and materials was involved in these projects."

China's limited financial and scientific resources forced leaders to reassess the Ten-Year Plan critically. It was decided that the top priority should be agriculture, the foundation of the economy, followed by light industry, which could meet domestic demands and earn foreign exchange, and then heavy industry. Capital investment in agriculture was increased from $26 billion (Ch$40 billion) to $59 billion (Ch$90 billion), and light and export industries also received new allocations. Within heavy industry, steel production targets were slashed from 60 million to 45 million tons; but coal, electric power, petroleum, and building industries retained priorities for investments.[43] Projects that could be completed quickly and earn foreign exchange were encouraged, and bank loans rather than government appropriations were planned for future investment projects. On the other hand, projects requiring huge amounts of capital and facing problems in resources, raw materials, location, transportation, technical capabilities, or energy supply were delayed or suspended.

At the Fifth National People's Congress (second session, June 1979), Hua Guofeng announced a three-year period

(1979–81) for the "adjustment, reconstruction, consolidation, and improvement" of the national economy. Blaming Lin Biao and the Gang of Four for sabotaging the economy, he ruefully admitted: "We had not taken this into full account, and some of the measures we adopted were not prudent enough."[44]

The immediate effect of the retrenchment was the halting of 348 important heavy industrial projects (including 38 steel and metallurgical plants) and 4,500 smaller ones. Capital investment for 1979 was reduced to 34.8 percent of state expenditures. Specifically, investments in the steel, machinery, and chemical industries were most deeply cut, losing from 30–45 percent of their investment allotment in 1979–80.[45] Construction also suffered, with a 33 percent cut in Shanghai and a 40 percent cut for Inner Mongolia. Simultaneously, investment in agriculture increased from 10.7 percent of the state budget in 1978 to 14 percent in 1979 and 16 percent in 1980, while in textile and light industries investment rose from 5.4 percent in 1978 to 5.8 percent in 1979 and perhaps 8 percent in 1980.

The retrenchment was necessitated not only by China's limited foreign credit, financial resources, and absorptive power but also by the unexpectedly high cost of invading Vietnam in 1979. In addition, original estimates of oil production and its export potential were far too optimistic, and disappointing performance in the energy sector dampened China's hope of using oil exports to finance modernization. The 1978 budgetary deficit was $6.5 billion and climbed to $11.3 billion in 1979.[46] Clearly, more sophisticated and thorough economic planning was required. Saburo Okita, chairman of the Japan Economic Research Center and an architect of the Japanese economic miracle, was invited to China as a consultant.

Rearranging developmental priorities served to correct many of the causes of structural disequilibrium in the Chinese economy: (1) the imbalances within fuel, power, and raw material industries; (2) the imbalance between light and heavy industries; (3) the imbalance between agriculture and industry; and (4) the imbalance between capital investment and consumption.

As a result of retrenchment, the new scaled-down targets for 1985 and the actual output of the five major industries in 1985 appear as follows:[47]

	1978	*1979*	*1985 (Ten-Year Plan)*	*1985 (revised)*	*1985 (actual output)*
Steel (million tons)	31.8	34.5	60	45	46.66
Coal (million tons)	618	635	900	800	850
Crude Oil (million tons)	104	106.2	500	300	125
Electricity (billion kwh)	256.6	282	n.a.	n.a.	407
Cement (million tons)	65.2	73.9	100	100	142.46

Of note was the very small growth in coal and oil production, the two main energy sources. Coal output grew 12.3 percent in 1978 but only 2.75 percent in 1979. Crude oil registered a 1.9 percent increase in 1979 compared to 11 percent in 1978 and an annual 22.5 percent between 1957 and 1977. This vast decrease might suggest that oil output at current producing sites had already peaked, and thus indicated the necessity for new exploration. Electricity output also fell from an annual growth rate of 13 percent between 1957 and 1978 to 9.9 percent in 1979 and 2.9 percent in 1980.[48]

The overall view clearly showed that energy and transportation remained major obstacles in the modernization plan. Oil, coal, and electricity production fell far short of meeting new demands. While freight volume increased 9.7 times from 1950 to 1978, railway mileage increased only 1.4 times—transport lines were strained to the limit. Unless the energy and transportation bottlenecks were eased, China's modernization would be constrained. The small increase in oil output had drastically reduced China's ability to earn foreign currency to finance the purchase of foreign high technology. It was possible that some additional income might be acquired from the textile and light industries which could more easily meet consumer demands and earn foreign exchange. As a result of increased state investment, bank loans, and better material, textile output rose 30 percent in the first quarter of 1980 over the same period in 1979, and light industry rose by 21 percent.[49] But it was questionable whether these sources would generate enough funds to hasten materially the date of modernization.

PROFIT, MATERIAL INCENTIVE, AND STRUCTURAL REORGANIZATION

It came as an odd realization that everyone in socialist China was interested in profit and openly talked about making more money. People who worked half-heartedly under Mao's regime were now enlivened by hopes of improving their lives through increased earnings. The new leadership had encouraged these hopes in the interest of increasing production. Indeed, the government had promoted workers' incentives and initiatives by giving material rewards, reforming the industrial organization, and appointing experts with proven managerial skills as plant directors. It was hoped that these reforms would increase the efficiency and output of existing plants as new ones would take time to build and contribute little to the economy for several years. Hua pointed out in 1979: "In the next eight years, and especially in the next three, our existing plants must be the foundation for the growth of production." China invited Western and Japanese firms to invest in renovating these plants, but most preferred to invest in new plants rather than to put money into obsolescent factories.

The government recognized material reward as a powerful

incentive for increased production. It was noted that during the First Five-Year Plan (1952–56) when wages rose 7.4 percent annually, productivity increased correspondingly with gross industrial production rising 18 percent per annum. During the Cultural Revolution the bonus system and wage increases were abolished, and the result was decreased production and increased absenteeism. In 1977, after more than a decade, a 10 percent wage increase was granted to 64 percent of the nonagricultural workers, and bonus and piece rate systems were restored in 1978.[50]

Toward industrial reorganization, farm machinery corporations were established in the Six Economic Regions to coordinate efforts at modernization and to reduce duplication and waste. Each province had a tractor motor company, an instruments and meter company, a ball bearing factory, and a machinery export company. To improve management, Maoist worker-participation-in-management and cadre-participation-in-labor schemes were rejected in favor of expert, professional management, with the hope of insuring efficiency and accountability. Economic norms were set up to measure an enterprise's output, including variety, quality, cost, profit, resource allocation, and productivity. Each enterprise had a fixed quota for output, personnel, materials, capital assets, and liquid capital; in return, the enterprise guaranteed the quantity and quality of products, labor and production costs and expected state profit. Surpassing production quotas entitled the enterprise to a part of the profit. Thus profit and material reward were officially used as the means to raise production and efficiency.

In addition, the government was streamlining the industrial infrastructure as well as the management and control system. In the past, the system usually worked from the top down with an overconcentration of decision-making power at the central level causing duplication, waste, and a lack of initiative and enthusiasm among workers. In 1979 the government consolidated some 25,000 to 50,000 marginal enterprises into 970 specialized companies, each with decision-making powers to suit local requirements. Each was allowed to: (1) prepare production plans and sell above-quota products to other units; (2)

keep 5 percent of profits on quota production and 20 percent on above-quota production; (3) reward more work with more pay and allow workers to control their own welfare and bonus funds; and (4) receive bank loans for investment.[51] In addition, five special economic regions have been established in Beijing, Shanghai, Tianjin, Guangdong, and Fujian, with power to negotiate with foreign concerns and keep part of their foreign currency earnings.[52]

The new system, borrowing heavily from Yugoslavian and Romanian models, combined central planning with local initiative and market mechanisms to form a blend of capitalist and socialist structures. To say that capitalism had returned to China was an oversimplification; rather, some capitalist management techniques and an emphasis on profit margins had appeared in hopes that those enterprises operating in the red could be made profitable.

Although "private enterprise" had not returned, "individual economic undertakings" were on the rise. Thus, an energetic citizen called Yen converted a tea room into a booming Multi-Service Center selling 500 items and grossing $9 million a year. A Mrs. Liu, with the help of two sons, operated a family restaurant with such success that reservations had to be made days ahead, and waiting lines were a common scene. The economic atmosphere was freer today than at any time in the past thirty years.

THE CONSEQUENCES OF RAPID MODERNIZATION

Just as there were problems in achieving modernization, there were also problems created by its accelerated achievement. First and foremost was inflation, which was almost nonexistent in earlier periods when the government deliberately adopted a policy of low wages and low commodity prices. When the people had little purchasing power, the demand for goods was kept low and prices were stable. With the increase in wages and government procurement prices for farm products (up 20–50 percent by 1977–79), the state correspondingly raised sale prices on various commodities creating inflation officially computed at 5.8 percent in 1979 but more likely reaching 15 percent. The upward spiral of price increases had continued unabated reaching an annual rate of 15–30 percent in 1980, while the light industry growth was only 9.7 percent. When prices increased faster than productivity, an inflationary psychology set in, resulting in a black market and speculation. Government budgets also revealed growing deficits: $11.3 billion in 1979, $10–12 billion in 1980, and $6 billion in 1981. To offset the deficits, the Ministry of Finance decided in the spring of 1981 to issue $3.3 billion in ten-year maturity bonds at 4 percent interest per annum. Government enterprises, administrative organizations, communes, and the army were urged to buy according to their ability, but individuals seemed free to purchase the bonds as they chose.[53] The floating of bonds indicated the financial difficulties China was facing.

Another immediate consequence of inflation and overzealous spending was the decision to cut back major construction projects by 40 percent in 1981. Many large projects involving foreign companies were abruptly terminated. The Japanese, who entered the China market early fared the worst: total Japanese losses were estimated at $1.5 billion including the Baoshan steel complex and three petrochemical projects. The Germans fared less badly while the Americans, who entered the China market late, suffered the least. The Chinese simply explained that they could not afford to go ahead with these costly projects at this time and agreed to compensate for losses incurred without setting definite figures.[54] Foreigners understood China's financial dilemma but had to question the nation's international credibility when agreements entered into in good faith were unilaterally cancelled. There was no doubt that China's reputation as a reliable trader had been affected.

Cancellations of construction projects led to the layoff of numerous workers, intensifying the already serious unemployment problem. China once boasted that its socialist system guaranteed employment for every able body, declaring proudly that there was no unemployment in China—there were only those awaiting job assignment! Semantics aside, overstaffing was common and a job requiring one was frequently shared by three at low wages. But construction cancellations and modernization of factories demanded a reduction in personnel resulting in the loss of many jobs. While $10 billion had been invested in new foreign-style plants, relatively few new jobs had been created. Meanwhile, an estimated 10 to 15 million new workers entered the labor force annually. In the past, surplus human labor was forcibly dispersed to the countryside or hinterlands, but during 1979–82 this practice had been relaxed, and many who were previously so dispersed had managed to return to their home towns. About 80 percent of the over one million youths who were "sent downward" (*xia-fang*) from Shanghai had furtively returned. Although half of them had found some employment, others seemed to have lost all hope. Unemployment in China was estimated at around 20 million in 1981.

Another anomalous phenomenon of modernization was the emergence of new classes in a so-called classless society. Modernization had given new prestige to the scientists, engineers, technicians, plant managers, writers, artists, and other intellectuals who would lead China's "Great Leap Outward." There was a new feeling that "among all activities, only science and technology are lofty." Scientists and intellectuals along with high party members now constituted a privileged upper class; urban workers of productive enterprises and lower echelon cadres formed the second class, with farmers and those living in the countryside at the bottom of the totem pole. The selective sending of scholars and students abroad for advanced education, many of whom were blood relatives of high party members, further strengthened the elitist trend and widened the class cleavages.

Another deepening problem arose from the increasing disparity between the city and the countryside and among various industrial enterprises themselves. Since the government had opted for an "enclave" strategy of locating key industries in selected urban areas, these areas were more likely to enjoy the fruits of modernization—higher wages, greater upward mobility, and a higher standard of living. An average industrial worker in 1981 earned about $40 a month with an additional bonus, while the average monthly cash income of a peasant was only $5–7. It was not unusual for a city worker to earn six to eight times more than a peasant, and scientific or technical personnel over ten times more. Within the industrial sector, the profit was vastly uneven: in 1978 the oil industry enjoyed a 40 percent profit margin; electricity, 31 percent; metallurgy, 13 percent; and coal mining, only 1 percent. Since profit decides not only levels of investment but also the size of bonuses and fringe benefits, it deeply affected the worker's life-style. Differences in rewards led to different degrees of enthusiasm for work.

A further conflict existed between the production enterprises and the state commercial departments. In the past, vital materiel for enterprises was supplied by the Ministry of Material Allocation. Now each enterprise was allowed to sell some materials and products to consumers, competing with the government's commercial departments for profit. With the authorization to engage in foreign negotiations and trade, five provincial-municipal organizations set up offices in Hong Kong and Shanghai to sell their products directly to foreign traders, causing jealousy, competition, price wars, and confusion.

Beneath all the adverse consequences of rapid modernization lay what may be the most serious of China's problems—a crisis of confidence. After thirty years of socialist construction, the country remained poor and backward. Past reports of achievements had often been exposed as pure propaganda, and many, especially the young, had lost faith in the superiority of socialism. There was a conspicuous lack of confidence in achieving a true modernization. Young people were especially critical of the party cadres' privileged status and of bureaucratism, and on the basis of past performance doubted both their capability and sincerity in implementing modernization programs. Indeed, many middle- and lower-echelon party members in responsible positions but lacking scientific expertise were threatened by the new demands of modernization. They secretly resisted, sabotaged, and slowed new undertakings which ran counter to their interests.[55] There was a popular saying: "The two ends are hot, but the middle is cold"—meaning the leaders and the people wanted modernization but the middle-level bureaucrats resisted change. Chinese newspapers and journals openly discussed China's triple crises: a lack of faith, confidence, and trust in the party and the government.[56]

FOREIGN VALUE AND CHINESE ESSENCE

Modernization had been a goal in China for more than a century. The late Qing court, the Nationalist government, and the Communist leadership all had tried to launch China on the road to modernization. Mao Zedong, in spite of his emphasis on peasants and grass root involvement, was an ardent supporter of industrialization though he knew little of economic planning. It was under Mao that China received from the Soviet Union the "most comprehensive technology transfer in modern history": 11,000 Russian experts worked in China during the 1950s and 15,000 Chinese were trained in the Soviet Union. China imported 157 complete plants from Russia and Eastern Europe representing 27 percent of total investment in machinery and equipment. The Sino-Soviet split in 1960 caused an abrupt termination of Soviet assistance, and during the Cultural Revolution other foreign technological and educational acquisitions virtually ceased. While the alternative to Soviet and Eastern European aid was Western capitalist technology and equipment, learning from the West and Japan was considered highly dishonorable. In September 1975 a spokesman for the Gang of Four proclaimed:

> Politically, "wholesale Westernization" meant loss of sovereignty and national humiliation, a total sell-out of China's independence and self-determination. . . . Ideologically, "wholesale Westernization" was meant to praise what is foreign and belittle what is Chinese. . . . Economically, "wholesale Westernization" was aimed at spreading a blind faith in the Western capitalist material civilization so as to turn the Chinese economy into a complete appendage of imperialism.[57]

Thus the Maoists advocated self-reliance. Mao recognized China's backwardness as much as he was aware of its limited resources. He feared the effects of modernization on such sensitive issues as income distribution, worker status, and the revival of elitism and bureaucratism at the expense of egalitarianism. Yet self-reliance and the rejection of foreign technology for nearly two decades (1958–76) left China in an undeveloped abyss of poverty, while other countries through technological innovations charged ahead by leaps and bounds. Pragmatic leaders realized the dangers inherent in Mao's policy, but none dared oppose it.

With Mao's death and the demise of the Gang, the way was cleared for a new start to make up for lost time. A crash program for modernization had been launched, with Hua in the lead and Deng as the main spirit of the New Leap Outward. They assumed that science, technology, and the dynamics of technological change were basically politically neutral and classless, and that they could be transplanted without injury to Chinese social and cultural institutions.[58] They had opted for a concentrated development of selected areas in key sectors of the Chinese economy through the imposition and internal development of science and technology. This "enclave" approach would undoubtedly result in encapsulated regions of progress to the detriment of a more general technological assimilation.

In the zealous spirit of the post-Gang period, there seemed to be an obsession with the notion that in little more than two decades, science could save China, rescue it from backwardness and poverty, and elevate it into the front ranks of the advanced states. The aim was worthy, but the grandiose targets and the stringent timetable seemed unrealistic. High technology was extremely expensive, and its absorption and dissemination required both time and properly trained personnel. Problems with the industrial infrastructure, scientific management, specialization, standardization, and serialization were not considered in the original Ten-Year Plan. It would be years before scientific methods of operation and new techniques could filter down to the masses of workers, creating the necessary ability and enthusiasm for a national modernization drive.

Chinese leaders proclaimed that they did not intend to ape the West but would forge a "Chinese-styled modernization." Yet the knowledge and skills associated with foreign technology would inevitably influence the thinking and behavior of those who acquired them. The late Qing debate on the "fundamentals versus application" (*tiyong*) dichotomy would reappear in a different form. Western scientists in China and "returned" students trained in advanced countries would undoubtedly exert new influences on Chinese life and thinking.

The cultural consequences of contact with foreign ideology, institutions, and ways of life could not be totally contained, despite party admonitions and exhortations to the contrary. It was hoped that the Chinese could achieve a happy medium whereby they would become modern in thought and in their specialties without sacrificing the distinctiveness of their Chinese origin. While the meeting of a particular timetable for China's modernization could not be assured, the leadership's increasingly pragmatic goals seemed to point toward the eventuality of the successful modernization of the Chinese nation— perhaps fifty years into the next century.

NOTES

1. The Chinese government has never disclosed the complete blueprint of the Ten-Year Four Modernizations Plan. It is only from various reports on the work of the government, interviews, and scattered reports that we piece together the general outlines of the Plan.
2. Chao Yu-shen, "Chinese Communist Attempt to Modernize Industry," in *Chinese Communist Modernization Problems* (Taipei, 1979), pp. 29–30 (hereafter to be cited as *Modernization Problems*).
3. 1. "On General Guidelines of the Party's Nationwide Activities."
   2. "Summary Outlines of the Academy of Sciences' Activity Reports."
   3. "Certain Issues Concerning Accelerated Industrial Development."

4. *The New York Times*, Jan. 2, 1976, pp. 1, 4.
5. *Renmin Ribao* [People's Daily], May 8, 1977. Tr. mine.
6. Li Tien-min, "Teng Hsiao-p'ing's Past and Future," in *Modernization Problems*, pp. 90–91.
7. Liu Keng-sheng, "Modernization of Peiping's Science and Technology," in *Modernization Problems*, p. 64.
8. *Renmin Ribao* [People's Daily], March 9, 1978, pp. 1–5.
9. Chu-yüan Cheng, "The Modernization of Chinese Industry," in Richard Baum (ed.), *China's Four Modernizations: The New Technological Revolution* (Boulder, 1980), p. 26.
10. Chen Ting-chung, "Agricultural Modernization on the Chinese Mainland," in *Modernization Problems*, p. 16.
11. "Report on National Conference on Fundamental Farm Construction," *Renmin Ribao* [People's Daily], Aug. 8, 1977.
12. Hu Qiaomu, "Observe Economic Laws, Speed Up the Four Modernizations," *Peking Review*, No. 47, Nov. 24, 1978, p. 18.
13. Chen Ting-chung, pp. 19–21. These figures are based on various mainland Chinese sources.
14. In Taiwan, it took US$11,000 to create a job opportunity during 1967–71. If Beijing could manage to create a job opportunity with half the amount, relocation of 100 million would cost $50 billion. *Ibid.*, p. 24.
15. *Ibid.*, p. 25.
16. These 27 fields include natural resources, agriculture, industry, defense, transportation, oceanography, environmental protection, medicine, finance, trade, culture, and education, in addition to a number of basic and technical sciences.
17. According to a study of the Royal Institute of International Affairs, London, by Lawrence Freedman entitled *The West and the Modernization of China* (London, 1979), p. 5, Chinese armed forces consisted of the following main units:

> STRATEGIC FORCES: medium-range ballistic missiles: 30–40 CSS–1, 600–700 miles; intermediate-range ballistic missiles: 30–40 CSS–2, 1750 miles;
> [long-range ballistic missiles: some CSS–3, 3500 miles, first tested in 1976, and a small number of CSS-X-4, 6000–7000 miles, first tested in May 1980—author].

> ARMY: 3,250,000 men, 10 armored divisions, 121 infantry divisions, and 150 independent regiments.

> NAVY: 300,000 men, 30,000 Naval Air Force with 700 shore-based aircraft, 38,000 Marines, 23 major surface combat ships, and a rather large number of submarines and destroyers with missile-launching capability.

AIR FORCE: 400,000 men, 5,000 combat aircraft including some 4,000 MIG 17/19, and a small number of MIG 21 and F-9 fighters.

18. Cited in Freedman, p. 6.
19. Jonathan Pollack, "The Modernization of National Defense," in Baum (ed.), p. 247.
20. *Ibid.*, pp. 249–50.
21. Jeffrey Schultz, "The Four Modernizations Reconsidered," in Baum (ed.), p. 280.
22. Almon R. Roth, "Commentary on National Defense Modernization," in Baum (ed.), p. 262.
23. Pollack, pp. 255–56.
24. Hua Guofeng, "Report on the Work of the Government," *Peking Review*, No. 10, March 10, 1978, p. 23.
25. Pollack, p. 243.
26. Freedman, pp. 19–20.
27. *Ibid.*, p. 19.
28. The former figure given by Vice-Premier Li Xiannian, and the latter by Deputy-Premier Deng Xiaoping.
29. Sun Yih, "Peiping's Plan for Defense Modernization," in *Modernization Problems*, p. 59.
30. *China: Economic Indicators* (Washington, D.C., 1978), p. 1.
31. Chu-yüan Cheng, in Baum (ed.), p. 37.
32. Hua Guofeng's report to the Fifth National People's Congress, First Session, Feb. 26, 1978, *Renmin Ribao* [People's Daily], March 9, 1978.
33. Shannon R. Brown, "China's Program of Technology Acquisition," in Baum (ed.), p. 167.
34. *Ibid.*, pp. 165–66.
35. *American Banker*, April 19, 1979, quoted in Baum (ed.), p. 271.
36. Chu-yüan Cheng, in Baum (ed.), p. 38.
37. Cheng Chen-pang, "Tough Knots in Peiping's Four Modernizations," in *Modernization Problems*, pp. 80–81.
38. Zhou Peiyuan, president of Peking University and a vice-president of the Chinese Academy of Sciences.
39. Sun Yih, pp. 58–59.
40. Rudi Volti, "The Absorption and Assimilation of Acquired Technology," in Baum (ed.), p. 188.
41. Chu-yüan Cheng, "Industrial Modernization in China," *Current History*, Sept. 1980, p. 24.
42. *Peking Review*, No. 47, Nov. 24, 1978, pp. 17–21.
43. Chu–yüan Cheng, in Baum (ed.), p. 41; *Los Angeles Times*, May 10, 1979.
44. *Renmin Ribao* [People's Daily], June 19, 1979; *Beijing Review*, No. 25, June 22, 1979, p. 11.

45. Chu-yüan Cheng, *Current History*, p. 25.
46. John Bryan Starr, "China's Economic Outreach," *Current History*, Sept. 1979, pp. 50–51.
47. Chu-yüan Cheng, *Current History*, p. 26.
48. *Ibid.*, p. 27.
49. *Ibid.*, p. 27.
50. *Renmin Ribao* [People's Daily], Nov. 22, 1977.
51. Cheng Chu-yüan, "Chung-Kung Hsien-tai-hua ti tun-ts'o chi chan-wang" (The frustration of and prospect for Communist China's modernization), *Hai-wai hsüeh-jen* [Overseas scholars], Sept. 1980, p. 29.
52. *U.S. News & World Report*, March 23, 1981, pp. 56–58.
53. *Far East Times*, San Francisco, March 10, 1981.
54. *The Christian Science Monitor*, Feb. 20, 1981. Reportedly, the Japanese firm Mitsubishi Heavy Industries asked for an $84 million reparation.
55. *Hongki* [Red Flag], Beijing, No. 14, 1980, pp. 25–27.
56. *Renmin Ribao* [People's Daily], July 1, 1980; Nov. 11, 1980; Feb. 24, 1981; *Guangming Daily*, March 28, 1981.
57. Liang Xiao, "The Yang Wu Movement and the Slavish Comprador Philosophy," *Historical Research*, No. 5, Oct. 20, 1975.
58. Genevieve C. Dean, "A Note on Recent Policy Changes," in Baum (ed.), p. 105.

FURTHER READING

Andors, Stephen, *China's Industrial Revolution: Politics, Planning, and Management, 1949 to the Present* (New York, 1977).
Baum, Richard (ed.), *China's Four Modernizations* (Boulder, 1980).
Bennett, Gordon, "Issues in China's Commercial and Financial Policy, 1978," *Contemporary China*, II:3:99–108 (Fall 1978).
Braybrooke, George, "Recent Development in Chinese Social Science, 1977–79," *The China Quarterly*, 79:593–601 (Sept. 1979).
Chang, Arnold, *Painting in the People's Republic of China: The Politics of Style* (Boulder, 1980).
Chen, Kuan-I, "Agricultural Modernization in China," *Current History*, 77:449:66–70, 85–86 (Sept. 1979).
Ch'en, Ting-chung, "Peiping's Ten-Year Economic Development Plan," *Issues & Studies*, XV:4:36–46 (April 1979).
Cheng, Chu-yüan, *China's Petroleum Industry: Output Growth and Export Potential* (New York, 1976).

————, "Industrial Modernization in China," *Current History,* 9:458:24–28, 43–44 (Sept. 1980).

————, "Chung-Kung hsien-tai-hua ti tun-ts'o chi chan-wang," (The frustration of and prospect for Communist China's modernization), *Hai-wai hsüeh-jen* [Overseas scholars], Sept. 1980, pp. 25–32.

Chinese Communist Modernization Problems (Taipei, Taiwan, 1979).

Chinn, Dennis L., "Basic Commodity Distribution in the People's Republic of China," *The China Quarterly,* 84:743–54 (Dec. 1980).

Chou, S. H., "Industrial Modernization in China," *Current History,* 77:449:49–52, 87–88 (Sept. 1979).

Dean, Genevieve C., *Science and Technology in the Development of Modern China: An Annotated Bibliography* (London, 1974).

————, and Fred Chernow, *The Choice of Technology in the Electronics Industry of the People's Republic of China: The Fabrication of Semiconductors* (Palo Alto, 1978).

Deng, Liqun, "Gongchan zhuyi shi qianqiu wandai de chonggao shiye" (Communism is a lofty calling for a myriad of generations), *Guangming Daily,* March 28, 1981.

Eckstein, Alexander, *China's Economic Revolution* (Cambridge, Eng., 1977).

————, *China's Economic Development: The Interplay of Scarcity and Ideology* (Ann Arbor, 1975).

Englesberg, Paul, "Education in Shanghai, 1976–1978," *Contemporary China,* III:2:69–78 (Summer 1979).

Field, Robert Michael, "A Slowdown in Chinese Industry," *The China Quarterly,* 80:734–39 (Dec. 1979).

Freedman, Lawrence, *The West and the Modernization of China,* Chatham House Papers (The Royal Institute of International Affairs, 1979).

Fureng, Dong, "Some Problems Concerning the Chinese Economy," *The China Quarterly,* 84:726–36 (Dec. 1980).

Gelber, Harry G., *Technology, Defense, and External Relations in China, 1975–1978* (Boulder, 1979).

Godwin, Paul H. B., "China and the Second World: The Search for Defense Technology," *Contemporary China,* II:3:3–9 (Fall 1978).

————, "China's Defense Dilemma: The Modernization Crisis of 1976 and 1977," *Contemporary China,* II:3:63–85 (Fall 1978).

————, *PLA-Military Forces of the PRC* (Boulder, 1981).

Goldman, Merle, "Teng Hsiao-p'ing and the Debate over Science and Technology," *Contemporary China,* II:4:46–69 (Winter 1978).

Hardy, Randall W., *China's Oil Future: A Case of Modest Expectations* (Boulder, 1978).

Harrison, Selig S., *China, Oil, and Asia: Conflict Ahead?* (New York, 1977).

Ho, Ping-ti, "China in the 1980's: Midway Toward Modernization," in Peter P. Cheng et al. (eds.), *Emerging Roles of Asian Nations in the Decade of the 1980's: A New Equilibrium* (Lincoln, 1979), pp. 8–46.

Howe, Christopher, *China's Economy: A Basic Guide* (New York, 1978).

Hu, Qiaomu, "Observe Economic Laws, Speed Up the Four Modernizations," Pt. I, *Peking Review*, 45:7–12 (Nov. 10, 1978); Pt. II, *Peking Review*, 46:15–23 (Nov. 17, 1978); Pt. III, *Peking Review*, 47:13–21 (Nov. 24, 1978).

Huang, Zhijian, "Jiujing yingdang ruhe renshi zhei yidai qingnian" (How shall we recognize this generation of youths?), *Renmin Ribao* [People's Daily], Beijing, Feb. 24, 1981.

Huang, Philip C. C. (ed.), *The Development of Underdevelopment in China* (White Plains, N.Y., 1980).

"Integrating Moral Encouragement With Material Reward," *Peking Review*, 16:6–7 (April 21, 1978).

Klatt, W., "China's New Economic Policy: A Statistical Appraisal," *The China Quarterly*, 80:716–33 (Dec. 1979).

———, "China Statistics Up-dated," *The China Quarterly*, 84: 737–43 (Dec. 1980).

Kokubun, Ryosei, "The Politics of Foreign Economic Policy-making in China: The Case of Plant Cancellation with Japan," *The China Quarterly*, 105:19–44 (March 1986).

Lardy, Nicholas R., "China's Economic Readjustment: Recovery or Paralysis?" in Robert B. Oxnam and Richard C. Bush (eds.), *China Briefing, 1980* (Boulder, 1980), pp. 39–51.

———, *Economic Growth and Distribution in China* (Cambridge, Eng., 1978).

——— (ed.), *Chinese Economic Planning: Translation from Chi-hua ching-chi* (White Plains, N.Y., 1979).

Li, Honglin, "Xinyang huiji shuoming liao shimo?" (What does the crisis of confidence mean?), *Renmin Ribao* [People's Daily], Beijing, Nov. 11, 1980.

Li, K. T., "Mainland China's Economic Modernization: An Evaluation Based on Taiwan's Development Experience," *Issues & Studies*, XV:1:13–21 (July 1979).

Liu, Charles Y., "Problems in Estimating PRC Grain Production," *Contemporary China*, II:3:128–42 (Fall 1978).

MacDougall, Colina, "The Chinese Economy in 1976," *The China Quarterly*, 70:355–70 (June 1977).

Marwash, Onkar, and Jonathan D. Pollack (eds.), *Military Power and Policy in Asian States: China, India, Japan* (Boulder, 1979).

Myers, Ramon H., *The Chinese Economy: Past and Present* (Belmont, Calif., 1980).

National Foreign Assessment Center, *China: Economic Indicators* (Washington, D.C., Dec. 1978).

———, *China's Economy* (Washington, D.C., Nov. 1977).

———, *China: Gross Value of Industrial Output, 1965–77* (Washington, D.C., June 1978).

———, *China: In Pursuit of Economic Modernization* (Washington, D.C., Dec. 1978).

———, *China: Post-Mao Search for Civilian Industrial Technology* (Washington, D.C., 1979).

———, *China: The Continuing Search for a Modernization Strategy* (Washington, D.C., April 1980).

———, *China: A Statistical Compendium* (Washington, D.C., July 1979).

———, *China: The Steel Industry in the 1970s and 1980s* (Washington, D.C., 1979).

Nelsen, Harvey, *The Chinese Military System* (Boulder, 1981).

Pannell, Clifton W., and Christopher L. Salter (eds.), *China Geographer*, No. 11, *Agriculture* (Boulder, 1981).

Pollack, Jonathan, "The Modernization of National Defense," in Richard Baum (ed.), *China's Four Modernizations* (Boulder, 1980), pp. 241–61.

Prybyla, Jan. S., *The Chinese Economy: Problems and Policies* (Columbia, S.C., 1978).

———, "Feeding One Billion People: Agricultural Modernization in China," *Current History*, 79:458:19–23, 40–42 (Sept. 1980).

Reardon-Anderson, James, "Science and Technology in Post-Mao China," *Contemporary China*, II:4:37–45 (Winter 1978).

Segal, Gerald, and William Tow (eds.), *Chinese Defense Policy* (Champaign, Ill., 1984).

Sigurdson, Jon, *Rural Industrialization in China* (Cambridge, Mass., 1977).

Smil, Vaclav, *China's Energy Achievements, Problems, Prospects* (New York, 1976).

———, "The Energy Cost of China's Modernization," *Contemporary China*, II:3:109–114 (Fall 1978).

Stavis, Benedict, *Making Green Revolution—The Politics of Agricultural Development in China* (Ithaca, 1974).

Stover, Leon E., *The Cultural Ecology of Chinese Civilization: Peasant Elites in the Last of the Agrarian States* (Stanford, 1979).

Suttmeier, Richard P., *Research and Revolution: Science Policy and Societal Change in China* (Lexington, Mass., 1974).

────── et al., *Science and Technology in the People's Republic of China* (Paris, 1977).

──────, *Science, Technology and China's Drive for Modernization* (Stanford, 1981).

Swetz, Frank, *Mathematics Education in China: Its Growth and Development* (Cambridge, Mass., 1974).

Ullerich, Curtis, *Rural Employment and Manpower Problems in China* (White Plains, N.Y., 1979).

Unger, Jonathan, "China's Troubled Down-to-the-Countryside Campaign," *Contemporary China*, III:2:79–92 (Summer 1979).

Volti, Rudi, *Science and Technology in China* (Boulder, 1981).

Wang, K. P., *Mineral Resources and Basic Industries in the People's Republic of China* (Boulder, 1977).

Wiens, Thomas B., "China's Agricultural Targets: Can They Be Met?" *Contemporary China*, II:3:115–127 (Fall 1978).

Young, Graham (ed.), *China: Dilemmas of Modernization* (Dover, N.H., 1985).

5

The End of the Maoist Age

THE TRIAL OF THE GANG OF FOUR
AND THE LIN BIAO GROUP

An unprecedented legal and political event took place in China from November 1980 to January 1981: the trial of the Gang of Four and the associates of Lin Biao. In the past, political dissidents or opponents defeated in power struggles were summarily purged, imprisoned, liquidated, or made "non-persons." But the new leadership, anxious to project an image of proper regard for the rule of law, established a special court to try the Jiang Qing and Lin Biao groups for crimes allegedly committed against the state and the people. It was extremely difficult to prepare for the trial because of its political ramification, yet the leadership decided to proceed in order to symbolize the beginning of a new order.

The four-year interval between the arrest of the Gang and the opening of the trial indicated the sensitivity and complexity of the issues at stake and the intensity of intraparty debate over the wisdom of and procedure for such an undertaking. The crux of the matter was Mao's intimate involvement in the rise of the Gang and its activities. Should he be implicated in the trial it would be necessary to have an official party assessment of his role during and after the Cultural Revolution in order to get at the truth of the matter. Yet no quick consensus could be reached due to vast differences in the opinions held by various leaders; to await such an assessment would further delay the trial. In addition, the position of Chairman Hua Guofeng was extremely sensitive due to his role as minister of public security (and later premier) while the Gang held sway over national policies. It was entirely possible, even inevitable, that he would be named as a witness at the trial. Thus, the question of separating Mao and Hua from the trial became a key issue in the high councils of state, one which could not be resolved without prolonged debate, intense negotiating, and many compromises.

Pretrial Politics

After their arrest in October 1976, the Four were repeatedly interrogated by government investigators in hopes of collecting evidence, confessions, and any relevant information as a basis for formal charges. But all Four were crafty politicians and skillfully dodged questions, passing all responsibility for their actions to Mao. In May 1980 the party held a secret pretrial hearing of the Four. Jiang Qing vigorously protested her innocence by insisting that her every act was carried out under express orders from Mao with the approval of the party Central Committee. Mao's only mistake, she said, was his choice of Hua as premier, for it whetted Hua's appetite for higher positions; and in the end he betrayed Mao's teaching and surrendered to capitalist countries in the manner of Li Hongzhang a century earlier. She insisted that Hua had been not only fully aware and supportive of her activities but was actually deeply involved (as minister of public security) in the suppression of the April 5, 1976, Tian An Men Square Incident; hence he must be called as a witness at the trial.[1]

Wang Hongwen and Zhang Chunqiao likewise attributed all responsibility for their actions to Mao, indicating further that Hua, as an insider, knew the full story. Yao Wenyuan's defense differed only slightly, holding the party center responsible and criticizing the current leadership for deviation from Mao's line in pursuing the Four Modernizations with the cooperation of foreign capitalists. In short, all four involved Mao and Hua in their defense.

Within the party leadership two lines of thought quickly emerged. General Secretary Hu Yaobang and party Vice-Chairman Chen Yun argued that only by first assessing Mao's contributions and mistakes could the crimes of the Gang be properly fixed. If Mao had not ignored "party democracy" and sponsored the Gang's rise to power, how could the Four have done such atrocious harm to the country? On the other hand, Hua and his supporters argued that any assessment of Mao's responsibility before the trial would lighten the responsibility of the Gang for its crimes; the inevitable inference would be that Mao and the party would bear the ultimate burden. They asked for an assessment of the Gang's crimes before an assessment of Mao.

To avoid further delay, the leadership finally decided that the trial should go ahead as announced without first making an assessment of Mao's role. Several guiding principles were adopted, the most basic of which was, according to Vice-Chairman Deng, to distinguish "political mistakes or misjudgments" from the actual crimes of murder, illegal detention, and torture. Mao's role in the Cultural Revolution was seen as a "mistake," not a "crime"; hence he could not be indicted. The other principles adopted were:

1. The trial was to be held in secret in order to prevent the disclosure of "state secrets" that might be revealed during the proceedings.
2. Great effort would be made to separate Mao from the Gang; the less he was mentioned the better. The crimes of the Four would be determined first so as to retain flexibility in the assessment of Mao.
3. Although the Four behaved as a group and committed similar crimes, the degree of responsibility varied and hence their penalties must be graded. Jiang Qing was the chief

culprit, followed by Zhang Chunqiao and Yao Wenyuan, while Wang Hongwen, a young upstart who joined the Gang seeking rapid promotions (and who showed repentance during interrogation) was assessed last in the order of crimes and punishments.[2]

Even without a pretrial assessment of Mao, Hua remained in a most uncomfortable position. Although Hua, after Mao's death and in conjunction with party and military leaders, had engineered a "palace revolution" to topple the Gang, he was nonetheless a beneficiary of the Cultural Revolution and had been favored by Mao in his naming as premier and then as "anointed successor." Therefore he was not anxious to hold the trial and dreaded being called as a witness, but he could not openly oppose the trial. His tactics were to delay it as long as possible while secretly working out an "understanding" with the other power holders. Reportedly, he demanded that these four conditions be met:

1. The trial should not implicate Wang Dongxing and his associates in the crimes of the Cultural Revolution. (In other words, Hua would not appear as witness.)
2. The trial should not involve the Tian An Men Square Incident.
3. The trial should not involve the "Criticize Deng, Antirightist Deviationist Campaign."
4. No sentence of immediate execution should be given to Jiang Qing.[3]

These conditions seemed sufficient to protect Hua from the worst of the predictable criticisms that the trial might stir up.

With these guidelines and "understandings" established, the leaders were ready to open the trial. A Special Court of thirty-five judges was created in which there were two sections: a civil tribunal for the Gang of Four and a military tribunal for the six associates of Lin Biao. Since the Lin group was accused of plotting against Mao, while the Gang was charged with usurping state power and party leadership under the aegis of Mao, the logic of combining the two groups in one trial seemed questionable. But the government rationalized that the two groups had conspired together during the Cultural Revolution in an attempt to overthrow the proletarian dictatorship, and in doing so they severely hurt the country, the people, and the present leaders. Ironically, both groups happened to have been favored by Mao at one time or another, and both had failed in attempts to seize supreme power.

Like the Nuremberg and Tokyo Trials after World War II, the trial in question was in fact a "victor's trial" held in response to a popularly felt need for justice.[4] What remained to be seen was whether the court was in fact a court of law or just a legal arm of the Politburo.

The Trial

On November 20, 1980, the long-awaited trial was formally opened by Jiang Hua, chief justice of the Supreme Court. The other thirty-four judges included military men, politicians, and well-known intellectuals;[5] seven of them had no legal training but were "special assessors" brought in to express the people's condemnation of the Cultural Revolution and the Gang. No foreign correspondents were admitted, and only 880 selected Chinese representatives chosen from provincial and government organizations, the party, and the army were admitted in a system of rotation.

The spotlight, of course, was on the star defendant, Jiang Qing, sixty-seven, who strode into the courtroom haughtily. Wearing a shiny black wig, she was immaculately clothed in black—a color said to symbolize the injustice that had been inflicted upon her, and perhaps also her grief over the demise of the leftist ideology she had once personified. Of the remaining Gang members, Zhang Chunqiao, sixty-three, looked weary, defiant, and older than his years; Yao Wenyuan, forty-nine, had grown fatter; while Wang Hongwen, forty-five, appeared hesitant, perhaps a result of his cooperation with the prosecution in what might be called "plea bargaining." Other co-defendants included Chen Boda, seventy-six, Mao's former political secretary who defected to Lin Biao and was purged in 1970, and five generals associated with Lin.[6] Sitting behind the iron bars of the prisoner's dock with downcast faces and uneasy demeanors suggesting long years in prison, they looked unkempt, haggard, and old. Only Jiang Qing appeared proud and strong, staring at the judges and prosecutors with utter contempt.

First, Special Prosecutor Huang Huoqing, head of the State Procuratorate, named six deceased persons who, if alive, would have been prosecuted as co-defendants: Lin Biao, his wife and son, a follower killed in the 1971 air crash, Kang Sheng (Mao's former security head), and his successor, Xie Fuzhi. Pointedly unnamed was Mao, who nevertheless was viewed by many as an "unindicted defendant" of a "Gang of Five."

Then Huang read a 20,000-word indictment charging the defendants with usurpation of state power and party leadership. Their chief crimes fell into four major categories:

1. Framing and persecuting party and state leaders and plotting to overthrow the proletarian dictatorship.
2. Persecuting, killing, and torturing a large number of cadres and masses in excess of 34,375 people.
3. Plotting an armed uprising in Shanghai after Mao's death, with Wang Hongwen in charge of distributing 300 cannon, 74,000 rifles, and 10 million rounds of bullets to the militia in August 1976.
4. Plotting to assassinate Mao and to stage an armed counter-revolutionary coup.

The first two categories applied to all ten defendants; the third to the Gang, and the fourth to the Lin Biao group. Forty-eight specific charges of crimes as legally defined, which did not include ideological or political mistakes, were made.[7]

During the trial, Jiang Qing rejected the services of three government-appointed lawyers on the grounds that they disagreed with her line of defense and could not properly represent her. She chose to speak for herself, and this former actress came close to the best performance of her life. She assumed a studied posture of innocence and composure mingled with a pride and arrogance that suggested a "regal" disdain for the entire proceedings. She tried to project the image of a revolutionary martyr—a Chinese Joan of Arc—whose only crime was defeat in a political struggle. All her actions, she insisted, were carried out on the express orders of Mao with the approval of the Central Committee. How else could she have done as she did? Many Chinese who called her a "witch" and "the most hated in the world" secretly agreed with her, and even conceded in private that she had an "indomitable spirit." Mao was the real culprit, they reasoned, for without him she could never have become what she was.

Jiang was accused of being the chief instigator of a plot to send Wang Hongwen to see Mao in October 1974 to falsely accuse Premier Zhou Enlai of suspicious meetings with other leaders and to block his appointment of Deng as first vice-premier. She responded to the charge contemptuously: "No, I don't know (anything about that). How would I know that?" The prosecutor then called Wang to testify. He admitted that the Four did meet at Jiang Qing's residence in Beijing (the Angler's Guest House) in October 1974 to plot the defamation of Zhou and Deng, adding, "It was Jiang Qing who called (us) together and the purpose was to prevent Deng from becoming first vice-premier." Wang further implicated Yao Wenyuan by stating that Yao pressed him to tell Mao that the situation in Beijing then was critical, much like that at the August 1970 Lushan Conference when Lin Biao attempted a coup. Yao did not deny his part, but emphasized that it was Jiang Qing who organized the plan to frame Zhou and Deng. The other witnesses, Mao's niece Wang Hairong (a vice-minister of foreign affairs) and Nancy Tang (Mao's favorite English translator), testified that Jiang Qing had asked them to defame Zhou and Deng before Mao, but they had refused.

Jiang Qing's response to all this was a look of utter unconcern. At one point, she declared that the charges against her involved a "contradiction among the people," i.e. an outcome of political differences and not of criminal or counterrevolutionary activities. But the chief justice accepted the prosecution's argument that the evidence was "sufficient" and "conclusive" that the Jiang Qing Group (now replacing the term

Jiang Qing at the Trial of the Gang of Four.

the "Gang of Four") framed Zhou and Deng to create favorable conditions for themselves to usurp party leadership and state power.

The Group was also accused of illegally prosecuting three-quarters of a million people and killing 34,375 of them during the decade 1966–76. To prove the crimes, the prosecution projected on a large screen grisly pictures of the badly bruised corpse of a former minister of coal mining and played chilling tape recordings of screaming, wailing, and moaning from intellectuals who refused to cooperate with Jiang Qing and were abused in her private torture chamber.[8]

Chen Boda, assumed dead since his purge in 1970, appeared feeble and old. He admitted having plotted with Jiang Qing and Kang Sheng in July 1967 the purge of Liu Shaoqi and his death in prison. Chen further confessed to ordering the purges of Deng Xiaoping (then party general secretary), Tao Zhu (Canton party leader), and Lu Dingyi (party Propaganda Department head). In late 1967 Chen even had pressed false charges against Zhu De, the co-founder of the Red Army and chairman of the National People's Congress. In all, Chen was charged with wrongful persecution of 84,000 people and the deaths of 2,950 during the Cultural Revolution.

Under repeated questioning, Jiang Qing broke down and admitted that she wrote letters to a group in charge of the persecution of Liu Shaoqi, instructing that Liu be hounded to death.[9] This irrefutably incriminating testimony enabled the prosecution to score a major breakthrough in the trial.

As time wore on Jiang Qing was increasingly affected by the pressures of the trial and began to lose her studied composure. When Wang Hongwen told the court that Mao had warned him "Don't hang around with Jiang Qing," she visibly squirmed. When party writer Liao Mosha, former director of the Beijing Municipal United Front Department purged in 1968, sobbingly testified that he had been imprisoned for eight years and subjected to brutal and inhuman tortures on false charges of being a "fierce secret agent," Jiang Qing angrily shouted at him: "Stop acting! You are a renegade!" When the judges ordered her to stop shouting, she jeered, "I have already spoken. What are you going to do about it?" For her contempt of court, an ejection order was issued. The female bailiffs pushed and pulled her down the aisle, while the spectators broke into thunderous applause.[10]

December 23 saw another stormy session of shouting matches. The witness, Ah Jia, former deputy director of the Beijing Opera Theater, accused Jiang Qing of stealing his opera "The Red Lantern," turning it into one of her own revolutionary model productions, and then persecuting him as a counterrevolutionary so that he could not reveal her plagiarism. He turned to Jiang Qing in court and said: "You were once very high but you are low and despicable. . . . Your heart is vicious and your means are ruthless. You have a sordid soul." Jiang Qing totally lost control, shouting at Ah Jia and calling the judges and the prosecutors "fascists" and "legal quibblers" and everyone else members of the Kuomintang.

In a final move to prove Jiang Qing's guilt, the prosecution produced a list of Central Committee members prepared by her for purge during the Cultural Revolution: Liu Shaoqi, Deng Xiaoping, Marshal He Long, Marshal Peng Dehuai, and Mayor Peng Zhen of Beijing. History showed that all of them had been forced out of office, the prosecution asserted, and all on false charges brought by Jiang Qing.

As regards the six defendants of the Lin Biao Group, all pleaded guilty to the charge that they plotted the murder of Mao while he was touring the country in September 1971, on orders from Lin. The oldest of them, Chen Boda, expressed the sentiments of all six when he said that he had nothing to say in his own defense, but that he asked for mercy from the party.

After twenty-seven days of trial and many recesses extending nearly two months, the court concluded its work on December 29, 1980, without announcing a verdict. Eight of the ten defendants admitted their guilt as charged, but Zhang Chunqiao consistently refused to cooperate and Jiang Qing remained unrepentant to the end. At the final session she broke into a blaze of rhetoric, defending the Cultural Revolution, her role as Mao's wife for thirty-eight years, and her obedience to the orders of Mao and of the Central Committee. It was the present leadership, she charged, that deviated from the socialist line and practiced revisionism. "When you vilify me, you are vilifying Chairman Mao and the Cultural Revolution in which millions of people participated," she proclaimed, hoping to rally the support of opponents of the current leadership. She condemned the judges, the prosecution, and political leaders as reactionaries, counterrevolutionaries, and fascists.[11]

Prosecutor Jiang Wen asked that Jiang Qing be given a severe penalty (though not necessarily death) in view of her "particularly serious, particularly wicked" counterrevolutionary activities. He came close to condemning Mao when he said, "The people of all nationalities throughout the country understand that Chairman Mao was responsible, so far as his leadership was concerned, for their plight during the Cultural Revolution, and that he was also responsible for failing to see through the Lin Biao and Jiang Qing counterrevolutionary cliques." Nonetheless, the prosecutor was quick to add, Mao made great contributions toward overthrowing imperialism, feudalism, and bureaucratic-capitalism, and was responsible for the founding of the People's Republic and for pioneering the socialist cause in China. Echoing the views of Deng, the prosecutor said that Mao's achievements were primary and his mistakes secondary.[12]

Still feisty, unrepentant, and haughty, Jiang Qing shouted in the court: "Fine. Go ahead! You can't kill Mao—he is already dead—but you can kill me. Still I regret nothing. I was right!" Declaring it would be more glorious to have her head chopped off than to yield to her accusers, she told the court: "I dare you to sentence me to death in front of one million people in Tian An Men Square."

Ultimately, just as the trial was political, so the verdict had to reflect the views of the present leadership; and a consensus was not reached for three weeks. From the legal standpoint, Article 103 of the new criminal code prescribes death for those who commit "serious crimes" against the state, but from the political standpoint, was execution the best course to take? Pragmatic leaders such as Deng and Hu and most of the public seemed to favor immediate execution to clear the air, to repudiate the Cultural Revolution and the Mao cult, to satisfy all those who had been victimized by the Gang, and to use the occasion to mark a new dedication to the drive for modernization. Hua Guofeng (who had announced a year earlier that there would be no execution) opposed the death sentence, and large numbers of Maoists considered executing the widow of the founder of the People's Republic too great an affront to Mao.

A compromise solution was offered by party Vice-Chairman Chen Yun, who argued that execution would lift Jiang Qing's position to that of a Maoist revolutionary martyr and perhaps goad the 18 million party members who had joined during and after the Cultural Revolution into a second cultural revolution, creating the danger of a party split and large-scale disturbances. Chen reminded the party that at sixty-seven Jiang Qing would not have many more years to live. A suspended death sentence followed by a long period of confinement in a high security prison would gradually obliterate her from people's memories. The party leaders, who had long been wrestling with this complex dilemma, accepted this approach.[13]

On January 25, 1981, the Special Court announced the death sentence for Jiang Qing and Zhang Chunqiao, but with a two-year suspended execution. Jiang Qing, apparently surprised at the verdict or misunderstanding the meaning of a suspended sentence, immediately denounced the judges, shouting, "To rebel is justified; revolution is no crime! Down with revisionists headed by Deng Xiaoping!" Armed female bailiffs quickly snapped handcuffs on her and hustled her out of the court.

In spite of Wang Hongwen's cooperation and the original low assessment of his responsibility and punishment, he was given life imprisonment. Yao Wenyuan received twenty years; and Chen Boda, eighteen years imprisonment. The other five generals were sentenced to sixteen to eighteen years in jail. With the exception of Yao, forty-nine, most were not likely to survive the long sentences.

Looking at the excruciatingly long time that it took the leadership to reach their verdict, one could only be reminded of the still powerful influence of the patriarch Mao. In life he sponsored the rise of his wife, and in death he shielded her from immediate execution. Jiang Qing seemed to know the present leadership dared not repudiate Mao and the Ninth and

Tenth Party Congresses without severely discrediting the party itself. Indeed, her main line of defense was never directly refuted by the prosecution. But her role in the persecution and deaths of 34,375 people and her maintenance of a private torture chamber were irrefutable crimes, for which even a death sentence seemed too charitable. Yet the verdict, like the trial itself, was politically motivated and would be politically decided. The specter of Mao inhibited the present leadership from killing her.

Some Questions About the Trial

Legal practice, procedure, and terminology in China were very different from those of the West. A defendant in the West is presumed innocent until proven guilty. In China, law has always operated on the assumption that unless a man were guilty of something he would not be arrested in the first place. Western legal terminology clearly differentiates between a "suspect" and a "criminal"; in China an apprehended man is often referred to as a criminal even before judicial determination of his involvement in a crime. Thus, in the present trial the ten defendants were called "major criminals" (*zhufan*) in the indictment, implicitly connoting a prejudgment.

Furthermore, the role of the Special Court was never clearly defined. Was it to determine the guilt or innocence of the defendants, or to fix the degree of guilt of each, or to carry out the orders of the party? From the start everybody knew that the trial was legal in form but political in reality; hence the arguments of the prosecution and the final verdict of the court had to reflect the views of the political leadership. Moreover, while a trial without a jury is quite common in China, the fact that the thirty-five judges outnumbered the defendants by three to one was most unusual even by Chinese standards.

In the political context, the government leaders who wanted the trial and the court president and the chief prosecutor had all been victims of the Cultural Revolution. Could the trial of their former oppressors be impartially carried out without personal vengeance? In the West these judges and prosecutors would most likely have disqualified themselves on the grounds of a "conflict of interests."

In terms of judicial procedures, seven of the thirty-five judges had no legal training at all, raising the question of their qualification. Several of them were called "special assessors" and acted as "silent jurors" rather than judges. The Chinese legal profession, suppressed since 1957, had only recently been revived, and it is understandable that there was a shortage of properly trained legal personnel. But to fill judgeships with persons who had no legal training was a questionable judicial act.

Another procedural question involved the criminal code in which the charges were based, which came into effect on January 1, 1980. Was it legal to apply it retroactively to crimes committed ten to fifteen years earlier?

Finally, the major political obstacle in the trial was the role of Mao. Though unnamed in the indictment, from the final statement of the prosecution it was clear that Mao was largely responsible (as the national leader) for failing to recognize the evil work of the two accused groups and of their effect on the people. It was a tactful way to suggest that Mao was too great to be indicted openly, yet too involved to be dismissed completely. As a young Chinese put it, "It really should be the Gang of Five, but we cannot afford to defile the father-figure yet."[14] This statement contained much truth and probably expressed the feeling of a great many people.

In a sense, the trial could be viewed as an indirect trial of Mao, with Jiang Qing serving as his surrogate. To probe still deeper, one might say that the trial was an indictment of the entire system which allowed Mao to overpower the Central Committee and allowed his wife's group to drive the country to the brink of anarchy and economic disaster. The net effect of the trial was a further erosion of the image of Mao and the effectiveness of the system he created.

The implied censure of Mao's role in his later years pointed up China's current crisis of a lack of "faith, trust, and confidence" in both leaders and party. Chinese youths who lived through the Cultural Revolution became alarmingly cynical and disillusioned, as one ex-Red Guard recalled: "They told us [the Cultural Revolution] was a class struggle. . . . It was not until this year that I realized the Cultural Revolution was really a power struggle, not a class struggle."[15] One writer confided to a foreign correspondent: "To have done things really fairly, the whole Central Committee would have to go on trial, since it approved of the Cultural Revolution. The worst criminal [in this] was Mao."[16]

In spite of all its shortcomings, the trial was a positive step forward—to quote government leaders, a "milestone" in the gradual emergence of a rule of law. It was important for people to see that one could differ with the government without facing a firing squad; at the same time, it satisfied a widely felt need to censure the leadership and excesses of the Cultural Revolution.

A not unexpected repercussion of the trial was its adverse effect on the future of Chairman Hua. As minister of public security during the heyday of the Gang, he signed warrants authorizing arrests, prison sentences, and even deaths for enemies of the Gang, for which some said he should be held responsible. During the trial, dialogues occasionally went beyond the prescribed script and implicated him in the "Criticize Deng, Antirightist Deviationist" Campaign and in the suppression of the Tian An Men Square Incident as well. The Dengists were quick to exploit the situation by accusing him of practicing "personality cultism" after the smashing of the Gang and of mismanaging modernization programs by stressing revolutionary zeal over solid economic planning. The Dengists saw Hua's leadership as a continuation of "wrong" Maoist policy which might provide a future rallying point for disaffected ultraleftists to oppose the course of the present leadership. Great pressure was exerted on him to resign.

Reportedly, Hua offered to resign as party chairman at the November 1980 meeting of the Politburo, to be effective at the next plenum of the party Central Committee in June 1981. Though still chairman until then, Hua had been reduced to a figurehead. The real power of the party fell into the hands of General Secretary Hu Yaobang, and Deng Xiaoping became the de facto chairman of the Military Commission. While no one denied Hua's key role in smashing the Gang, Chinese newspapers increasingly reported that credit for such an exploit "should not go to individuals but to the rules of historical development and to the will of the people."[17] With the phasing out of Hua, the Maoist age came closer to an end.

The main lesson of the trial was that Chinese leadership had to take heed of the defects in their system which allowed one of the gravest misfortunes in Chinese history to occur. Unless corrective measures were devised to prevent its recurrence, instability would continue to plague Chinese politics and block genuine progress. China could not afford to lose any more time in its drive to become a modernized state.

ASSESSMENTS OF MAO

Few issues in Chinese politics had caused such deep dissension as the assessment of Mao. The pragmatic leaders, the victims of the Cultural Revolution and the Gang of Four, and a considerable number of youths favored a candid and critical assessment of Mao's achievements and failings. They regarded his legacy as unfit for the new mission of modernization and cited his failure to lift China from poverty as proof of the inadequacy of his approach. On the other hand, a large number of party and military leaders and cadres who owed their status to Mao's revolution, particularly the "old-timers" and those who rose during the Cultural Revolution, considered such an assessment tantamount to a defamation of the man who led the revolution to success, founded the People's Republic, and pioneered the socialist cause in China. Sympathetic to this latter view were many others who grew up under the influence of ceaseless indoctrination that Mao saved China from imperialism, feudalism, and capitalism, and gave the people a new life. These people could not easily renounce their habitual reverence of the Leader.

In the vortex of such conflicting views, consensus was difficult to reach; the closest thing to it was Vice-Chairman Deng's statement that Mao's achievements were primary and his mistakes secondary. The party adopted the principle of separating Mao's Thought from Mao's leadership qualities. Mao's Thought was said to represent the sum total of the Chinese revolutionary experience: all the contributions made by all the participants in that revolution. Hence it did not reflect Mao's thinking alone but was the legacy of all Chinese, and they had to continue to treasure it. On the other hand, Mao as a leader made many contributions as well as some very serious mistakes. To assess his achievements and errors impartially was to seek truth from facts and to learn from past experiences. Despite its compromising nature, the party's critical position was unacceptable to some. The elder statesman and military leader Ye Jianying, for example, showed his displeasure by leaving Beijing for Guangzhou in late 1980 on "sick leave." He still retained considerable influence among the military and might have used it to affect the assessment of Mao.

General Huang's View

The first open assessment of Mao came in April 1981 from General Huang Kecheng, who as chief of general staff of the Liberation Army had been purged in 1959, along with Defense Minister Peng Dehuai, and had not been rehabilitated until 1977. Now an executive secretary of the party's Central Commission for Inspecting Discipline, he made an assessment perhaps according to the army view. It was a generous and sympathetic review of Mao's accomplishments vis-à-vis his mistakes and a eulogy to the Thought of Mao. The prominence with which Huang's article was published suggested that a party-approved compromise had been reached between military and political leaders and that the pragmatists had made certain concessions in order to reach a consensus. Huang's long article might well have been a preview of the formal party assessment, published in advance to test public reactions.

General Huang enumerated Mao's achievements, beginning with the Autumn Uprising in 1927, to the founding of the Red Army and the Chinese Soviet government, the Long March, ending with the ultimate seizure of power in 1949. He pointed to these achievements as evidence of Mao's major role in founding the party and the People's Republic and in steering the revolution through many crises. As Deng had stated, "Without Mao the Chinese people would have had to grope in the dark for a much longer time." However, the assessment did not deny the contributions of others, or suggest that Mao was China's "savior."

In General Huang's assessment, after Liberation, Mao correctly launched the land revolution, entered the Korean War to fight American aggression, implemented the three major transformations (agriculture, handicrafts, and capitalist industry and commerce), and initiated the socialist revolution and construction of the nation.

Yet, in his later years Mao committed many mistakes, and Huang viewed two as particularly serious. The first was that having established a socialist government and completed the three major transformations, Mao failed to decisively shift the major task of government and party to socialist construction. Simultaneously, he was rash and reckless in seeking unrealistic results in socialist revolution and construction. Secondly, he blurred the two distinct types of contradictions, treating those within the party as if they were enemies outside it: thus class struggle was carried to the extreme, and opportunities were created for bad elements to exploit divisions and initiate the disastrous Cultural Revolution.

In Huang's view, however, these mistakes were not Mao's alone, but should be shared. During the Great Leap of 1958, many comrades were guilty of setting unrealistic targets and exaggerating facts and figures, and they were responsible for exacerbating the already serious problems. The Central Committee itself must also be held responsible for the many erroneous rsolutions it passed. If the old comrades shared Mao's glory in good times, they must also share the burden of his mistakes. While Mao, as chairman, should be assessed the ultimate responsibility, it would be grossly unfair to heap all the blame on one man alone. Only by learning from past mistakes could the living carry on the unfinished task of Mao to serve the country and the people.

Huang diagnosed several reasons for Mao's failures. First, to build socialism without experience in a poor, backward, and extremely populous country was a most difficult task. Even today, the Chinese were still groping for solutions to many problems, and new mistakes were inevitable. In addition, in Mao's later years he became less prudent, less democratic, and less aware of the masses and the reality of the country. Having worked all his life for revolution, he was tired and overwrought, and therefore prone to mistakes and a distorted sense of proportion. Mao was racing against time, hoping to accomplish in a few decades what would normally take several hundred years to achieve. While the result was confusion and failure, his intentions were good; hence he must be viewed with sympathy and understanding. To defame him would defame the party and the socialist motherland.

In conclusion, Huang delved into a long discourse on Maoism as a spiritual weapon not to be discarded lightly. Neither Confucianism, nor the Three People's Principles, but only the Thought of Mao could serve socialist China; for it was the creative transmutation of Marxism-Leninism to the specific conditions of China and as such had distinctive Chinese characteristics. Moreover, the Thought of Mao had been repeatedly affirmed in party constitutions; to negate it would violate the constitution. To be sure, not every word of Mao's was correct and not every concept up-to-date, but the essence of the Thought should serve as a spiritual guide, to be continuously enriched and developed by later generations.[18]

General Huang's assessment was significant for its omissions as well as its content. Mao's successful dealings with the Soviets were omitted, including the very substantial aid program that resulted in one of the largest technological transfers in modern history and was the foundation of early Chinese industrialization. Nor was there any acknowledgment of his skillful recovery of the Soviet Manchurian "loot" and claims to joint ventures in Xinjiang. These substantial diplomatic gains should hardly be ignored, regardless of current Sino-Soviet enmity.

In the assessment, nineteen paragraphs are devoted to a recital of Mao's successes before 1949, compared with a three-line paragraph on his later achievements. The long list of Mao's achievements from 1927 to 1949 was never doubted; he was universally recognized as the greatest revolutionary of the mid-twentieth century. What was in question was his statemanship and the quality of his leadership after 1949. Chinese leaders had frankly admitted that only the first seven years of the People's republic were "good" years and that the next twenty were chaotic.[19] Even in those early years, the decision to enter the Korean War was at best questionable, for it cost China dearly at a time domestic reconstruction needed capital desperately.

The Antirightist Movement of 1957, which sacrificed hundreds of thousands of intellectuals and devastated China's cultural and artistic development, marked the beginning of Mao's erratic leadership. The Great Leap was precipitous. The introduction of communes was premature, forcing farmers into unfamiliar ways of production and driving millions to starvation. The fight with Defense Minister Peng in 1959, a storm in a teapot, held disastrous implications of the Leader's omnipotence, while the power struggle with Liu Shaoqi, dignified under the name of Cultural Revolution, opened the way for a decade of disorder and the disastrous rise of the Gang of Four. Suffice it to say that an impartial assessment should have taken into account these occurrences, good intentions notwithstanding, and critically discussed the glorification of the Thought of Mao which had obstructed the prevention of such mistakes. Moreover, one must question Huang's emphasis on the "spiritual weapon" in a system dedicated to dialectical materialism.

Mao's position in history, as viewed by present party leadership, was revealed in a *Renmin Ribao* [People's Daily] article (March 19, 1981)entitled "Patriotism as a Great Spiritual Power in Building Socialism" which listed "outstanding personalities" in Chinese history. The list included the philosophers Lao-zih, Confucius, and Mencius; Tang poets Li Bo and Du Fu; and the emperors Liu Bang, Tang Taizong, and Genghis Khan.

Among modern personalities, Emperor Kangxi, Hong Xiuquan, Kang Youwei, and Sun Yat-sen were mentioned with more recent leaders such as Li Dazhao, Qu Qiubai, Mao Zedong, Zhou Enlai, Zhu De, and Peng Dehuai. Thus, in what might be called the Chinese Communist "Hall of Fame," Mao's historical model, the First Emperor of Qin, was absent, and Mao himself ranked third among Communist leaders, preceded by the dubious character Qu and followed by Marshal Peng whom Mao had disgraced.

The Party Assessment

The long-awaited party assessment of Mao finally came at the Sixth Plenary Session of the Eleventh Central Committee held between June 27 and 29, 1981. In a leadership reshuffle, the plenum accepted Hua Guofeng's resignation, naming Hu Yaobang chairman of the Central Committee, and Deng Xiaoping chairman of the Military Commission, thereby breaking the tradition of one man holding both posts. Another personnel change was the appointment of Premier Zhao Ziyang as a vice-chairman of the party, forming a "collective triumvirate" with Hu and Deng. Hua Guofeng became the most junior of the six vice-chairmen, a powerless but nevertheless respectable position.[20]

The plenum adopted a 35,000-word "Resolution on Certain Questions in the History of Our Party Since the Founding of the People's Republic," which detailed the party's accomplishments in the past sixty years, especially since 1949. However, a major point of the document was the Cultural Revolution and Mao's role in it. The party's stand was unequivocally critical: "The 'Great Cultural Revolution' from May 1966 to October 1976 caused the most devastating setback and heavy losses to the party, the state, and the people in the history of the People's Republic, and this 'Great Cultural Revolution' was initiated and led by Comrade Mao Zedong."

The movement, said the party, was neither in conformity with the Thought of Mao nor with Marxism-Leninism or the realities of China. Indeed, the assertion that the "Great Cultural Revolution" was a struggle against revisionism and capitalism was, in retrospect, groundless. False accusations were prevalent: the "capitalist roaders" who were knocked down were in fact leaders from different levels of the party and the government who were the core force of socialist construction; the so-called "Liu-Deng Bourgeois Headquarters" never really existed. The persecution of "reactionary intellectual authorities" sacrificed countless talented and accomplished scholars. Moreover, the Cultural Revolution was conducted in the name of the masses but was actually divorced from both the party and the masses. Pointedly, the document stated: "Comrade Mao's leftist mistakes and personal leadership actually replaced the collective leadership of the party center and he became the object of fervent personal worship." The prominence of Mao's errors made a critical assessment absolutely necessary, for "to overlook mistakes or to whitewash them is not only impermissible but is in itself a mistake." The verdict was:

> Practice has shown that the "Great Cultural Revolution" did not in fact institute a revolution or social progress in any sense, nor could it possibly have done so. It was we and not the enemy who were thrown into disorder by it. Therefore, from beginning to end, it did not turn "great disorder under heaven" into "great order under heaven." . . . History has shown that the "Great Cultural Revolution," initiated by a leader laboring under a misconception and capitalized on by counter-revolutionary cliques, led to domestic turmoil and brought catastrophe to the party, the state, and the whole people. . . . Comrade Mao . . . far from making a correct analysis of many problems . . . confused right and wrong and the people with the enemy. . . . Herein lies his tragedy.

The party document also assessed Hua Guofeng; and while it gave him due recognition for his constructive role in the smashing of the Gang and certain economic works, it criticized him for leftist thinking. Hua was branded a "Whateverist"— supporting *whatever* decisions *Mao* made and implementing *whatever* instructions he issued—thereby perpetuating leftist errors. Hua took part in the "Anti-Deng" campaign, and after becoming party chairman blocked moves to correct the wronged cases, including the rehabilitation of victimized cadres and the Tian An Men Square Incident. He even practiced "personality cult." Worse, at the August 1977 Eleventh Central Committee meetings he obstructed attempts to assess the Cultural Revolution critically and instead used his influence to affirm it; later he was also responsible for proceeding with hasty, leftist economic policies. The document concluded: "Obviously, for him to lead the party in correcting the leftist errors, and particularly in reestablishing the fine tradition of the party, is an impossibility."[21]

A terse and crisp assessment of Mao was made by Chairman Hu in his first major address celebrating the sixtieth anniversary of the founding of the party (July 1, 1981). Where General Huang's assesment and the party document had eulogized Mao's accomplishments from 1927 to 1949. Hu's praised the 1911 Revolution and highlighted the "Four Great People's Revolutionary Wars," which included the Northern Expedition (1926-27), the land revolution, the Japanese War (1937-45), and the War of Liberation. It appeared that Hu was making a special effort to conciliate the Nationalists by openly recognizing their role in the Northern Expedition and the Japanese War.

After the establishment of the People's Republic, Hu announced, the party led the people in defeating imperialism, hegemonism, and various attempts to destroy the independence and security of the country, and achieved national unification with the exception of Taiwan and several small islands. The elimination of an exploitative class system from a country of one quarter of humanity signified a dramatic social revolution for China and an international victory for Marxism.

Mao's greatest contribution, Hu stated, was his early rejection of the "childish sickness" of worshipping foreign (Soviet) experience in the 1920s and 1930s. He creatively integrated Marxist universal principles with concrete Chinese revolutionary conditions to form a new synthesis that suited the Chinese situation. The Thought of Mao was the "crystallization of the collective wisdom of the party and a record of the victories of the great struggles of the Chinese people," and its creativeness had enriched the storehouse of Marxism. As such, Hu said, it "was, is, and shall be" the guiding principle of the party. Having complimented Mao, Hu then made the official criticism:

> Comrade Mao, like many great historical figures of the past, was not free from shortcomings and mistakes. The principal shortcoming occurred during his later years when, due to long and ardent support by the party and by all the people, he became smug and increasingly and seriously lost contact with realities and the masses. He separated himself from the collective leadership of the party, often rejecting or even suppressing the correct views of others. Mistakes thus became inevitable. A long period of comprehensive, serious mistakes led to the outbreak of the "Great Cultural Revolution," which brought the most severe misfortune to the party and the people. Of course, we must admit that neither before nor after the outbreak of the "Great Cultural Revolution" was the party able to prevent and turn Comrade Mao from his mistakes. On the contrary, it accepted and approved some of his erroneous proposals. We who are long-time comrades-in-arms with Comrade Mao, his long-time followers and students, must realize deeply our own responsibility and resolutely accept the necessary lessons.

Nonetheless, though Comrade Mao committed serious errors in his late years, it is clear that from the perspective of his entire life his contributions to the Chinese revolution far outweigh his mistakes. . . . He was both a party founder and the principal creator of the glorious People's Liberation Army. After the establishment of the People's Republic under the leadership of the party center and Comrade Mao, China was able to stand on its feet and pioneer the socialist cause. Even when he was making serious mistakes during his last years, Comrade Mao still vigilantly guarded the independence and security of the motherland, correctly assessed new developments in world politics and led the party and the people to resist all the pressures of hegemonism, opening a new direction for our foreign relations. During the long period of struggle, all party members absorbed wisdom and strength from Comrade Mao and his Thought. They nurtured the successive generations of our leaders and cadres, and educated our people of different nationalities. Comrade Mao was a great Marxist, a great proletarian revolutionary, theorist, strategist, and the greatest national hero in Chinese history. He made immense contributions to the liberation of all oppressed peoples of the world and to human progress. His great contributions are immortal.[22]

Since Hu's speech commemorated the party's sixtieth anniversary, he appropriately praised other outstanding leaders: Zhou Enlai, Liu Shaoqi, Zhu De, Peng Dehuai, and earlier figures such as Li Dazhao, Qu Qiubai, and Li Lisan along with a number of intellectuals, scientists, two Nationalist generals who joined the Communist cause, and several foreign friends.

It was noteworthy that in the entire speech Hu never once referred to Mao as chairman but only as comrade. The "Great Cultural Revolution" was mentioned in quotes, implying his refusal to recognize its legality. The praise of Liu Shaoqi, Peng Dehuai, and Li Lisan, all Mao's enemies, revealed what the present leadership really thought of Mao.

A Historian's View

In an objective assessment of Mao, historians who seek truth from facts will be among the first to recognize Mao's greatness as a revolutionary leader, founder of the People's Republic, and pioneer of the socialist cause in China. But they would be remiss if they overlooked his various policy blunders and their consequences. First and foremost was his rejection of any population control. Experts, including Beijing University President Ma Yinchu,[23] warned of the serious economic and social consequences of a population explosion, but Mao argued that population problems existed only in capitalist societies. The Soviet Union had no population control and did not suffer any negative consequences—why should China be different? Mao dismissed Malthusian population theories in the naïve belief that more people could do more work—more work meant more production and faster economic development. The result was an uncontrolled increase in population from 500 million in the early 1950s to over a billion today, while arable land, rather than increasing, actually decreased due to national disasters, increased industrial use of land, and the removal of trees for fuel by the poor.

The task of feeding, clothing, and providing shelter and employment for a billion people was a gigantic burden which no other country on earth faces. It drained much of the national resources which otherwise could be used for economic development. With 80 percent of the huge population based in the countryside, improvement of agricultural production was basic to China's socialist construction. Yet Mao followed the Soviet model of investing heavily in heavy industry and lightly in agriculture, resulting in extremely low agricultural productivity. Mao did not heed the Marxist dictum that the foundation of a society lay in the agricultural laborer's productive rate exceeding the individual needs of the laborer, creating a surplus to support the other sectors of the state. For thirty years, China's agricultural sector was neglected and semi-independent, necessitating the importation of food to meet domestic needs, and thereby consuming a considerable amount of scarce foreign exchange reserves. In 1978–79 per farm capita production amounted to only $50 a year—pitifully below any surplus that might support economic growth and improve the standard of living. Unless agricultural conditions were vastly improved and birth control was strictly enforced, China's march toward modernization would, at best, be slow and labored. In retrospect, Mao's population and agricultural policies had created the most serious obstacle to rapid modernization.

The second major policy blunder was the enforced isolation of the country. Except for the 1950s when Sino-Soviet cooperation was in full swing, China had been virtually cut off from the outside world for twenty years. Under the ideology of self-reliance Chinese science, technology, arts, education, and other aspects of culture were deprived of the benefits of developments in other countries. It was exactly during the decades of the sixties and seventies that phenomenal progress was made in the West and Japan, while China preoccupied itself with civil strife and class struggle. The cost of this isolation was practically incalculable.

The third policy blunder was "leftist blind actionism" and "adventurism" in economic development. At a central work conference in December 1980, party Vice-Chairman Chen Yun, an economist, pointedly declared: "Since the founding of the People's Republic, the main mistake in economic development was 'leftism.' The situation before 1957 was relatively good, but after 1958 'leftist' mistakes became increasingly serious. It was a principal mistake . . . and the main source of that mistake was leftist leadership thinking."[24] An obvious manifestation of this "wrong thinking" was an overfondness for quick results, in total disregard of objective economic realities, which resulted in "taking fantasy as truth, working stubbornly according to self-will, and carrying out work today that might be possible for the future." Such "leftist adventurism" severely undermined the productive relations in the economic structure. Furthermore, the doctrine of uninterrupted revolution led to reckless "blind actionism" which set up unrealistic economic targets supported by a level of investment that far exceeded the country's ability to pay. What followed was an unending flow of falsified figures to deceive the leadership, and the twin evils of adventurism and blind actionism together drove the people to the brink of bankruptcy.[25]

Although knowledgeable persons recognized the irrationality of these policies, in speaking out they risked being branded as anti-Maoist or antirevolutionary—therefore the country was thrust unrestrained into one economic crisis after another. Three of the most obvious crises were: (1) the Great Leap (1958–60) which caused a loss of $66 billion and widespread starvation; (2) the disastrous Cultural Revolution (1966–76) which saw investment reach a dangerous 33 percent of the national income in 1970, resulting in government deficits for three years thereafter and an economic dislocation which threatened total collapse; and (3) the grandiose Ten-Year plan of 1976–85, which allocated to construction projects 31.1 to 36.6 percent of the national income in 1976–78, rates which came close to those of the catastrophic years of the Great Leap. Chen Yun concluded that these mistakes occurred because "our thought and action lost contact with the basic conditions of China."[26]

Mao's fourth major mistake was his assumption of an unquestionable superiority within the party, destroying party democracy and collective leadership, and opening the way for "one-man rule." As the revolutionary leader and founding father of the People's Republic, Mao endowed himself with the status of a patriarch (*jia zhang* 家長), tolerating no opinion except his own (*yi yan tang* 一言堂). His actions reflected the feudalistic notion that he who conquered the country controlled it as a family possession (*jia tian xia* 家天下). Thus, official documents frequently started with the phrase "the Chairman, and the party center . . . ," suggesting one man towering above the party, mocking the collective leadership affirmed in the Eighth Party Congress. Sycophants such as secret service head Kang Sheng whetted Mao's appetite by asserting that a party history mentioning the contributions of other leaders belittled Mao and created a rival center. Thus, the party history became a chronicle of the Leader's continuous feuds with others until, one by one, he had knocked them all down.[27] Like the emperors of the past, Mao was a patriarch, Helmsman, and even god-hero, who could do no wrong. He acted with total impunity in "designating" his successor and sponsoring the rise of his wife far beyond her worth. It appears that the Actonian dictum "power corrupts and absolute power corrupts absolutely" holds true even in a dictatorship of the proletariat!

In addition to granting him absolute control, Mao's political style became an example for party secretaries in the provinces and districts to follow; they behaved like small patriarchs and smaller patriarchs in their respective jurisdictions. Nothing could be done without their approval, establishing a highly bureaucratic and privileged class throughout the country.[28]

How could the party allow all this to happen? The Chinese themselves were hard put to find a proper explanation but finally came up with two interpretations. The first stated that in China, as in other Communist countries, the leader of the revolutionary party was empowered with great discretionary authority and freedom of action during the seizure of power. Once success was achieved, the concentration of power had a tendency to become a tradition; and due to the obviously great contributions of the leader, his followers readily accepted his exalted status. His status eventully became institutionalized, and he received lifelong tenure as *the* Leader, as well as credit for the fruits of others' labor.

The broader official explanation concerned the profound impact of China's feudal past on the thought and action of all. The vestiges of the distinction between high and low, of the rank and grade system, and the role of the family head could be seen everywhere. Farmers and small producers were unaccustomed to controlling their own fates, relying instead on the graces of the emperor as "savior," giving in return their loyalty and gratitude. Thus, there was a powerful social precedent for the high concentration of authority in one man. Even the party itself reflected this feudal influence, permitting the emergence of a situation in which no one dared criticize the patriarch. Consequently, collective leadership and democratic centralism became meaningless: in the former, one was "more equal" than others, and in the latter, centralism prevailed over democracy.[29]

These explanations were certainly valid, but they omitted one key element: it was Mao's firm control of the army, the secret police, the security apparatus, the 8341 unit, and the network of intelligence and investigatory agencies, which made opposition to him virtually impossible. Those who dared to criticize him risked their futures and even their lives.

In conclusion, historians would agree that Mao was extremely successful as a revolutionary but disappointingly erratic as a nation builder. His great achievements before 1957 were a source of inspiration to others, but his serious mistakes thereafter must serve as a lesson to all.

A NEW LEADERSHIP AND A NEW ORDER

With the delicate assessment of Mao finally out of the way and the party's guilt recognized, a heavy psychological burden was lifted. The new power structure put Hu, Deng, and Zhao firmly in control of the party, the military, and the government, and cemented their plans for China's future. They were committed to a revolution of modernization. Lest there be any misunderstanding, Hu impressed upon the nation the following six points in his speech commemorating the sixtieth anniversary of the founding of the party:[30]

1. All party members must dedicate themselves to modern construction of Chinese socialism regardless of personal sacrifice, and serve the people with all their hearts and minds.
2. Under the new historical conditions, we must advance Marxism and the Thought of Mao Zedong. [Hu reaffirmed the importance of the four basic principles: the socialist line, the proletarian dictatorship, the leadership of the Communist Party, and Marxism-Leninism and the Thought of Mao.]
3. We must further strengthen the democratic life of the party and tighten the party discipline. . . . We must forbid any form of individual worship. . . . All important issues must be decided after collective discussions by appropriate party committees. No one man should have the final say. All members of the committees involved must abide by such decisions. At all levels of party organization, we must implement collective leadership . . . with emphasis on quality and efficiency. [To enhance party democracy,] any member has the right to criticize party leaders at party meetings, even including the top leaders at the center, with impunity. [But no one is allowed to create his own independent kingdom.]
4. We must regularly dust ourselves off in order to insure revolutionary youthfulness permanently within the political framework of the government. [Very pointedly Hu admitted] in the past excessive struggles resulted in a counter-

productive situation in which no one dared to make self-criticism or offer criticism. We must rectify this unhealthy style of behavior.

5. We must select young and vigorous cadres of character and knowledge for different levels of leadership.

6. We must persist in supporting internationalism and share the breathings and the lives of the proletarian class and people all over the world. . . . In dealing with strong and rich countries we must preserve our national dignity and independence, never permitting any cowering or toadying action and thought. We must be determined to unite all people including those on Taiwan in the sacred struggle for the return of Taiwan to the motherland.

It was clear that Mao's political work style and approach to economic development would not be followed: there would be no more personal worship, no suppression of free expression in party meetings, and no penalty for criticizing the leaders. However, all cadres were to be subordinated to orders from above to carry out economic construction, without feigning compliance while secretly resisting implementation. Also rejected were Maoist ideas of class struggle, disdain for intellectuals and foreign contacts, and opposition to limited private enterprise.

To ensure the success of socialist modernization, which was "a great revolution in itself," Hu called for intraparty and party-citizen unity as well as international exchanges in economics, culture, and science and technology, in order to develop a "prosperous, strong, highly democratic, and highly cultured modern socialist power," which would ultimately lead China to the communist utopia.

Hu's speech, together with the communiqué and resolution of the Sixth Plenum, was a crowning testimony to the victory of the pragmatists. In the spirit of unity, stability, conciliation, pragmatism, democracy, and realistic economic development, a new order was born under new historical conditions. With this, the Maoist era had come to an end.

From the perspective of China's long history, every sixty years formed a cycle, and the history of the Chinese Communist Party seemed to be no exception. The monumental changes now unfolding were a promising sign of the nation's viability, and the people of China welcomed the beginning of a new age with rising expectations.

CHINESE COMMUNISM: A THIRTY-FIVE-YEAR REVIEW

On October 1, 1949, standing atop the Gate of Heavenly Peace to proclaim the establishment of the People's Republic, Mao shouted triumphantly: "The Chinese people have stood up!" What a heroic voice, what an auspicious beginning! Foreign imperialism and domestic opposition had been swept away, and the country was unified in a way unknown since the mid-nineteenth century. China was a blank canvas for the artist Mao; and his revolutionary romanticism, vision, idealism, and egalitarianism had caught the imagination of millions inside and outside China. The charismatic leader's articulation of a national purpose and the promise of the future reinforced the desire of 500 million people to rebuild their country. The galaxy of talents surrounding Mao and contributing to the success of the revolution seemed to ensure China's goals of domestic security, international respectability, and eventual emergence as a world power.

That these goals had been met at least in part was obvious. The greatest accomplishments had been the unification of China (except Taiwan) under one central government, the attainment of the status of a major participant in world affairs, the elimination of the curse of landlordism, the laying of a foundation for industrialization, the improvement of public health, the selective development of science and technology (especially in nuclear power and rocketry), the improvement of literacy, and significant archeological finds that could result in new interpretations of ancient Chinese history. The provision of subsistence-level food, housing, clothing, and employment for over a billion people answered a challenge no other country on earth has ever had to meet. Finally, statistics showed considerable increases in total industrial and agricultural productions and in social services.

Yet recent Chinese leaders had openly acknowledged that despite selective progress, the country remained in a state of dire poverty and scarcity (*yi qiong er bai*). The physical complexion of the country and the livelihood of the people had not substantially changed in twenty years;[31] the gap between China and advanced countries was probably wider today than in 1949 due to phenomenal progress in science, technology, and economic development in other countries. What was it that kept China from making greater progress in the three and one-half decades following liberation?

The chief deterrents within China had been political instability and the destruction of the principle of democracy within and without the party. Except for seven years (1949–56) of revolutionary momentum and the euphoria of building a new order, China's recent history had been plagued with such upheaval and strife that the country had been nearly destroyed. Political turmoil had resulted in the loss of much able talent, interruptions in economic development, and devastation of intellectual and artistic creativity.

In considering the source of Chinese political instability, the Eighth Party Congress of 1956 was generally viewed as the Rubicon in political development. This Congress, like the previous one, stressed party democracy and free discussion of issues. The Second Plenum of the Seventh Congress had explicitly enjoined the development of a "personality cult" by forbidding the glorification of leaders through literature, birthday celebrations, or renaming cities and streets after them. Throughout the Seventh Congress (1949–56) participants expressed their views freely, creating what might be called "A Hall of Many Voices" (*Qun yan tang*). Party democracy and collective wisdom seemed to assure the new nation's progress.

The Eighth Congress likewise stressed collective leadership and a democratic style of work, while opposing bureaucratism and worship of the individual, characteristics already apparent in the party hierarchy. Liu Shaoqi delivered the keynote report which enumerated the great successes of Chinese socialism in eliminating former class conflicts.[32] In view of these socialist transformations, Liu maintained that the conflict between the capitalist and proletarian classes had been largely resolved, and current contradictions existed only between the productive forces of advanced socialism and those of "backward" socialism. The Congress resolved that henceforth the focal point of the party and the government should be "the transformation of our country from a backward agricultural state to an advanced industrial state as fast as possible." It called for the modernization of industry, agriculture, communications, and national defense. While science and technology were not specified, they were recognized as basic to all other development. The Congress reflected China's bright future under the collective leadership of Mao, Liu, Zhou, and Zhu De; and the period from 1956 to early 1957 was regarded as a "springtime" in party history.

Into this springtime Mao introduced the Hundred Flowers Campaign. When intellectuals criticized sharply certain party policies, Mao responded as though Chinese communism itself were endangered by the criticism, and launched the Antirightist Campaign which adversely affected as many as one million people. Mao overthrew the decisions of the Eighth Congress, proclaiming that "the decisions of the Eighth Party Congress referring to the major contradiction between the productive forces of advanced and backward socialism is incorrect," and that capitalist-proletarian class conflict and capitalist-socialist line struggle remained the principal contradictions in Chinese society. From then on Mao enlarged the scope of class struggle which caused ceaseless turmoil. Rejecting collective leadership, the concept of patriarchal rule gained ascendancy and the party center became "The Hall of One Voice" (*Yi yan tang*). When Defense Minister Peng Dehuai expressed his views on the Great Leap in 1959, he was dismissed and disgraced as a "rightist opportunist." Thereafter, no one dared speak out. Party democracy was shattered, and the tenets of the Eighth Congress were negated.[33]

Once Mao's "omnipotence" was demonstrated, opportunists and intriguers crowded around him, gaining power by controlling access to him. Their power struggles reverberated throughout the nation in intensified class struggle and in the Cultural Revolution. The dominance of Kang Sheng, Lin Biao, and the Gang of Four turned the proletarian dictatorship into a fascist one, with the added features of feudalism and revisionism.[34]

Political instability and the disappearance of party "democracy" inevitably affected economic development and the peoples' lives. On July 1, 1979, an editorial in the *People's Daily* commented:

> In the past thirty years whenever party democracy was relatively sufficient and democratic centralism relatively healthy, party leadership in economic work was in tune with reality. When problems arose, they were discovered and corrected easily, bringing about rapid socialist economic development. Whenever there was a lack of democracy in the party, nobody dared to speak out or speak the truth. Blind obedience was prevalent and the party's economic policies frequently lost touch with reality and objective laws. Socialist economic development then slowed, stagnated, or even retrogressed.[35]

Chinese statistics show that economic development was marked by three periods of growth (1949–57, 1963–65, 1977–88) and two periods of decline (1958–62, 1966–76). During Mao's twenty-seven-year rule, only 1952–57 were years of genuine growth. The following statistics summarize development in the past thirty-five years.

China's erratic development demonstrates that revolutionary leaders who were skillful in political struggle were not necessarily knowledgeable in economic matters. Mao in particular would not heed the advice of economic experts or act according to economic laws and the realities of the country. In the fifties he adopted the Soviet model for development and emphasized heavy industry over agriculture and light industry, when the concrete situation in China suggested the reverse as more logical. When the Soviet model proved ill-suited, he precipitously resorted to the Commune and the Great Leap. What followed for the next decades was the familiar saga of "leftist

Periods of Recovery and Growth

	1949–52	1953–57	1963–65	1977	1978–86
Industry	36%	19.2%	7.9%	14.1%	134.3%
Agriculture	14%	4.5%	11.1%		67.2%
National Income	n.a.	n.a.	14.5%		

Periods of Decline

	1958–62	1967	1968	1974	1976
Industry	+3.8%	−13.8%	−5%	+0.3%	+1.3%
Agriculture	−4.3%		−2.5%		
National Income	−3.9%				

(Figures from the *Journal of Philosophy and Social Sciences,* Nanjing University, No. 3:1–8 (1979). See also CIA, "China-Economic Policy and Performance in 1987," (Washington, D.C., 1988).

adventurism," which caused waste of time, energy, capital, and valuable talents. Consequently, Chinese per capita income of $300 ranked last among the socialist countries, and productivity lagged far behind that of Hong Kong and South Korea.[36]

Yet in spite of political instability and erratic economic performance, substantial progress was registered in agricultural and industrial productions. The former averaged a 2 to 3 percent annual growth rate, and the latter, a 9 to 10 percent rate. Between 1952 and 1987, grain grew from 163.9 million metric tons to 402 million tons; coal, from 66.4 million tons to 920 million tons; steel, from 1.35 million tons to 56.22 million tons; crude oil, from 440,000 tons to 134 million tons; and electric power, from 7.3 billion kwh to 496 billion kwh.[37] However, many of the benefits of increased productions were compromised by the population explosion from 570 million to 1.08 billion, resulting in an extremely low standard of living for most Chinese.

The lessons to be learned from the past thirty-five years were many. First and foremost, there must be political and social stability to enable the government to carry out orderly reforms and development. Second, population control must be strictly enforced so as to achieve a zero growth rate. Third, international cooperation must be strengthened in all areas including science, technology, education, and the arts. Fourth, war must be avoided if possible, for it is the biggest waster of financial and human resources. Fifth, the political system must be reformed to prevent the recurrence of patriarchal rule and to ensure democracy within and without the party. Bureaucratism, lifelong tenure of cadres, and special privileges for the few must be drastically reduced, if not eliminated, with the institution of a benevolent retirement system. Sixth, economic development must be neither "leftist" nor "rightist" but "centrist," based on realities and economic laws. Last but not least, the party must take note of the Actonian dictum that "power corrupts and absolute power corrupts absolutely." It must rid itself of widespread corruption and stamp out the rampant inflation. Unless these serious problems are effectively addressed, the party's credibility before the people would be in question.

NOTES

1. *Central Daily News*, Nov. 16, 1980. Based on Nationalist intelligence reports.
2. *Ibid.*, Aug. 12, 1980. Intelligence reports.
3. *Ibid.*, Jan. 29, 1981. Intelligence reports.
4. *The Christian Science Monitor*, Jan. 16, 1981.
5. Including the famous sociologist Fei Xiaotong.
6. The five generals were: Huang Yongsheng, 70, former chief-of-staff of the Liberation Army; Wu Faxian, 65, former air force commander; Li Zuopeng, 66, former political commissar for the Navy; Qiu Huizuo, 66, former head of the army logistics department; and Jiang Tengjiao, 61, former air force commander in Nanjing.
7. Full text of indictment in *A Great Trial in Chinese History* (Beijing, 1981), pp. 18–26, 148–49.
8. The coal minister was Zhang Linzhi. Eleven professors and acquaintances of Liu Shaoqi were tortured and three of them died. See *A Great Trial*, pp. 43–45, 56–57.
9. *A Great Trial*, p. 39.
10. *Central Daily News*, Dec. 13, 1980.
11. *The Christian Science Monitor*, Dec. 30, 1980.

12. *A Great Trial*, p. 105.
13. *Central Daily News*, Jan. 11 and 12, 1981. Nationalist intelligence reports.
14. Interview by a University of California student, Mark Dowie, "China's Differing Moods on the Gang of Four," *Daily Nexus*, Jan. 8, 1981.
15. *Ibid.*
16. *Time* Magazine, Jan. 12, 1981, p. 28.
17. *The Christian Science Monitor*, Dec. 18, 1980.
18. Full text of Huang's speech in the *Renmin Ribao* [People's Daily], April 11, 1981. Tr. in quotes are mine. There is an abridged version of English translation in *Beijing Review*, No. 17, April 17, 1981.
19. Remarks by Vice-Chairman Chen Yun in the *Renmin Ribao* [People's Daily], April 9, 1981.
20. "Communiqué of the Sixth Plenary Session of the 11th Central Committee of CPC," adopted June 29, 1981, *Beijing Review*, No. 27, July 6, 1981, pp. 6–9.
21. Chinese text of the "Resolution" in the *Renmin Ribao* [People's Daily], July 1, 1981. Tr. mine. An English version, somewhat less literal than mine, may be found in *Beijing Review*, No. 27, July 6, 1981, pp. 10–39.
22. Chinese text of Hu's speech in the *Renmin Ribao* [People's Daily], July 2, 1981. Tr. mine.
23. And others such as Chen Da and Wu Jingchao.
24. "Leadership Thinking in Rectifying Economic Work: On the Leftist Mistakes in Economic Construction," by a special commentator of the *Renmin Ribao* [People's Daily]. Chinese text in *Renmin Ribao*, April 9, 1981. Tr. mine.
25. *Ibid.*
26. *Ibid.*
27. *Renmin Ribao*, Sept. 18, 1980, p. 5.
28. "On the Necessity of Reforming the Leadership System," by a commentator of the *Hongqi* [Red Flag] Magazine. Chinese text in *Hongqi*, No. 17, 1980, pp. 2–4.
29. *Ibid.*, pp. 5–8.
30. Full text in the *Renmin Ribao* [People's Daily], July 2, 1981. Tr. mine.
31. According to Hu Qiaomu, president of the Chinese Academy of Social Sciences. See his article, "Observe Economic Laws, Speed Up the Four Modernizations," *Peking Review*, No. 47, Nov. 24, 1978, pp. 18–19.
32. 1. Elimination of bureaucratic-comprador-capitalist class.
    2. Liquidation of landlord class and disappearance of rich peasants.

3. Transformation of bourgeoisie class from exploiter to workers.
4. Transformation of individual peasants and workers into collective workers.
5. Working class assuming leadership positions.
6. The reform of intellectualism to serve socialism.
33. Lu Zhongjian, "Sanshi nian di jiaoxun" (The lessons of thirty years), *Zhengming* Magazine, Hong Kong, No. 24, Oct. 1, 1979, pp. 8, 11.
34. *Ibid.*, 14.
35. *Renmin Ribao*, [People's Daily], July 1, 1979. Tr. mine.
36. Lu Zhongjian, p. 6.
37. Xue Muqiao (ed.), *Almanac of China's Economy, 1985/1986* (Hong Kong, 1986), p. 26; State Statistical Bureau, Beijing, Feb. 23, 1988; *Beijing Review*, March 7–13, 1988.

FURTHER READING

A Great Trial in Chinese History (Beijing, 1981).

"Aiguo zhuyi shi jianshe shehui zhuyi di juda jingshen liliang" (Patriotism is a great spiritual power in building socialism), *Renmin Ribao* [People's Daily], March 19, 1981.

Bonavia, David, *Verdict in Peking: The Trial of the Gang of Four* (London, 1984).

"Communiqué on Fulfillment of China's 1980 National Economic Plan," issued on April 29, 1981, by the State Statistical Bureau, *Beijing Review*, 19:23–27 (May 11, 1981); 20:17–20 (May 18, 1981).

"Communiqué of the Sixth Plenary Session of the 11th Central Committee of CPC," adopted on June 29, 1981, *Beijing Review*, 27:6–8 (July 6, 1981).

"Comrade Ye Jianying's Speech—At the Meeting in Celebration of the 30th Anniversary of the Founding of the People's Republic of China," *Beijing Review*, 40:7–32 (Oct. 5, 1979). Complete Chinese text in *Renmin Ribao* [People's Daily], Sept. 30, 1979.

"Duanzheng jinji gongzuo di zhidao sixiang: Lun jinji jianshe zhong di zuoqing cuowu" (The leadership's thinking in rectifying economic work: On the leftist mistakes in economic construction), *Renmin Ribao* [People's Daily], Peking, April 9, 1981.

Han, Suyin, *Wind in the Tower: Mao Tse-tung and the Chinese Revolution, 1949–1975* (Boston, 1976).

Hsiung, James C. (ed.), *Symposium: The Trial of the "Gang of Four" and Its Implication in China* (Baltimore, Md., 1981).

Occasional Papers/Reprint Series in Contemporary Asian Studies, University of Maryland, School of Law.

Hu Yaobang, "Speech Commemorating the 60th Anniversary of the Founding of the Chinese Communist Party," Chinese text in the *Renmin Ribao* [People's Daily], July 2, 1981; English tr. in *Beijing Review*, 28:9–24 (July 13, 1981).

Huang, Kecheng, "How to Assess Chairman Mao and Mao Zedong Thought," *Beijing Review*, 17:15–23 (April 27, 1981).

Johnson, Chalmers, "The Failure of Socialism in China," *Issues & Studies*, XV:7:22–33 (July 1979).

Kallgren, Joyce K. (ed.), *The People's Republic of China after Thirty Years: An Overview* (Berkeley, 1979).

Li, Honglin, "Kexue he mixin" (Science and superstition), *Renmin Ribao* [People's Daily], Peking, Oct. 2, 1978.

———, "Chinese Communist Party Is Capable of Correcting Its Mistakes," *Beijing Review*, 25:17–20 (June 22, 1981).

Li, Victor H., *Law without Lawyers: A Comparative View of Law in the United States and China* (Boulder, 1978).

"Lingdao zhidu bixu gaige" (The leadership system must be reformed), *Hongqi* [Red Flag], 17:2–4, (1980). Written by a commentator of the journal.

Liu, Kwang-ching, "World View and Peasant Rebellion: Reflections on Post-Mao Historiography," *The Journal of Asian Studies*, XL:2:295–326 (Feb. 1981).

Lu, Zhongjian, "Sanshi nian di jiaoxun" (The lessons of thirty years), *Zhengming* Magazine, Hong Kong, 24:5–15, (Oct. 1, 1979).

Lu, Shi, " 'Mao xuan' wujuan yingdang chongshen chongbian" (Vol. 5 of Mao's *Selected Works* should be reexamined and reedited), *Zhengming* Magazine, Hong Kong, 24:16–17 (Oct. 1, 1979).

Morath, Inge, and Arthur Miller, *Chinese Encounters* (New York, 1979).

Oxnam, Robert B., and Richard C. Bush (eds.), *China Briefing, 1980* (Boulder, 1980).

Pye, Lucian W., *Mao Tse-tung: The Man in the Leader* (New York, 1976).

"Quanli buneng guofen jizhong yu geren" (Power should not be overly concentrated in one man), *Hongqi* [Red Flag], 17:5–8 (1980). Written by a special commentator of the journal believed to be one close to Vice-Chairman Deng Xiaoping.

"Resolution on Certain Questions in the History of Our Party Since the Founding of the People's Republic of China." Adopted June 27, 1981, at the Sixth Plenary Session of the Eleventh Central Committee of Chinese Communist Party. Chinese text in *Renmin Ribao* [People's Daily], July 1, 1981; English translation in *Beijing Review*, 27:10–39 (July 6, 1981).

Shao, Yü-ming, "Shih-lun Chung-Kung cheng-ch'üan tsai Chung-kuo chin-tai-shih shang ti kung-kuo" (An appraisal of the achievements and failures of the Chinese Communist regime in modern Chinese history), *Hai-wai hsüeh-jen* [Overseas scholars], Taipei, 99:6–20 (Oct. 1980).

Wilson, Dick (ed.), *Mao Tse-tung in the Scales of History* (Cambridge, Eng., 1977).

Witke, Roxane, *Comrade Chiang Ch'ing* (Boston, 1977).

Yahuda, Michael, "Political Generations in China," *The China Quarterly*, 80:793–805 (Dec. 1979).

"Yao gongkai di kexue di ping Mao" (Mao should be openly and scientifically assessed) *Zhengming* Magazine, Hong Kong, 24:4 (Oct. 1, 1979), editorial.

6

Building Socialism
with Chinese Characteristics

The party conference of December 1978 (Third Plenum, Eleventh Central Committee) was a major landmark in the political and economic life of the post-Mao era. It signaled the rise of Deng Xiaoping as the paramount leader and adopted the key decisions of accelerating economic development and opening the door to the outside world. Deng became the architect of a new socialist transformation that promised to lift China out of her poverty and developmental stagnation.

THE VISION OF DENG XIAOPING

Initially, Deng had no master plan. He had only the pragmatic sense that, in order for any transformation to be successful, socialist construction in China must have Chinese characteristics and that Marxism-Leninism must be integrated with Chinese realities. In this, he was not unlike Mao, who early recognized that a successful Communist revolution in China depended on the same integration. History will take note of Mao's revolution and Deng's construction as two of the most powerful events in China, and to a degree in the world—during the second half of the 20th century. As such, both of them will receive due recognition.

As the year following the conference passed, Deng gradually evolved a clearer vision of his plans for the future of China. In December 1979, when the visiting Japanese Prime Minister, Masayoshi Ōhira, asked: "What is the aim of your Four Modernizations?" Deng readily replied that it was to quadruple the then current gross national product (GNP) of $250 billion to $1 trillion by the end of the century, with a per capita GNP of $1,000. Later, he clarified his statement by taking into consideration the inevitable population increase from one billion to 1.2 billion and lowered the goal of a per capita GNP to $800 by A.D. 2000, while leaving the gross GNP goal unchanged at $1 trillion. Once this target was reached, China would have a solid foundation from which further gains could be made. It could then join the ranks of the more advanced nations within 30 to 50 years. The figure of $1 trillion by A.D. 2000 quickly caught on and became a national fixation.[1]

Reaching the goal, of course, would require the dedication of the entire nation; accelerated economic growth; and the absorption of foreign capital, science and technology, and managerial skills. Hence, it was essential to adopt the dual policy of economic reform and opening up the country to the outside world. Since 80 percent of the people lived in the countryside, invigorating the rural economy and raising farm income and the peasants' standard of living became the first order of business. Successful rural reforms would be followed by industrial reforms in the urban areas. Meanwhile, a long-range open-door policy was launched to increase foreign trade; to promote tourism; and to absorb foreign capital, technology, and managerial skill. It was stressed that the open-door policy was necessary for China to advance: the closed-door policy from the mid-Ming period to the Opium War (1840) and the unfortunate period 1958–76 resulted in years of ignorance and backwardness.[2]

Deng assured his fellow citizens that their fear that the Open-Door represented a capitalistic erosion of socialism was unfounded. The mainstays of the Chinese economy would remain socialistic: China would maintain the socialist principle of distribution, and the state still owned the means of production and all the basic economic structures. Influx of foreign capital could not undermine the socialist economic foundation as joint ventures with foreigners would be at least 50 percent Chinese. To be sure, the open-door policy would have some negative effects, but it would not lead to a capitalistic revival. Even with a per capita GNP of several thousand dollars, there should be no fear of the rise of a new capitalist class. Deng asked, "What's wrong with increasing the wealth of the country and the people?"[3]

Deng was realistic enough to know that different regions of the country were endowed with different natural and human resources, so that no two areas could develop at the same pace. He would permit some regions and people to get rich first as examples for others to emulate. The city of Suzhou, 70 miles from Shanghai, was a source of inspiration, for it had already reached the level of affluence represented by a per capita GNP of $800. Curious about the quality of life there—which might give an inkling of what China would be like in A.D. 2000—Deng made a visit in 1983. He found the local people well clothed, well fed, living in more spacious quarters than other places (on average 20 square meters per person), enjoying television, and willing to invest in local education. The crime rate was low, and the local inhabitants exuded a spirit of well-being and confidence. Their life-style was characterized by a deep love for their native locality and a conspicuous lack of desire to move to large cities such as Beijing and Shanghai.[4]

Deng became more and more confident that his dream could be realized. On October 1, 1984, on the occasion of the 35th anniversary of the founding of the People's Republic, he confidently announced to the nation that the annual economic growth rates of 7.9 percent during the period 1979–83 and 14.2 percent in 1984 surpassed the 7.2 percent needed to quadruple the GNP to $1 trillion by the year A.D. 2000. If the growth rate continued, China could reach the projected target.

The World Bank also seemed to agree with this.[5] Deng's pragmatic strategy was "one step at a time; watch out and keep the momentum going."

AGRICULTURAL REFORM

Traditionally, argiculture was the foundation of the Chinese state and economy. Therefore, it was considered essential to institute radical reforms in agriculture first. For the 20 years between 1957 and 1978, agriculture had been in a sorry state, with the annual growth of grain production only 2.6 percent; and of cotton, 2.1 percent.[6] China had had to import large quantities of grain to feed its growing population. The rural economy was listless, if not lifeless. The standard of living on farms had not improved for two decades, and a strong incentive to work was almost nonexistent.

Everybody knew that the most serious obstacle to the reinvigoration of the rural economy was the commune system. Since it was the kingpin of the Maoist rural economic structure, nobody dared criticize or tamper with this sacrosant institution as long as Mao lived. Now it was recognized that nothing less than a fundamental reform could inject new life into the stultified rural economy, rekindle enthusiasm for work, release the vast potential of the peasant masses, and improve their standard of living.

The party conference of December 1978 adopted the drastic decisions of using greater material incentives and loosening the control mechanisms that had heretofore constrained growth in the rural sector. In the months that followed, discussions between local and central government leaders led to the adoption of what was described as the "Responsibility System," or *baogan daohu,* meaning literally "full responsibility to the household." Under this system, land remained public, but each household received a plot for cultivation and negotiated a contract with the commune production team or economic cooperative. The contract specified quantities of crops to be planted and the quota of output to be handed to the production team or cooperative as payment for the use of the land. This payment also covered such common expenses as irrigation fees, health care, and welfare. Each household had full control of its labor resources and could either keep or sell in the free market the products that exceeded the contracted quota. The farming household assumed full responsibility for the entire process of production—from the selection of seeds, choice of fertilizer, labor allocation, work schedule, and preparation of soil, all the way to the final product.

The Responsibility System, which began in 1979, gradually spread through the provinces in the period 1980–81 and the process accelerated during the 1982–83 period, so that by 1984 some 98 percent of farm households came under it. A plot of land was initially assigned to each household for a season or a year. But later, in 1984, the assignments were extended to 15 years to encourage long-term planning and investment in the land. The longer contracts were in consideration of such agricultural concerns as the intensity of farming, choice of crops—especially slow-maturing fruit trees—and development of soil fertility.[7] More recently, the land contract was made inheritable, as was the house on the land, to encourage further long-range investment. However, cancellation of contracts could occur in cases of nonfulfillment of the original terms.

The government also encouraged rural workers to specialize in crops, livestock, forestry, fisheries, or other diverse sidelines. This was in contrast to Mao's heavy emphasis on grain production. Gradually, "specialized households" (*zhuanye hu*) emerged, which did not till the land but engaged exclusively in noncrop production. Between the specialized households and the ordinary farming households were the "key households" (*zhongdian hu*), which tilled the land but were primarily occupied with noncrop activities such as fishery and animal husbandry. These two types of households amounted to some 24 million by October 1984, or 13 percent of total rural households.[8]

The expansion of the *Baogan* Responsibility System increasingly superseded the functions of the commune until the latter was all but extinct. Today only a few models are left as historic landmarks or as showpieces for foreign visitors and students of Chinese social and economic history. In 1984 a further significant restructuring came when the individual household was allowed to transfer the contracted land to another household with the approval of the local cooperative unit. This was instituted to allow for times when a household might be beset with sickness, death, or other problems that would prevent it from utilizing its parcel of land. In 1987, the Thirteenth Party Congress further liberalized the sale of right to land utilization by one household to another. Theoretically, it is not inconceivable that one household could have acquired the right to cultivate the contracted land of two or three or more neighbors. Some critics pointed to this possibility as a case of incipient capitalism, but such occurrences were rare. In any event, land remained public and chances for renewed capitalism seemed small.

As a result of the argicultural reforms, both yield and productivity rose sharply. In 1987, rice and wheat yields had risen 50 percent over those obtained under the commune system. More importantly, the farmer spent only an average of 60 days a year on the crops, compared with 250 to 300 days a year in the field in the days of the farm collectives. The time saved was spent on sideline activities aimed at profit. Cash income quadrupled and the standard of living vastly improved. This newfound prosperity was soon reflected in new brick houses; new televisions and furniture; and new, more colorful clothes for the participating households. In Sichuan and many other provinces, the contracted quota accounted for approximately one-sixth of the total output, and although most plots were less than one acre in size, there was enough food raised for each household. The farmers led an ownerlike life, and quite a few of them earned incomes in excess of 10,000 yuan annually (*wanyuan hu*).[9]

Thus, the dismantling of the commune was not abrupt but took place over a period of five years. Now a new type of township-collective-household rural structure emerged, which assumed some of the former functions of the commune, but, with a clear-cut division of labor. The township concerned itself with government and administrative affairs, the party committee did party work, and the economic collectives performed such functions as signing the responsibility contracts with the individual households. Not infrequently, the former commune production brigades and teams became new economic cooperatives, and many former commune departments were transformed into "village and township enterprises" engaged in production, processing, transportation, marketing, and service industries.[10]

The results of the reforms were nothing less than spectacular. The growth rate in annual grain production rose from 2.1 percent during the period 1957–78 to 4.9 percent during the period 1979–84, with record harvests of 407 million metric tons in 1984, compared with the previous 305 million metric tons. Per capita grain production also surpassed the high 302 kilograms achieved in 1957 and even the pre-Liberation production peaks. Total production of crops and livestock increased 49 percent between 1978 and 1984.[11]

The remarkable advance in agricultural output changed China from being a net importer to an exporter of grains, soybeans, and raw cotton. China achieved a trade surplus of $4 billion in agricultural products between 1980 and 1984, the largest gain in 35 years.[12] Per capita farm income rose from Y134 in 1978 to Y310 in 1983 and Y463 in 1987. Success came not only through hard work and good planning, but also from

Major Farm Products (in million tons)						
	1952	*1957*	*1965*	*1978*	*1980*	*1984*	*1987*
Grain	163.42	195.05	194.53	304.77	320.56	407.31	402.41
Cotton	1.30	1.64	2.09	2.16	2.07	6.25	4.19
Oil-bearing Crops	15.25	4.19	4.19	3.62	5.21	7.69	11.91
Sugarcane	7.11	10.39	13.39	21.11	22.80	39.51	46.85

Sources: Xue Muqiao (ed.), *Almanac of China's Economy, 1985/86* (Hong Kong, 1986), p. 19; State Statistical Bureau figures, Feb. 23, 1988; *Beijing Review*, March 7–13, 1988.

the higher procurement prices the government paid for farm products (a dramatic 50 percent increase between 1978 and 1983), as well as noncrop sideline income from livestock, as well as fishery, and forestry enterprises. The success was all the more remarkable in light of a reduction of some 50 percent in state agricultural investment between 1978–79 and 1981–82. However, the slack was partially taken up by an increase in credit offered by the People's Bank and by private investments in machine tools, tractors, and housing, with housing totaling Y15.7 billion in 1982 and Y21.4 billion in 1983.[13]

The dismantling of the commune resulted in a progressive neglect of large projects formerly serviced by the commune, such as the mechanized pumping of the irrigation system and the use of heavy tractors for preparation of the land. Social services, health care, and primary education also suffered. Moreover, the state incurred a heavy new burden because it paid higher prices for farm products but could not raise commodity prices in the city for fear of inflation and public anger. State subsidies to cereals and oils grew from Y4 billion in 1974 to Y20 billion in 1983.[14]

There were other agricultural problems as well. First, there were limits to what hard work and material incentive could achieve; beyond a certain point, saturation was reached, and no amount of hard work or willpower would make a difference. Greater government investment in agriculture was needed to improve productivity power, but government finances were tight, and the amount budgeted for agricultural investment actually decreased from 13.3 percent of the national expenditure in 1978 to 6.8 percent in 1983 and to 5.6 percent in 1985. Secondly, decline in collectivization resulted in deferred maintenance of irrigation, reduction of mechanization, and greater use of low-grade chemical fertilizers. The ability of the farm units to deal with natural calamities had been vastly reduced. Thirdly, low prices for grains resulted in a low profit margin compared with other production activities. In 1985 a farmer in the relatively well-off Feng District of Jiangsu Province earned Y650 annually, compared with Y2,375 for an animal husbandry or fishery worker, Y4,199 for an industrial worker, Y4,033 for a construction worker, and Y4,762 for a communications worker. On the average, a nonagricultural worker earned 4.1 times more than a grain producer.[15] It is little wonder that a number of grain producers turned to other lines of work for support or turned farm work into a mere sideline activity. Fourthly, loss of productive farm land continued owing to national appropriation of such land for industrial uses; for new farm housing; and for the development of timber, livestock, and fisheries. In 1985 alone the loss amounted to 15 million *mou* (2.5 million acres) of land. Fifthly, such perennial problems as high illiteracy; lack of agricultural technicians (1 in 4,000 farm households); and periodical flooding, drought, and fire persisted.

A much more fundamental challenge was the burgeoning population explosion, which threatened to consume most, if not all, of the increased agricultural and industrial production, thereby neutralizing the benefits of the reforms. To check the population from getting out of control, the government initiated a "one-child-per-family" policy, supported by material rewards for those who observed it (i.e. job security, promotion, favorable housing and school assignments) and by penalties for those who did not (demotion, monetary fines, food rationing, etc.). Given vast publicity during 1982, the policy was a success in the cities but less so in the countryside. The farmers still preferred male offspring as potential helpers and heirs and would often resort to female infanticide in order to win a second chance for a male issue. More recently, economic affluence on the farm led many farmers to defy the governmental orders by deliberately having a second or third son while paying the fines willingly. In China today, children from one-child families have often become so spoiled by doting parents and grandparents that they behave like "little emperors." These children, usually the center of a family's affection, attention, and social life, are increasingly becoming more steeped in egoism and individualism than in Marxist-Maoist ideology. It will be of great interest to follow the development and maturation of this new generation of Communist brats.

In spite of all these problems, grain production in 1986

reached 390 million tons, an increase of 10 million tons over 1985; and average farm income reached Y425 in 1986, a 7 percent increase over the previous year. In 1987 grain production rose further to 402.41 million tons, an increase of 2.8 percent.[16]

All in all, the first five years of agricultural reform released such vast hidden potential in the argicultural sector that the government was encouraged to tackle industrial reform in the urban areas as well. Here the problems were much more complicated.

INDUSTRIAL REFORM

Chinese industrial growth had averaged a respectable 9.8 percent annually from 1952 to 1983.[17] But efficiency, productivity, and work incentive were all hampered by numerous "irrational practices," as Western economists would call them. The industrial structure built by Mao in the early 1950s was modeled after the Soviet system, which was characterized by central planning and emphasis on the development of heavy industry. As the owner, operator, and employer, the state planned, directed, and funded all public enterprises. The state provided land, plants, equipment, basic materiel, working capital, managers, and everything else throughout the entire process of production. It also set the prices of the finished goods regardless of their cost and quality. There was no recognition of the "law of value" or the principle of supply and demand. State enterprises were required to remit to the central government all their profits and depreciation funds.

Under this system, enterprises received state support regardless of their performance records, and the workers received their standard wages regardless of the quality of their work. A saying went, "Every enterprise eats from the Big Pot of the state, and every worker eats from the Big Pot of the enterprise." The system worked at first because of the momentum of revolution, patriotism, and personal dedication to the building of a new socialist society. But as time went on, it became clear that the merits of an enterprise or of a worker were immaterial. The reward would remain the same in any case: the plant would receive the same allotted funding; and the worker, the same low pay. The socialist boast of full employment virtually guaranteed lifelong job security, and dismissal of indolent workers was well nigh impossible. Attempts by a manager to dismiss a worker would likely result in the disgrace of the manager for unsympathetic leadership rather than the dismissal of the worker. Similarly, penalties for inefficiently run state enterprises or debt-ridden plants were rare or unheard of. In the period 1979–80, roughly 25–30 percent of state enterprises operated at a loss.[18] Pricing structure was even more "irrational": the state set the prices of all commodities without regard to production cost or quality. Not infrequently, an article cost more to produce than it could be sold for, and a low-quality product would sell for more than a similar item of higher quality.

Irrational as this system was, the country had become accustomed to it over the previous 30 years. Reform of any part of it would disrupt the balance that had existed in the vast interlocking network of planning, management, production, marketing, and pricing. Millions of cadres were involved in the process, and any change in any part of it would adversely affect their lives. The worst fear was price decontrol, which raised the dreaded specter of inflation. The central government wanted to avoid any action that would arouse public anger or unrest. It took one step at a time, tested the reaction, evaluated the results, and then either proceeded or took a step back.

The First Phase

The spirit of the industrial reform during the period 1978–84 was to rekindle work enthusiasm, to unleash the full potential of the workers, to "enliven" the industrial structure, and to raise the living standard. The method used was none other than material incentive—the most disdained of values in the Maoist revolutionary days.

Beginning in the period 1978–79, various profit retention

schemes were experimented with in Sichuan and other selected areas. When improvements were achieved, they were extended throughout the country. The heart of the reform was the institution of an Industrial Responsibility System whereby a state enterprise signed a "profit and loss contract" (*yinkui baogan*) with its supervisory body, agreeing to remit a quota of profit to the state but retain a share of the "basic profits" above the quota. By 1980 some 6,600 state enterprises had come under this system. Profits so retained could be used for bonuses, employee welfare benefits, and further industrial innovations.[19] It was decreed that more work would yield more pay and that different types of work (skilled vs. unskilled, intellectual vs. manual) should command different renumerations. Work enthusiasm returned overnight.

In the period 1981–82, the profit retention system was refined to allow a larger share of profit above the quota for the enterprises and also partial retention of budgetary savings through reduced losses. The retention rates averaged 10 percent for high-profit industries, 30 percent for low-profit ones, and 20 percent for all others. By the end of 1982 all industrial enterprises had come under the Responsibility System. They were made responsible for all their economic decisions, as well as their return of a profit or loss. Plant managers could hire and fire employees, determine wages and bonuses, and set prices within a state-approved price range. But the managers themselves were no longer given lifelong tenure. Effective January 1, 1985 they were appointed for four-year terms, renewable up to three times.[20]

One immediate repercussion of the Responsibility System was the vast reduction of funds the state received from the enterprises, with the corresponding increase in funds kept by the enterprises and the localities, which were used for capital construction without central control or coordination, to the tune of Y42 billion by the end of 1982.[21] The state was dealt the double blow of budgetary deficits and loss of control over local investments. A construction boom led to shortages of building materials and inflation.

On June 1, 1983, the government substituted a new income

tax for profit remission (*yi shui dai li*). Large and medium-sized state enterprises were required to pay 55 percent of their profit as tax, and small enterprises paid according to an eight-grade progressive tax schedule, thus severing the direct relationship between the state enterprises and the government business bureaus.[22] In addition, three different kinds of taxes were to be phased in gradually, and their relative share of the total profit was as follows: (1) product tax, 40 percent of profit; (2) income tax, 33 percent; and (3) adjustment tax or a surtax for the better developed coastal areas, 12 percent. The amount of profit retained by the state enterprises amounted to some 15 percent. In addition, there were two other exactions imposed on a local level: a capital user's fees and a municipal tax for the use of land, roads, housing, and urban services.[23]

The introduction of income tax in a Communist system was an epochal event. Formerly, the plants, as public properties, paid no rent on land, little or no interest on working capital, and little or no amortization on fixed capital investments provided by the state. They retained high profits even though many operated inefficiently or in the red. Now industrial profits became a source of tax revenue, and the income taxes had the temporary effect of adjusting price distortions—a kind of substitute for price reforms.[24]

These new measures had indeed brought improvement to the industrial sector in the form of a higher standard of living, new business bonuses, and a construction boom; but there was little evidence of improvement in the efficiency of the enterprises. The performance of Chinese industry had not become more effective as first expected.[25] In fact, in 1982 some 30 percent of enterprises still operated in the red with a loss of Y4 billion, or 4 percent of the state budget revenue. Some 42,000 industrial enterprises were consolidated or amalgamated between 1983 and 1985.[26]

Perhaps the most visible result of the economic reforms was the mushrooming of private businesses and free markets in both rural and urban areas. Private businesses grew in number from 100,000 in 1978 to 5.8 million in 1983 and 17 million by

1985, with some making impressive profits in the capitalist fashion.[27] The service industry, considered a tertiary sector, also made great strides. Its share in the GNP grew from 18.7 percent in 1980 to 21.3 percent in 1985, and as of 1985, it employed 73.68 million people.[28] Rural free markets numbered some 40,000 by 1985, and urban free markets totaled some 3,000. Together they accounted for 6.6 percent of total retail sales in 1978, 9.5 percent in 1979, 10.2 percent in 1980, and 11.4 percent in 1981. These free markets and private businesses constituted a lively sector in the vast sea of state-owned enterprises.[29]

The most sensitive issue involved in the urban economic reform was the introduction of a realistic pricing system that would ultimately obviate the need for government subsidies for consumer goods. Gingerly the government lifted price controls on selected articles to minimize the effect on the market. Between 1979 and 1982, prices of coal, iron ore, cigarettes, and liquor increased whereas those of machinery and tires decreased. In 1983 price changes affected 100,000 items with a total value of Y40 billion, including increases in the prices of chemical products by 20 to 50 percent, in railway freight transport by 20 percent, and in light industry consumer durables such as electric fans and color television sets by 8–17 percent. People complained of inflation, which outpaced both wage increases and cost-of-living adjustments. Inflation was officially put at 4 percent in 1979, 6 percent in 1980, 2.4 percent in 1981, and 1.9 percent in 1982,[30] though the unofficial estimates ranged from 15 to 20 percent or more annually. In October 1984, when the party announced its accelerated program of urban reform, people flocked to the banks to withdraw money to purchase merchandise suspected to be in short supply in an effort to beat price increases. Confusion, fear, and disbelief were prevalent. Having experienced the hardships caused by the hyperinflationary period of 1945–49, the Chinese dreaded any sign of its recurrence.

The urban reforms of the 1979–84 period were not intended to create a free market system. They were only a patchwork, designed to amend the inefficient old structure with some economic realism and market mechanisms in hopes of breathing life into an otherwise ossified body. In the process, the government backed away from the bureaucratic command economy characterized by central planning and directives (*zhilinxing jihua*) to a position of planning through guidance (*zhidaoxing jihua*). By 1984, only 30 to 40 percent of industrial production could be attributed to central planning measures, 20 percent to the market economy, and 40 to 50 percent to locally planned or guidance-planned output.

The Second Phase

Encouraged by the success of agricultural reform and progress made in the industrial sector, the party, on October 20, 1984, passed a new "Resolution on the Reform of the Economic System" to accelerate the pace of urban reform. This was a curious and interesting document in that it was not a blueprint for reform but an optimistic statement of intent and principles for the guidance of the 44 million party members. It exuded confidence of future success, coming as it did in the wake of a string of good news: record grain production (407 million tons), unprecedented foreign reserves (US $20 billion), and exceptional performance by Chinese athletes at the Summer Olympics in Los Angeles (32 gold, silver, and bronze medals). Moreover, the gross industrial and agricultural output surpassed the grand psychological mark of Y1 trillion for the first time in Chinese history.[31]

There was yet another favorable development that bolstered China's new confidence. This was the successful negotiations with Britain for the return of Hong Kong. For more than two years the two countries had been discussing the future of three pieces of territory that China had ceded and leased to Britain in the 19th century under the unequal treaties: (1) the island of Hong Kong, ceded by the Treaty of Nanking in 1842; (2) the southern part of the Kowloon peninsula and Stonecutters Island, ceded by the convention of Peking in 1860; and (3) the New Territories and 235 nearby islands, which comprise

92 percent of the land area of Hong Kong, leased in 1898 to Britain for 99 years until June 30, 1997.

In view of the impending expiration of the lease, both Britain and China desired an amicable negotiated settlement. In this, the British hoped to retain some administrative role beyond 1997 so as to ensure Hong Kong's continued stability and prosperity. The Chinese, on the other hand, insisted on the complete restoration of sovereignty over all three territories. After British Prime Minister Margaret Thatcher's visit to Beijing in September 1982, substantial progress was made in accommodating the Chinese wish. On September 26, 1984, an agreement on the future of Hong Kong was reached, under which Hong Kong would become a Special Administrative Region of China after June 30, 1997, but would still retain a high degree of autonomy in its legal, educational, and, most importantly, its economic and financial structures, including its free enterprise system.[32] China pledged not to interfere with Hong Kong's socioeconomic systems for 50 years beyond 1997, in effect, creating a "One Country, Two Systems" arrangement, which Deng Xiaoping also wished to someday apply to Taiwan.

The initialing of the agreement in October 1984 and its formal signing in December by Margaret Thatcher and Premier Zhao Ziyang marked an epoch-making triumph for China. It signaled an end to the last vestiges of foreign imperialism in China. This triumph was all the more satisfying because the British Prime Minister twice came to China in connection with the settlement, and, for the first time in history, the British Crown was scheduled to visit China.

It was in this state of euphoria that the second stage of urban reform was launched. What was wrong with the existing economy? Premier Zhao stated that it was stultified because the government and economic enterprises were not treated as separate entities and that the former controlled the latter too tightly. Disregard of proper interaction between commercial production, the law of value, and market forces caused imbalances that had to be redressed. In distribution there was too much emphasis on "averageism" (*pingqun jui*), resulting in everyone eating from the same "Big Pot" of the state and nobody wanting to work hard. The enterprises and the workers had lost their initiative and creativity, lapsing into a general state of paralysis. On top of this malaise was the "leftist" tendency, in force since 1957, to deprecate any effort to develop a commodity economy as a revival of capitalism. Zhao admitted that it would require a bold liberation of thought to correct such ossified thinking: "The basic function of socialism is to develop the productive power of the society, ceaselessly to increase its wealth, and to meet the increasing material and cultural needs of the people. Socialism wants to end poverty; pauperism is not socialism."[33]

Zhao's method of injecting life into the economy was to loosen state control of the large and medium-sized enterprises. Public ownership need not be equated with direct state control: ownership and management were two separate functions. Within the framework of state governance, Zhao felt, enterprises should be granted enough autonomy to make their own decisions about supplies, sales, capital utilization, hiring and firing, salaries, wages, and bonuses and about the prices of the finished products as well. An enterprise should be made to function legally as an individual person, responsible for its own profit and loss.

> We must break loose from the traditional concept that a planned economy and a commodity economy stand opposed to each other and recognize clearly that, under socialism, the planned economy must spontaneously rely on and utilize the law of value to build a planned commodity economy on the basis of public ownership. The full development of a commodity economy is an indispensable step in the development of a socialist economy. It is a necessity in the modernization of our economy. The difference between a socialist and a capitalist economy does not lie in the existence of a commodity economy or in the functioning of the law of value, but in the ownership system, in the existence or not of an exploiting class, and in whether the workers are the masters of the house.[34]

Zhao considered the gradual lifting of price control to be the heart of urban economic reform, for it would enable the state to withdraw its subsidies and allow prices to float according to the law of value and the market forces of supply and demand. But fluctuation in prices had to be kept within limits and people's salaries and wages adjusted according to inflation. Profit in an economic enterprise should come from better management, not from individually determined price increases, which could only distort market conditions. To fight the debilitating effects of "averageism," Zhao reaffirmed the principle of reward based on work: "Those who labor more shall receive more and those who labor less shall receive less." The much abused practice of equal pay for all was a chief stumbling block in increasing the productive power of society.

Zhao declared that to equate "common wealth" with "equal wealth for all at the same speed" was not only impossible, but would lead to common poverty. Certain regions, enterprises, and people should be allowed to grow rich first so as to exert a ripple effect on others. But China would not allow exploitation by a small number of people to plunge the majority into poverty.[35]

Finally, Zhao approved the continued growth of private enterprise to supplement the public ownership system and also the leasing or contracting of small and medium-sized state enterprises to private operation to enrich the variety of economic life. Such developments would not jeopardize the socialist foundation, but were seen as necessary to the progress of socialism.

Even as the resolution was being passed, the economy was charging ahead. The gross output value of agriculture and industry increased at an annual rate of 10 percent between 1978 and 1986, and the national income grew at a rate of 8.7 percent annually. Particularly impressive were the sharp increases in capital construction outside the state budget, from 16.7 percent of total investment in 1978 to 57 percent in 1984. The construction boom was evident everywhere. Capital investment rose 25 percent in 1982, 23.8 percent in 1984, and 42.8 percent in 1985. The level of investment was the highest since the disastrous Great Leap of 1958–60.

However, this pace was clearly unsustainable, creating with

it shortages of construction materials, waste, confusion, and inflation. With such high capital investment, industrial growth naturally was fast, at 14 percent in 1984, and 18 percent in 1985; but only the most strenuous effort kept the 1986 rate to 9.2 percent. In 1987, the rate rose again to 16.5 percent, achieving a total industrial output value of almost Y1.4 trillion.[36]

The overheated economy created many adverse effects on the long-term interests of the state. The following were among the most obvious:

1. State budgetary deficits between 1978 and 1985 came to Y100 billion, largely owing to excessive capital investment and large subsidies.
2. Large trade deficits amounted to US$ 28 billion in 1985 and 1986.
3. High inflation rates of 12.5 percent in 1985, 7 percent in 1986, and 8 percent in 1987 prevailed although unofficial figures put the rates between 15 and 20 percent annually.
4. Widespread economic crime and corruption occurred, especially among the children and relatives of high cadres who exploited their special positions to practice favoritism and other business irregularities.
5. Fast growth took place in durable consumer goods in 1986 such as washing machines (9 million units), electric fans (33 million), and refrigerators (2.85 million).
6. An energy bottleneck was caused by the slow growth of primary energy supplies (2.9 percent in 1986), which could not sustain the demands of the rapidly expanding industrial growth (9.2 percent), forcing many plants to operate only four days a week.
7. There was a rapid development of village industry to 820,000 units in 1985, with a total value of Y137.5 billion, accounting for 15.7 percent of total industrial output. But the quality of rural industrial products was frequently low.
8. Cultivated land was lost at the rate of 20 million *mou* or 3.29 million acres annually owing to increased industrial use, new housing, and an annual population growth of 14 million.[37]

Facing the serious problems of rapid industrialization, conservative leaders clashed with the pragmatists over the direction, speed, and scope of economic reform; and the former attacked the open-door policy as a source of foreign "spiritual pollution" of Chinese life. The clash resulted in the retrenchment policy of January 1986, which highlighted four key concepts: (1) to *consolidate* the gains already made and to solidify the foundation of reforms, (2) to *digest* the changes made necessary by price reforms and wage adjustments and to tackle the problems of reform in line with the financial and physical capacities of each unit, (3) to *supplement* and amend the imperfect and unhealthy links in the chain of reform so as to improve coordination, and (4) to *improve* the macroeconomic controls so as to achieve a better balance between supply and demand.

		Output of Major Industries					
	1952	*1957*	*1965*	*1978*	*1981*	*1984*	*1987*
Coal (100 mill. tons)	0.66	1.31	2.36	6.18	6.22	7.89	9.20
Crude Oil (1 mill. tons)	.14	1.46	11.31	104.05	101.22	114.61	134.00
Natural Gas (100 mill. cubic meters)	0.08	0.7	11.00	137.30	127.40	124.30	140.15
Electricity (bill. kwh.)	7.3	19.3	67.6	256.6	309.3	377.0	496.0
Rolled Steel— Final Products (mill. tons)	1.06	4.15	8.81	22.08	26.70	33.72	43.91
Steel (mill. tons)	1.35	5.35	12.23	31.78	35.60	43.47	56.02
Pig Iron (mill. tons)	1.93	5.94	10.77	34.79	34.17	40.01	54.33

Sources: *Almanac*, 26; State Statistical Bureau, Feb. 23, 1988; *Beijing Review*, March 7–13, 1988; *Monthly Bulletin of Statistics*, China, March 1988.

The retrenchment policy, however, could not stop the momentum of economic expansion. In 1987 the agricultural output value climbed 4.7 percent to Y444.7 billion, and the industrial output grew 16.5 percent to Y1,378 billion—both new records. But the growth was uneven, as the energy and transportation sectors continued to lag behind, with coal production registering only a 2.9 percent increase and crude oil a 2.6 percent increase. The energy bottleneck would constrain the economic growth for years to come and inhibit a balanced development. Nevertheless, the general trend toward continued growth would persist, if only haphazardly.

THE OPEN-DOOR POLICY

During the first decade of the People's Republic (1949–59), China maintained diplomatic and commercial relations only with the Soviet Union and the Eastern European satellite states. There was no trade between China and the United States. After the Sino-Soviet split in 1960, China became extremely isolated in the international community, simultaneously facing both the Soviet Union and the United States as potential enemies. It was not until after the visit of President Richard Nixon to China in 1972 that limited commercial relations began. In 1972 American-Chinese trade amounted to only $92 million, but it rapidly grew to $1,189 million in 1978, $5,478 million in 1981, $8 billion in 1986, and an estimated $10 billion ($13 billion according to U.S. calculations) in 1988, amounting to approximately 10 percent of China's total foreign trade.[38]

The rapid growth of foreign trade after 1978 was the result of the new open-door policy adopted by the party in December 1978 (Third Plenum, Eleventh Central Committee). It was a complete reversal of the Maoist policy of seclusion that had been in force for the 20 years between 1958 and 1978. Deng Xiaoping and his pragmatic followers realized that China could not develop in isolation and that she must import foreign science, technology, capital, and management skills in order for her modernization to succeed.

Japan, Hong Kong, the United States, and West Germany were China's largest trading partners. In 1983, Japan's share came to $9,764 million; Hong Kong's $8,341 million; the United States', $4,425 million; and West Germany's, $1,743 million. The nature of the trade goods China imported and exported had changed substantially. Initially, Chinese imports consisted largely of raw materials such as agricultural products (primarily grains), synthetic fibers, lumber, and chemicals. But later, as China became almost self-sufficient in agricultural production, the focus of importation shifted to industrial machinery, finished manufactured goods, technology, office equipment, commercial aircraft, and services.

Japan enjoyed a special relationship with China because of her geographical proximity and a certain degree of cultural affinity. This gave Japan a deeper understanding of both Chinese psychology and her immediate economic needs, much more so than other foreign traders might have had. Japan's technological and financial successes in the world markets enabled her to offer concessional loans, grants, and preferential tariffs under the Generalized System of Preferences (GSP). Hong Kong also had a special place in China's opening world trade: it served as a link between China and the outside world. The United States and West Germany did not share these advantages, but the Chinese traditionally had great respect for American and German aircraft, machinery, and scientific products.

A prime objective of the foreign trade program was to generate sufficient foreign exchange to help finance modernization. To improve their competitive edge, the Chinese diversified their products, raised quality levels, devalued the yuan, and eagerly learned international business practices. In purchasing, they adhered strictly to the three criteria of good prices, good quality, and financing arrangements on concessionary terms. They wanted transfer of the latest technology; but they would also accept less sophisticated plants at bargain prices, as in the cases of the purchases of an older steel mill, a semiconductor line, and a textile mill in the United States during the 1982 recession.[39]

Through strict control of foreign currency, export expansion, and import restraint, China steadily built up a foreign currency reserve. When China encountered protectionism in the West against her textiles, she opened new markets in the Middle East, Latin America, Eastern Europe, and the Soviet Union, although the volume of trade in these areas remained limited. In early 1981 China crossed the line from being a debtor nation to being a creditor nation. By the end of 1983 her foreign currency reserve reached an unprecedented $20 billion, the tenth largest in the world and ahead of Britain's $18.2 billion. Part of the foreign earnings were used for domestic infrastructural projects in the long neglected areas of energy, transportation, communication, and light industries.[40]

One of the persistent difficulties with China's foreign trade system was the irrationality of her domestic pricing system, which made necessary government subsidies for both imports and exports. Domestic prices in China were out of line with world prices. Though it was profitable for China to export primary goods and to import manufactured goods, it was highly unprofitable to do the opposite at the official exchange rate of Y2.8 to the dollar. Before 1981, Chinese exports generally created losses and imports gains—a sure sign of overvaluation of the yuan, creating the need for government subsidy for exports. To counteract these pricing distortions, China devalued her currency to Y3.7 to the dollar in 1984, but it resulted in increased subsidies for many imports, again producing a loss.[41]

An unexpected source of foreign trade profit came from arms sales to the states of the Middle East through North Korea and Egypt, rising from almost nothing in 1980 to $1.5 billion in 1983 and $5 billion in 1987. Most famous among these arms were the Silkworm short-range missiles sold to Iran and the intermediate range (2,000 miles) CSS-2 missiles sold to Saudi Arabia. Arms were also sold to Iraq, Jordan, Egypt, Syria, and Israel.[42] Tourism provided another source of income, which came to $1.84 billion in 1987, up 20.3 percent from 1986.[43]

Except for the retrenchment years 1981–83, when importation of capital goods declined, Chinese foreign trade grew annually by 20 percent in imports and 10 to 15 percent in exports.[44]

To attract foreign capital and investments, China adopted a number of measures to improve the investment climate. The following were some of the more salient steps taken:

1. Opening four "Special Economic Zones" in 1979 (with preferential tax treatment) in Shenzhen, Zuhai (on the opposite banks of the Pearl River estuary close to Canton), Shantou (on the northern Guangdong coast), and Xiamen (formerly Amoy, on the southern Fujian coast). These were not "Export Processing Zones" (EPZ) as in Taiwan, but "laboratories" for transforming the Chinese economy.[45]

2. Opening 14 coastal sites and Hainan Island in 1984 to foreign investment, with preferential terms on taxes and import duties.

3. Hosting international conferences to advertise projects that needed foreign advice, capital, equipment, management, and marketing.

4. Permission given to local authorities to arrange foreign investments without central government approval, which resulted in a burgeoning of imports of foreign supplies—steel, nonferrous metals, lumber, plastics—with a substantial outflow of foreign reserve.

5. Passing laws and regulations on taxation, liability, patent protection, and foreign trademarks.

6. Clarification of arbitration procedures, labor compensation, and repatriation of foreign profit from China.[46]

China's success in attracting foreign investments was very limited. By the end of 1983, there were only 188 "equity" and 1,047 "contractual" joint Chinese-foreign ventures, with $6.6 billion pledged but only $2.3 billion paid in. Three of the largest American-Chinese ventures were the Great Wall Hotel ($11 million), the Jiangguo Hotel ($11 million), and American Motor's Beijing Jeep Corporation ($16 million). Atlantic Richfield took part in exploring and drilling gas fields near Hainan Island at a cost of $250–300 million.[47]

Foreigners found the Chinese environment unconductive to investment. Endless negotiations and long bureaucratic delays strained patience, and business and residential facilities were substandard. Many foreign firms had to set up offices in hotels and paid high rents and fees for Chinese services even though their Chinese employees received only a fraction of the foreign wages paid while the lion's share went to the government's business bureaus. Many foreign firms left out of frustration and lack of prospects for profit.

Sino-Japanese Trade

As China's leading trading partner, Japan was the largest supplier of modern plants and equipment and also of financial and technical assistance. In addition, Japan provided a market for Chinese exports of oil and other labor-intensive products. The

Japan's Trade with the People's Republic of China: Exports, Imports, and Shares of Total Trade, 1950–83, Selected Years
(in thousands of dollars)

	Japan's exports to the PRC	Japan's imports from the PRC	Japan's trade with the PRC as a percent of Japan's total trade	The PRC's trade with Japan as a percent of the PRC's total trade
1950	$19,633	$39,328	3.3	4.9
1956	67,339	83,447	2.6	4.8
1959	3,648	18,917	0.3	0.5
1966	315,150	306,237	3.2	14.6
1972	608,921	491,116	2.1	18.6
1973	1,039,494	974,010	2.7	20.4
1974	1,984,475	1,304,768	2.8	24.0
1975	2,258,577	1,531,076	3.3	26.0
1976	1,662,568	1,370,915	2.3	22.9
1977	1,938,643	1,546,902	2.3	23.2
1978	3,048,748	2,030,292	2.9	23.8
1979	3,698,670	2,954,781	3.1	22.6
1980	5,078,335	4,323,374	3.9	23.1
1981	5,097,189	5,291,800	3.6	24.1
1982	3,510,825	5,352,417	3.3	21.7
1983	4,912,334	5,087,357	3.7	23.0

China's Merchandise Exports to Japan by Commodity, 1980–83
(in thousands of dollars)

Commodity	1980	1981	1982	1983	1983 share (per-cent)
Animal products	297,108	316,311	272,910	262,467	5.2
Fish shellfish	181,979	188,042	138,042	131,314	2.6
Vegetable products	321,623	407,377	377,977	484,236	9.5
Mineral products	2,514,233	3,060,980	3,212,072	2,926,877	57.5
Coal	116,519	188,676	212,536	212,958	4.2
Crude oil	1,949,172	2,332,960	2,340,918	2,080,959	40.9
Textiles and textile articles	682,967	691,504	722,582	806,577	15.9
Silk/silk fabrics	171,611	116,587	153,262	158,487	3.1
Cotton/cotton fabrics	92,180	115,865	118,248	140,121	2.8
Garments	230,704	242,748	263,896	270,895	5.3
Others	507,443	815,628	766,876	607,200	11.9
Total	4,323,374	5,291,800	5,352,417	5,087,356	100.0

needs of the two countries complemented each other, and the Chinese were successful in keeping the trade deficit small with the strategy that what Japan could sell to China must be co-ordinated with what she could buy from China. The Japanese helped China develop exports needed to generate foreign exchange for the purchase of Japanese goods and also offered low-intrest concessional loans or grants. In 1983, Sino-Japanese trade reached $10 billion, with $4.9 billion in Japanese exports to China and $5.1 billion in Chinese exports to Japan. The two-way trade represented 23 percent of China's total foreign trade and 3.7 percent of Japan's.[48] In 1983 China's largest exports were crude oil (40.9 percent of total exports)—representing 5.2 percent of Japan's total petroleum imports—and coal, 4.4 percent of Japan's coal imports. Other Chinese exports included light manufactured goods, agricultural products, meats, fish, shell-fish, antiques, art work, and firearms.

Japanese exports to China were mostly metals and metallic articles (iron and steel), which accounted for 49.6 percent of

Japan's total exports in 1983. Heavy machinery and mechanical apparatus represented 28.5 percent; chemical goods, 11.0 percent; and textiles, 5.8 percent.

Some of the reasons for the Japanese success in China included the following: (1) geographical proximity, which cut transportation costs—Tokyo is 5,000 miles closer to Shanghai

Japan's Merchandise Exports to China by Commodity, 1980–83
[in thousands of dollars and percent]

Commodity	1980	1981	1982	1983	1983 share (percent)
Chemical goods	575,416	559,599	512,139	539,674	11.0
Chemical fertilizers	244,476	213,120	84,712	17,509	0.4
Metals and articles thereof	1,686,655	1,255,421	1,355,788	2,434,133	49.6
iron and steel and articles thereof	1,618,233	1,197,407	1,292,616	2,253,334	45.9
Machinery and mechanized apparatus	2,154,309	2,440,450	1,007,491	1,399,656	28.5
General machinery	1,164,226	1,440,696	399,967	545,107	11.1
Electrical machinery	422,428	554,861	203,868	264,502	5.4
Transport machinery	426,746	225,294	309,836	320,580	6.5
Scientific, optical, and precision apparatus	140,909	219,599	163,820	269,466	5.5
Textiles and textile articles	403,900	599,233	368,220	286,567	5.8
Man-made fibers	156,127	201,815	115,869	81,977	1.7
Others	258,055	242,486	197,817	252,304	5.2
Total exports	5,078,335	5,097,189	3,510,825	4,912,334	100.0

Source: U.S. Congress, *China's Economy Looks Toward the Year 2000* (Washington, D.C., 1986), II, pp. 460–63.

than San Francisco; (2) cultural affinity, which enabled the Japanese to gain a deeper understanding of Chinese psychology and taste, adapt their products to suit the Chinese life-style, and lobby the Chinese bureaucracy effectively with lavish promotional gifts and free trips to Japan; (3) Japanese businesspersons offered competitive prices and sales training, and the Japanese government offered preferential tariff rates under the Generalized System of Preferences (GSP) in addition to the Most-favored-nation treatment (FMN); (4) Tokyo offered concessional loans and credit in yen, at attractive, low interest rates; credit of ¥300 billion ($1.5 billion) at a 3 percent interest rate for the period 1979–83 and ¥470 billion ($2.1 billion) in 1984 at 3.5 percent interest to finance key development projects such as railways, ports, telephone equipment, and hydroelectric power stations; (5) between 1978 and 1982 the yen weakened against both the dollar and the Chinese yuan, making Japanese products highly competitive in price; after 1982 the yen gained in value against the dollar and the yuan, but the attractive concessional financial arrangements still stood Japanese products in good stead; and (6) the basic policy of helping China to develop resources to generate the needed foreign exchange to buy Japanese goods.[49]

Yet, in spite of these advantages, the Japanese did not score an unqualified success. The Chinese often complained of "second quality" and even shoddy Japanese products, nonconformity with the original orders, and the dubious business practice of sponsoring great "show-how" but withholding the genuine "know-how."

Sino-American Trade

The Americans did not have the same advantages as the Japanese, nor could they offer concessionary loans and credit. But they had a deep reservoir of goodwill among the Chinese, who preferred American aircraft, computers, electronics, telecommunication equipment, and oil-drilling tools for their reputed quality and durability. The Americans imported considerable quantities of Chinese textiles, apparel, and oil products and an assortment of hand tools, housewares, pharmaceuticals, furni-

Sino-United States Trade Balances, 1972–83
[Million US dollars, FOB]

	Two-way total	Chinese exports	Chinese imports	Chinese surplus or deficit	Chinese cumulative deficit
1972	92	32	60	−28	−28
1973	802	61	741	−680	−708
1974	931	112	819	−707	−1,415
1975	460	156	304	−148	−1,563
1976	337	202	135	67	−1,496
1977	374	203	171	32	−1,464
1978	1,189	324	865	−541	−2,005
1979	2,318	594	1,724	−1,139	−3,135
1980	4,814	1,059	3,755	−2,696	−5,831
1981	5,478	1,875	3,603	−1,728	−7,559
1982	5,187	2,275	2,912	−637	−8,196
1983	4,425	2,252	2,173	79	−7,797
1984 January–June	2,644	1,482	1,162	320	−7,805

Note: U.S. Customs Bureau statistics. Chinese customs statistics do not agree with U.S. data. For example, Chinese customs for 1983 show exports of $1.718 billion and imports of $2.763 billion, for a deficit $1.045 billion. Chinese data probably include some services and fees that are not counted in U.S. merchandise trade data. In addition, China lists imports CIF, thus including insurance and freight fees that are not included in analogous U.S. FOB export data.

ture, antiques, and art. In 1981, the Chinese-American trade temporarily peaked at $5.5 billion, which represented 14 percent of China's foreign trade and 3 percent of America's. Every year between 1972 and 1983, China sustained a trade deficit with the United States, resulting in a cummulative shortfall of $7.7 billion.[50]

As China progressed in her modernization, she would need more state-of-the-art technology, as well as fertilizers, chemicals, and timber products. Her 300,000 state industrial enterprises could use American advice on upgrading, management techniques, and infrastructure development. There was a great potential in the service industry sector, and the United States could offer advice and guidance in tree cultivation, insecticidal chemistry, water conservancy, food preservation, coal extraction, cargo handling, birth control, integrated circuits—and any number of developmental activities. The possibilities were limitless.[51]

Irritation and frustration within Sino-American trade was inevitable on both sides. The Americans were critical of the seemingly endless delays in negotiations, lack of a bilateral in-

Highlights of China's Exports to the United States
[Million U.S. dollars, FAS]

	1983		First half, 1984	
Category	Value	Share (percent)	Value	Share (percent)
Total	2,244	100.0	1,482	100.0
Manufactures	1,026	45.7	689	46.5
Apparel and accessories	774	34.5	499	33.7
Wicker, basketware	58	2.6	35	2.4
footwear	34	1.5	24	1.6
Fuels	430	19.2	263	17.7
Gasoline	309	13.8	149	10.1
Crude oil	79	3.5	62	4.2
Intermediate manufactures	390	17.4	272	18.4
Textile yarn and fabrics	241	10.7	184	12.4
Chemicals, related products	131	5.8	79	5.3
Fireworks	29	1.3	19	1.3
Pharmaceuticals	25	1.1	13	0.9
Food	112	5.0	78	5.3
Canned vegetables	34	1.5	30	2.0
Tea	10	0.4	8	0.5
Crude materials	97	4.3	55	3.7
Barium sulfate and carbonate	26	1.2	14	0.9
Down and feathers	8	0.3	6	0.4
Machinery, transport equipment	42	1.9	29	2.0
Miscellaneous	10	0.5	12	0.8
Beverages and tobacco	4	0.2	2	0.1
Beer	2	0.1	1	0.1
Animal/vegetable fats, oils	2	0.1	2	0.1

Highlights of China's Imports from the United States
[Million U.S. dollars, FOB]

Category	1983 Value	1983 Share (percent)	First half, 1984 Value	First half, 1984 Share (percent)
Total	2,173	100.0	1,162	100.0
Machinery, transport eqpt	586	27.0	284	24.4
Aircraft and parts	235	10.8	49	4.2
Construction, mining eqpt	52	2.4	45	3.9
Office eqpt	52	2.4	34	2.9
Food	541	24.9	284	24.4
Grain	536	24.7	283	24.4
Chemicals	354	16.3	265	22.8
Fertilizers	168	7.7	119	10.2
Plastics	92	4.2	73	6.3
Crude materials	300	13.8	173	14.9
Conifer logs	228	10.5	129	11.1
Manufactures	220	10.1	61	5.2
Aluminum	87	4.0	3	0.3
Paper	41	1.9	22	1.9
Miscellaneous	172	7.9	94	8.1
Electrical meters, controls	92	4.2	46	4.0

Source: U.S. Congress, *China's Economy Looks Toward the Year 2000* (Washington, D.C., 1986), II, pp. 336–40.

vestment treaty, and the difficulty of repatriating funds from China. The Chinese, on the other hand, were unhappy with American protectionism against Chinese textile imports and limitations on American hi-tech exports. As a Communist state, China came under the U.S. Export-Import Bank provision restricting loans exceeding $50 million, and the Generalized System of Preferences (GSP) excluded China from duty-free treatment. However, by joining the GATT (General Agreement on Tariffs and Trade), China came closer to the GSP status, which qualified her for lowered import tariffs and made Chinese goods more competitive in the American markets. Also, the United States' rule on merchandise's "country-of-

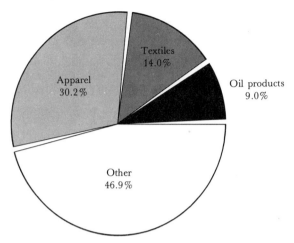

United States Imports from China, 1983.

origin" made the Chinese feel discrimianted against; moreover, the long delay in granting the most-favored-nation treatment generated a feeling among the Chinese of being less than equal. Finally, the very modest American investments in China caused deep disappointment. Irritations aside, the Sino-American trade was expected to continue to grow, estimated to surpass $10 billion ($13 billion according to U.S. calculations) in 1988, and reach several times that in the years to come.

FUTURE PROSPECT OF GROWTH

The economic and technological benefits of the reforms and opening were obvious. There was growing prosperity in the countryside and substantial improvement in the farmer's standard of living. Urban life had become more colorful, open, and relaxed; and commercial and scientific exchanges with foreign countries grew by leaps and bounds. The successful leadership of Deng Xiaoping was compared by foreign observers to that of Colbert of France, Frederick the Great of Prussia, and the leaders of the early Meiji period in Japan.[52] Others

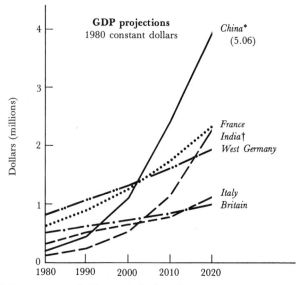

GDP Projections of China, India, and Certain Western European States, 1980–2020.

Source: *The Economist*, London, Dec. 21, 1985, 69.

forecast rosily that barring a catastrophic occurrence such as the outbreak of war with the Sovet Union or a major political upheaval on the scale of the Cultural Revolution, China's GNP, growing at a feasible annual rate of 8 percent, could surpass those of Italy and England before the year 2000 and soar past those of West Germany and France by A.D. 2020.[53]

The forecast was plausible statistically. Ten years into the reforms, China's economic indicators continued to skyrocket and showed no sign of slackening, but major catastrophes of the types mentioned could not be ruled out entirely. Destabilizing influences that could prove highly detrimental in the long run and that eluded statistics were already lurking in the background. Foremost among them were these: (1) the progressive erosion of faith in Marxism-Leninism-Maoism and in the leadership of the ruling party; (2) widespread corruption in the party and the government, which threatened a breakdown of public morality; and (3) raging inflation in the wake of price decontrol, causing massive discontent.

As the decade of reform and opening drew to a close, there were ominous signs of ideological confusion, economic imbalance, social unrest, and moral degradation. Serious challenges, as well as new opportunities, waited to test the leadership.

NOTES

1. Deng Xiaoping, *Building Socialism with Chinese Characteristics* (Beijing, Foreign Language Press, 1985), 35–40, 49–52, 58–59, 70–73.
2. *Ibid.*, 61.
3. *Ibid.*, 62.
4. *Ibid.*, 53.
5. *China: Long-Term Development Issues and Options* (Washington, D.C., The World Bank, 1985). The World Bank believes the goal of quadrupling the GNP is possible if China (1) invests efficiently in building its infrastructure at a rate of 30 percent of national income, (2) makes reasonable improvement in the use of energy and raw material, and (3) keeps its population to no more than 1.2 billion by A.D. 2000.
6. Nicholas R. Lardy, "Overview, Agricultural Reform and the Rural Economy," *China's Economy Looks Toward the Year 2000,* Joint Economic Committee, Congress of the United States (Washington, D.C., 1986), I, *The Four Modernizations*, 325, 331.
7. Frederick W. Crook, "The Reform of the Commune System and the Rise of the Township-Collective-Household System," *China's Economy Looks Toward the Year 2000*, I, 362–63.
8. Crook, 370.
9. *Los Angeles Times*, Nov. 25, 1987.
10. Crook, 364–65, 368–69.
11. Frederic M. Surls, "China's Agriculture in the Eighties," *China's Economy Looks Toward the Year 2000*, I, 338.
12. Lardy, 327.
13. *Ibid.*, 328–30. Procurement prices increased 22.1 percent in 1979, 7.1 percent in 1980, 5.9 percent in 1981, and 2.2 percent in 1982. See Nai-Ruenn Chen and Jeffrey Lee, *China's Economy and Foreign Trade, 1981–85* (U.S. Dept. of Commerce, 1984), 6.
14. Lardy, 333.

15. *Jingjixue zhoubao* (Economic Weekly), Shanghai, July 20, 1986. Article on food problems.
16. State Statistical Bureau, Peoples Republic of China, *Statistics for 1987: Socio-Economic Development,* issued Feb. 23, 1988. In *Beijing Review,* March 7–13, 1988.
17. Robert Michael Field, "China, The Changing Structure of Industry," in *China's Economy Looks Toward the Year 2000,* I, 505.
18. Nai-Ruenn Chen and Jeffrey Lee, *China's Economy and Foreign Trade,* 13. (Hereafter Chen and Lee).
19. Barry Naughton, "Finance and Planning Reforms in Industry," *China's Economy,* I, 608.
20. Christine Wong, "The Second Phase of Economic Reform in China," *Current History,* September 1985, 261, 278.
21. Chen and Lee, 13.
22. Field, 532.
23. Naughton, 612.
24. *Ibid.,* 611.
25. *Ibid.,* 608–9.
26. Chen and Lee, 14.
27. Song Tingming, "Review of Eight Years of Reform," *Beijing Review,* Dec. 22, 1986, 15.
28. Rongxia Li, "Tertiary Industry Takes Off in China," *Beijing Review,* Feb. 9, 1987, 18–19.
29. Chen and Lee, 15.
30. *Ibid.,* 8.
31. Zhao Ziyang, "Dangqian di jingji xinshi he jingji tizhi gaige" (On the economic conditions before us and the economic institutional reform), Report before the Sixth National People's Congress, March 27, 1985 (Hong Kong, 1985).
32. For details of the agreement, see *A Draft Agreement between the Government of the United Kingdom of Great Britain and Northern Ireland and the Government of the People's Republic of China on the Future of Hong Kong.* Hong Kong, Sept. 26, 1984. It should be noted that Portugal also reached an agreement with China in Oct. 1986 on the return of Macao on Dec. 20, 1999.
33. Zhonggong Zhongyang guanyu jingji tizhi gaige di juding (Third Plenum, Twelfth Central Committee, Chinese Communist Party, Resolution on the Reform of the Economic System), Oct. 20, 1984 (Hong Kong, 1984), 4–6, 17. Tr. mine.
34. *Ibid.,* 9–10. Tr. mine.
35. *Ibid.,* 17–18. Tr. mine.
36. Chu-yuan Cheng, "China's Economy at the Crossroads," *Cur-*

rent History, Sept. 1987, 272; State Statistical Bureau, Peking, Feb. 23, 1988, *Beijing Review,* March 7–13, 1988.
37. Chu-yuan Cheng, 272–73.
38. U.S. figures do not agree with Chinese data because the U.S. used the "country of origin" method in its calculation whereas the Chinese used their customs figures, which often include insurance and freight fees. In 1987 the Chinese figure for the total U.S.-China trade came to $8.5 billion, compared with the U.S. figure of $10.5 billion.
39. Helen Louise Noyes, "United States-China Trade," *China's Economy,* II, 343.
40. John L. Davie, "China's International Trade and Finance," *China's Economy Looks Toward the Year 2000,* II, 311–12, 323.
41. *Ibid.,* 319.
42. *Los Angeles Times,* May 4, 1988.
43. State Statistical Bureau, Beijing, Feb. 23, 1988.
44. Davie, 318.
45. Victor C. Falkenheim, "China's Special Economic Zones," *China's Economy,* II, 348–50; Y. C. Jao and C. K. Leung (eds.), *China's Special Economic Zones: Policies, Problems and Prospects* (Hong Kong, 1986).
46. Noyes, 340.
47. Davie, 324–25; Noyes, 341.
48. Dick K. Nanto and Hong Nack Kim, "Sino-Japanese Economic Relations," *China's Economy,* II, 454, 466.
49. *Ibid.,* 465–66.
50. Noyes, 335–37.
51. Davie, 324, Noyes, 342, 344.
52. Paul Kennedy, *The Rise and Fall of the Great Powers: Economic Change and Military Conflict 1500 to 2000* (New York, 1987), 448.
53. *Ibid.,* 455.

FURTHER READING

A Draft Agreement between the Government of the United Kingdom of Great Britain and Northern Ireland and the Government of the Peoples Republic of China on the Future of Hong Kong. Hong Kong, Sept. 26, 1984.

Bannister, Judith, *China's Changing Population* (Stanford, 1987).

Burns, John P., *Policy Conflicts in Post-Mao China* (Armonk, N.Y., 1986).

Barnett, A. Doak, and Ralph N. Clough (eds.), *Modernizing China: Post-Mao Reform and Development* (Boulder, 1985).

Chen, Nai-Ruenn, and Jeffrey Lee, *China's Economy and Foreign Trade* (Washington, D.C., 1984), Dept. of Commerce report.

China: Economic Policy and Performance in 1987 (Washington, D.C., 1988). A report by the Central Intelligence Agency presented to the Subcommittee on National Security Economics of the Joint Economic Committee, U.S. Congress.

China: Long-Term Development Issues and Options (Washington, D.C., 1985). The World Bank report.

"China and India: Two Billion People Discover the Joys of the Market," *The Economist*, Dec. 21, 1985, 65–70.

China's Economy Look Toward the Year 2000, 2 vols., Joint Economic Committee, U.S. Congress (Washington, D.C., 1986).

Ching, Frank, *Hong Kong and China: For Better or for Worse* (New York, 1985).

Chiu, Hungdah, Y. C. Jao, and Yuan-li Wu (eds.), *The Future of Hong Kong: Toward 1997 and Beyond* (New York, 1987).

Chow, Gregory C., *The Chinese Economy* (Hong Kong, 1986).

Cremer, R. (ed.), *Macau, City of Commerce and Culture* (Hong Kong, 1987).

Croll, Elisabeth, *The Family Rice Bowl* (Geneva and London, 1983).

Deng, Xiaoping, *Building Socialism with Chinese Characteristics* (Peking, 1985).

Griffin, Keith (ed.), *Institutional Reform and Economic Development in the Chinese Countryside* (Hong Kong, 1986).

Hinton, William, *Shenfan: The Continuing Revolution in a Chinese Village* (New York, 1984).

Ho, Samuel P. S., and Ralph W. Huenemann, *China's Open Door Policy: The Quest for Foreign Technology and Capital* (Vancouver, 1984).

Ishikawa, Shigeru, "Sino-Japanese Economic Cooperation," *The China Quarterly*, 109:1–21 (March 1987).

Jao, Y. C., and C. K. Leung (eds.), *China's Special Economic Zones: Problems and Prospects* (New York, 1986).

Joffe, Ellis, *The Chinese Army After Mao* (Cambridge, Mass., 1987).

Kelley, Ian, *Hong Kong: A Political-Geographic Analysis* (Honolulu, 1986).

Kirby, Richard J. R., *Urbanization in China: Town and Country in a Developing Economy, 1949–2000 A.D.* (New York, 1985).

Lardy, Nicholas R., *Agriculture in China's Modern Economic Development* (New York, 1983).

Lee, Ching Hua (Patrick), *Deng Xiaoping: The Marxist Road to the Forbidden City* (1985).

Leeming, Frank, *Rural China Today* (New York, 1985).

Madsen, Richard, *Morality and Power in a Chinese Village* (Berkeley, 1986).

Mathur, Ike, and Chen Jai-sheng, *Strategies for Joint Ventures in the People's Republic of China* (New York, 1987).

Parish, William L. (ed.), *Chinese Rural Development: The Great Transformation* (Armonk, N.Y., 1985).

Perkins, Dwight H., *China: Asia's Next Economic Giant* (Seattle, 1986).

————, and Shahid Yusuf, *Rural Development in China* (Baltimore, 1984).

Perry, Elizabeth J., and Christine Wong (eds.), *The Political Economy of Reform in Post-Mao China* (Cambridge, Mass., 1985).

Rabushka, Alvin, *Forecasting Political Events: Future of Hong Kong* (New Haven, 1986).

Saith, Ashwani (ed.), *The Re-emergence of the Chinese Peasantry: Aspects of Rural Decollectivisation* (London, 1987).

Shaw, Yu-ming (ed.), *Mainland China: Politics, Economics, and Reform* (Boulder, 1985).

Starr, John B. (ed.), *The Future of U.S.-China Relations* (New York, 1984).

Stavis, Benedict, *The Politics of Agricultural Mechanization in China* (Ithaca, N.Y., 1978).

Stephan, John J., and V. P. Chichkanov (eds.), *Soviet-American Horizons on the Pacific* (Honolulu, 1986).

Tam, On Kit, *China's Agricultural Modernization: The Socialist Mechanization Scheme* (Dover, N.H., 1985).

The Chinese People's Liberation Army 60 Years On: Transition towards a New Era, four articles, *The Chinese Quarterly*, 112: 541–630 (Dec. 1987).

Tsao, James T. H., *China's Development Strategies and Foreign Trade* (Lexington, Mass., 1987).

Tsou, Tang, *The Cultural Revolution and Post-Mao Reforms: A Historical Perspective* (Chicago, 1986).

Wesley-Smith, Peter, *Unequal Treaty, 1898–1997: China, Great Britain, and Hong Kong's New Territories* (New York, 1984).

Wik, Philip, *How to Do Business with the People's Republic of China* (Englewood Cliffs, N.J., 1984).

Youngson, A. J. (ed.), *China and Hong Kong: An Economic Nexus* (New York, 1985).

Zhao, Ziyang, "Dangqian di jingji xinshi he jingji tizhi gaige," (On the economic conditions before us and the economic institutional reforms"), Report before the Sixth National People's Congress, March 27, 1985 (Hong Kong, 1985).

Zweig, David, "Prosperity and Conflict in Post-Mao Rural China," *The China Quarterly*, 105:1–18 (March 1986).

7

China in Transition, 1986-88
The Cultural Impact
of the Open Door Policy

When the policy of opening China's doors to the outside world was first adopted in December 1978, the central leadership had hoped to import foreign science and technology without importing foreign culture and values. But ideas travel across boundaries like the wind; they cannot be stopped by decree. The cultural impact of the open-door policy went far beyond anything the CCP leadership had imagined, causing the conservative ideologues to decry the invasion of Western "bourgeois liberalism" as foreign "spiritual pollution." From the standpoint of ideological orthodoxy, the fears and accusations were understandable, but the fact remained that Westernization was a global phenomenon that could not be stopped.

In China's case, after 30 years of isolation from the West, the doors were suddenly flung open: foreign ideas, news, films, plays, music, literature, and popular culture swept in like a windstorm. In the 10 years that followed, 60,000 students and visiting scholars, as well as tens of thousands of officials and delegates, went abroad to study and visit, creating international exchange between China and the outside world such as had not been seen for decades.

The workings of Western democracy and the freedom of its people made a deep impression on Chinese visitors to the West. Particularly enlightening was seeing the functioning of institutional checks and balances; of the division of power in government; of judicial supremacy and the rule of law; political pluralism; and the freedoms of speech, of assembly, and of the press. Many Chinese came to believe that their country needed political democracy as the Fifth Modernization, without which a true modern transformation would not be possible. University students, in particular, felt a social responsibility to be the vanguard of such change.

Not only the West, but Japan and the Four Little Dragons of Asia—Hong Kong, Singapore, Taiwan, and South Korea— were sources of inspiration. Any comparison between them and China would lead to the inevitable questions as to whether Marxism-Maoism was the proper ideology for China's modernization and whether the Chinese Communist Party was the most effective agent to lead China into the 21st century. Doubts persisted on both counts among a number of social critics, writers, journalists, artists, professors, scientists, and college students, although most of them chose to remain silent.

The party itself was torn between the need for liberalization and the urgency of maintaining some level of orthodoxy. Ideology was in a state of flux. Many party members wondered whether a Communist system should adopt the capitalist devices of material incentives and market mechanisms based on supply and demand and the law of value, capitalist-style management, and private enterprise. Others asked whether the Four Cardinal Principles—the socialist line, the proletarian dictatorship, the leadership of the Communist Party, and Marxism-Leninism and the Thought of Mao—should not be downplayed to defuse both the demand for political pluralism and Taiwan's thrust as an alternative model of development.

China, from 1986 to 1988, was experiencing the growing pains of rapid economic development and the agony of changing values. Society was buffeted by student unrest, ideological confusion, a leadership crisis, widespread corruption, high inflation, and a loss of a clear sense of direction. If there were such a thing as a "misery index," the period of 1986–88 would have had the highest readings of any period since the end of the Cultural Revolution. Yet, within the depths of the chaos and turbulence, some promise of regeneration and a better future were dimly discernible.

STUDENT DEMONSTRATIONS

In December 1986 gigantic student demonstrations broke out in 15 major cities in China, which left the party and the government in deep disarray. One hundred thousand students from 150 colleges and universities marched in the streets to demand the freedoms of speech, assembly, and of the press, as well as democratic elections. Their message was clear: the Chinese youths wanted political liberalization.

Student activism was nothing new in modern Chinese history; many precedents existed for the incidents of December 1986. The May Fourth Movement of 1919 was the most famous of these. More recently, in September 1985, students had protested Japan's new economic aggression and the Chinese government's ingratiating attitude toward Japan. This protest had been timed to coincide with the 54th anniversary of the Japanese invasion of Manchuria on September 18, 1931. The protest also served as a vehicle for the students to air other grievances, such as rising prices, economic crimes, bureaucratic irregularities, and nepotism and favoritism for the children of high cadres. A demonstration planned by students of Beijing and Qinghua Universities on December 9, 1985, had been aborted owing to government intervention. The discontent, however, remained.

The first protest of December 1986 broke out in Hofei, in Anhui province, early in the month. The students of the Chinese University of Science and Technology, which is located within the city's electoral district, protested the local party secretaries' designation of eight prospective delegates to the National People's Congress without consulting the university. On December 1, 1986 a big poster appeared on the campus calling for a general boycott of the "faked" election scheduled for December 8. At a student-faculty meeting the following day, the renowned astrophysicist and Vice-President of the university, Fang Lizhi, called for decisive action to achieve a breakthrough in the struggle for political democracy. He repeated his much touted saying that democracy could not be bestowed from above but must be won from below—what was bestowed could be withdrawn, but what was won could not.

The students of the Chinese University of Science and Technology were joined in their protest by students from two other institutions of higher learning in the area.[1] In all, 3,000 students marched on the municipal government on December 5, demanding democratic elections, freedom of the press and of assembly, and immunity from persecution and insisting that the media be allowed to report their protest. They further demanded the formation of a Democratic Alliance of All Students of Higher Learning. The students aimed at breaking the party's control of the press and of the students. The local party authorities reluctantly agreed to assign four delegates to the university precinct and postpone the election to December 29.[2] The students continued to press for election reform, chanting: "We want democracy. We want liberty. We want freedom of the press. No democracy, no modernization."[3]

In Shanghai, there was a huge sympathetic response. On December 19 some 30,000 students,[4] joined by an estimated 100,000 workers, marched on the municipal government. This marked the high tide of the protest. In Beijing, 4,000 students marched on Tian-an-men Square and burned bundles of the party newspaper, the *Beijing Daily*. One of the protesters, watching the rising smoke, was heard to say elatedly: "Gone with the wind!"[5]

These demonstrators made it clear that, although they sought democratization, they were true supporters of Deng Xiaoping's policy of economic reform and an Open Door to the outside world. This prompted a sarcastic comment from the *Peking Daily* that they waved the Red Flag to attack the Red Flag.

Caught off guard, the party was unable to be decisive on the issue. The conservatives pressed for forceful repression, but

General Secretary Hu Yaobang took the enlightened attitude that youthful idealism should not be blunted but guided toward constructive goals. The Vice-Minister of the State Education Commission,[6] himself a demonstrator in his youth, said that most of the demonstrators, who constituted less than 2 percent of China's 2 million college population, were patriotic and well-meaning, but that they were misguided by Western liberalism. He said, "God allows young people to make mistakes. When we were younger, we basically did the same thing. . . . Our policy toward them is to educate them and to advise them and to give them a proper orientation." But he warned that the students must not violate the Four Cardinal Principles lest the country's hard-won stability and unity be compromised.[7]

Other authorities were likewise moderate in their reactions. The Mayor of Shanghai[8] acknowledged the student action to be "just, legal, and patriotic" and permissible under the constitution. He promised that there would be no retribution.[9] Police and public security agents conducted themselves with restraint. They took pictures of the demonstrators but avoided inflaming them lest the demonstration get out of control. Party newspapers urged the students to cherish China's material progress and the improvement in the quality of life made in recent years, including their educational privileges. A famed sociology professor[10] asked the students to air their grievances through the existing channels and offer their criticisms in the interest of stability and unity lest a good cause turn sour. The party authorities did not question the students' motives but feared that their actions might create traffic problems or disrupt economic production!

The more conservative leaders blamed Western bourgeois liberalism as the source of trouble. A small number of students were arrested, and most were soon released. However, a few remained in custody for months.[11] Time was on the government's side. Final examinations soon preoccupied the students, followed by the winter vacation. On the whole, the official position toward the students was initially lenient, but toughened later. In an effort to tighten further central control of

China's student population, the government reinstated military training and political indoctrination on campus and revived the unpopular policy of sending students to "grass roots" farms and factories for a year before being sent to their job assignments.[12] But the government's policy toward the workers had been very strict from the beginning: they were strictly prohibited from joining the demonstrations. The authorities were determined to keep a Polish-style union strike from happening in China.

General Secretary Hu's handling of the unrest raised the ire of the hard-line conservatives. They were impatient with his liberal approach and became increasingly critical of his leadership. A large group of them in the party, the army, and the government formed a grand alliance to denounce him before the paramount leader Deng Xiaoping. They blamed the Voice of America and Taiwan's Voice of Free China as outside instigators of the turmoil, but even more emphatically they attacked Western bourgeois liberalism as the source of discontent and disharmony. This conservative group held a number of secret meetings in the second half of December, and before the end of the month they had won Deng over. Decisions were made to clamp down on the student agitation, to deal with Hu sternly, and to fight Western liberalism. The *People's Daily* editorialized, "It's time to wake up. Bourgeois liberalism is indeed an ideological trend. It is in the process of poisoning our youth, imperiling our social stability and unity, interfering with our reforms and opening-up policy, and obstructing modernization's move forward. Can we afford to do nothing about it?" As the New Year approached, all party members were admonished to raise their vigilance against the spread of "bourgeois liberalization" in China.[13] The fate of General Secretary Hu hung in a precarious balance.

Bourgeois Liberalism

The student unrest was not an isolated and sudden outburst of youthful enthusiasm, but a movement several years in the making. Ever since the Third Plenum of the Eleventh Party

Congress in December 1978, when the policy of modernization and opening up was adopted, foreign news, contacts, and travel had swamped the Chinese public with cultural and political concepts once considered alien and inconceivable. A new vista was opened to the Chinese as to the nature of the modern world. Ideas such as human rights, democracy, free elections, free speech, free assembly, free press, division of power, and "loyal opposition" captured the Chinese imagination and won their deepest appreciation. Particularly admired was the idea that the governing bodies could be supervised by the govnered through a watchful press, the right to dissent, and political pluralism, all of which could serve as checks on the excesses of the government. These ideas, to the Chinese, symbolized the true character of a democracy dedicated to the fullest development of the human potential.

Several international events contributed to this state of mind among the reading public: the overthrow of the Marcos regime in the Philippines by "people's power" in February 1986; the expulsion of the Haitian dictator, Jean-Claude Duvalier, by a popular revolt; the political liberalization of Taiwan and, with it, the creation of the opposition Democratic Progressive Party; and the student strike in France against the adoption of an elitist educational policy.

Domestically, there were powerful stirrings in intellectual and cultural circles. Ever since the Third Plenum of December 1978, when the central focus of the party shifted from class struggle to economic development, intellectuals had been given higher status because modernization demanded knowledge and talent. Deng Xiaoping proclaimed the intellectuals to be part of the proletariat, deserving both respect and good treatment from the state—no longer the "stinking No. 9" at the bottom of the social heap as under Mao. Emboldened by their new status, independent-minded writers, artists, scientists, and thinkers began to speak their minds on pressing social and political issues.

These dissenters frequently touched a raw nerve in the party, which jealously guarded its right to rule and to be obeyed unquestioningly. Dissent was equated with defiance, disloyalty, and a challenge to the authority of the party. In 1979, when the "Democracy Wall" movement sprang up, the government condemned its leader[14] to a 15-year prison sentence. In 1983, when it perceived Western ideas, theories, and practices as invasive of the Chinese public consciousness, the party instituted an "Anti-Spiritual Pollution" movement to counter the inroads of "decadent" values.

When President Ronald Reagan visited China in April 1984, he was imbued with a mission to extol the virtues of American democracy, faith in God, freedom, individual initiative, free enterprise, and the spirit of progress. In a speech delivered at the Great Hall of the People before 600 Chinese social leaders, he declared:

> From our roots we have drawn tremendous power from two great forces—faith and freedom. America was founded by people who sought freedom to worship God and to trust in Him to guide them in their daily lives with wisdom, strength, goodness, and compassion.
>
> Our passion for freedom led to the American Revolution, the first great uprising for human rights and independence against colonial rule. We knew each of us could not enjoy liberty for ourselves unless we were willing to share it with everyone else. And we knew our freedom could not truly be safe unless all of us were protected by a body of laws that treated us equally.
>
> George Washington told us we would be bound together in a sacred brotherhood of free men. Abraham Lincoln defined the heart of American democracy when he said, "No man is good enough to govern another man without that other's consent. . . ." These great principles have nourished the soul of America, and they have been enriched by values such as the dignity of work, the friendship of neighbors, and the warmth of family.
>
> "Trust the people"—these three words are not only the heart and soul of American history, but the most powerful force for human progress in the world today . . . the societies that have made the most spectacular progress in the shortest period of time are not the most rigidly organized nor even the richest in natural resources. No, it's where people have been

allowed to create, compete, and build, where they've been permitted to think for themselves, make economic decisions, and benefit from their own risks that societies have become the most prosperous, progressive, dynamic, and free.[15]

These were strong and agitating messages for an atheistic and authoritarian society. Obviously taking offense, the Chinese leadership decided to censor what it did not want the people to hear during later media coverage. Chinese television audiences did not hear the statements on faith and freedom, nor the exhortation that "free people build free markets that ignite development for everyone." Presidential Deputy Press Secretary Larry Speakes stated that while the decision to censor was "an internal matter for the Chinese people to decide," he regretted the omission of "key passages dealing with the President's view of values that Americans cherish . . . which would have given the Chinese people a better understanding of our country and its people."[16]

Reagan repeated the same themes with special emphasis on human rights in a televised speech at Fudan University in Shanghai: "We believe in the dignity of each man, woman, and child. Our entire system is founded on an appreciation of the special genius of each individual—and of his special right to make his own decisions and lead his own life."[17] The Chinese allowed no translation of the text during the telecast, but there were enough people who could understand Reagan. The full texts of both speeches quickly appeared in the free markets and were snapped up instantly. Reagan got his message across, and the Chinese audiences secretly admired him for his audacity and "guts."[18]

The Chinese youths were strongly affected by their new exposure to Western political ideas, both abroad and through Reagan's visit. They came to feel that any political system that deviated from the ideals of the Western democracies inhibited the full development of individuals and must be condemned as backward, authoritarian, and out of touch with the modern era.

With the urban economic reforms in 1984, there were increasing instances of crime, corruption, inflation, and favoritism toward the children of the high cadres under the guise of promoting third-tier leaders. Seeing themselves as the conscience of the younger generation, the students felt a social responsibility to protest this degradation of morals. They wanted human rights; democracy; the rule of law; freedom of speech, assembly and the press; and prohibition of arbitrary arrests and ad hoc extrajudiciary proceedings.

Not only the students but also the general cultural, artistic and intellectual communities came under the impact of Western liberalization as well. Writers and artists demanded greater freedom in creative endeavors, and public-minded intellectuals longingly discussed such subjects as free elections, the three-way division of power, the right to dissent, and the multiparty system. A writer in Shanghai wrote: "Ideology should be free, emancipated, rich and pluralistic. . . . I have established for myself four basic ideological principles—to shake off ideological bonds, to free myself from following others blindly and from superstition, to think for myself, and to help my own ideology eventually jump from the realm of necessity to the realm of freedom."[19]

Fang Lizhi, the noted professor of astrophysics, was a tireless proponent of human rights and democracy. Dubbed the Chinese "Sakharov," he made frequent speaking tours and appeared at universities and before research institutes. His favorite topics were the rule of law, free elections, free speech, a free press, and political pluralism. Imbued with the conviction that scholars had a social responsibility to speak out on the vital issues of the day, he declared that he feared nobody and would accept the consequences of his actions. A research university, he stated, should honor science, democracy, creativity, and independence as the Four Basic Creeds. He advocated these in place of the Four Cardinal Principles, which he disparagingly compared with superstition, autocracy, conservatism, and dependency. He partook fully of the spirit and ideas of the May Fourth Movement—science, democracy, and complete Westernization. He considered Marxism to be obsolescent and held it responsible for keeping China backward and for sanctioning the party's unrestrained and inviolable exercise of power. The party's rule, he pointed out, was based on military conquest, not merit, and its overall record in the past 35 years could only be considered a failure. Fang urged the students to fight for their rights, but he never asked them to take to the streets.[20]

Liu Binyan, an investigative reporter for the *People's Daily,* and Wang Ruowang, a writer, were devastating in their exposé of the darker side of bureaucratism and official domination of literature and of the press. They particularly took exception to Mao's 1942 talk in Yanan, which stated that literature and journalism should serve politics.

A vice-chairman of the Chinese Writers Association, Liu Binyan ridiculed the Four Cardinal Principles and questioned the logic of insisting on socialism in China. He asked: if the socialism of the period 1953–76 under Mao was correct, what would the socialism of the period 1979–86 under Deng be? The two were so different. How could they both be correct? With contempt he asked:

> What is the essence of extreme leftism? It is mutual despite, mutual destruction, and mutual cruelty. It makes human inhuman. It makes a free man unfree. It turns a person of independent personality into a submissive tool. It turns man into beast. In the process, the conscience is lost, and the sense of self-reproof disappears. In their place, there is mutual hostility and hatred, and mutual suspicion and cruelty. Finally, fear fills the air—fear of brutal power, fear of leaders, and fear of authorities. . . . Hence, I must submit that the essence of leftism is inhumanism.

Liu chided his countrymen for delusion with four fantasies: (1) that socialism is perfect, (2) that the Communist party is infallible, (3) that Marxism-Leninism is eternal truth, and (4) that there is a deep chasm between socialism and capitalism and that nothing in the capitalist societies that took place in the past several hundred years should be given proper recognition. For these misconceptions, Liu stated, the country paid dearly in the form of wanton sacrifices and unnecessary losses. And all for what?[21]

The other critic, Wang Ruowang, a council member in the Chinese Writers Association, took on Deng himself in November 1986. Deng had agreed to an interview with the CBS journalist Mike Wallace and stated that Chinese socialism would permit some to get rich first but would prevent the rise of polarity between the very rich and the very poor. In any event, Deng believed that it would be difficult for anyone to become a millionaire under the Chinese socialist system and that there should be no concern for the rise of a new capitalistic class. The statement sounded innocuous enough, but Wang took issue with several points in this line of thinking. Polarity in a developing socialist society was unavoidable, Wang argued. The opposite of polarity would be egalitarianism or averageism ("Everybody eats from the same Big Pot"), which China had practiced for 30 years and which had brought on nothing but abject Communist poverty. To avoid polarity was to remove incentives for greater production and profit, Wang argued. To predict the impossibility of millionaires was to preset a limit to one's expectations and upward mobility. In a country as large as China, Wang suggested, even 3,000 or 5,000 millionaires would not be too many; and being products of Chinese socialism, they would be different from the capitalists of Marxist definition.[22]

It was not just intellectuals like Fang, Liu, and Wang who showed the influence of Western liberalism. In society at large, there was a craving for anything Western. Thousands would stand in line for hours to see a Picasso exhibit, a performance by The Royal Ballet, or an Arthur Miller play; but few would visit Mao's Revolutionary Military Museum. Almost anything foreign was attractive: political thought, social theories, futurology, novels, plays, art, fashion, and even such mundane things as Coca-Cola, Maxwell House Coffee, and Kentucky Fried Chicken. The most prized wedding gift of the time was a set of the Encyclopaedia Britannica in Chinese. The chairman of the translation and editorial board explained the public enthusiasm:

> For more than three decades, we treated Western culture as taboo and abandoned everything from the West. As a result, our knowledge of the West remained a blank. The works of Milton, Shaw, Rousseau, Balzac, Boccaccio, and Goethe, the music of Bach and Mozart, and the dramas of Shakespeare and Ibsen were considered 'bourgeois" and their publication and performance were forbidden. How many Chinese are there who don't even know about the stories in the Bible?[23]

There is no denying that Western influence was pervasive and growing stronger by the day.

In the party, reaction to the new trend was mixed. General Secretary Hu Yaobang took a laissez-faire attitude toward it in the belief that the information revolution of the world had brought countries closer to each other and that it was in China's interest to experiment with new ideas and to create a new image for Chinese communism. His liberal approach pained the conservative elders who considered Western liberalism to be a disturbing influence, a source of decadence and spiritual pollution in Chinese life. They were distressed by the growing popularity of disco music, rock 'n' roll, blue jeans, sexy movies, and foreign publications that suggested freedom and democracy. They concluded that the inroads of bourgeois liberalism prompted a loss of regard for the party, a lack of respect for the leaders, a questioning of the legitimacy of Communist rule, and a blind worship of Western values. If bourgeois liberalism were not stopped in time, they insisted, there would be no place for Communist orthodoxy. Hu, the supposed ideological leader of the party, was too soft to lead the fight. Only the hard-line ideologues could defend the purity of the Faith. Thus, the Long March generation septuagenarians and octogenarians assigned themselves the sacred duty of remaining in power to fight Western liberalism.

The clash between the orthodox ideologues and progressive reformers could only be resolved by the paramount leader, Deng. He was a curious mixture of economic progressivism and political conservatism, endowed with a gift for playing a balancing act as political necessity dictated. In a system where the rule of man superseded the rule of law, he was the supreme arbiter. In his mind, economic reforms and an open-door policy were but means by which to borrow foreign technology, capital, and managerial skills. These were seen as tools with which to strengthen the Communist rule, but never as steps to move the country toward a Western-style democracy. He ridiculed the three-way division of power as three governments in one country and considered political pluralism to be totally out of order. Only his Four Cardinal Principles, announced in March 1979, could ensure stability and order and provide the necessary environment for modernization. The country could not tolerate any disruption, such as the student turmoil, or any disturbing influence, such as Western liberalism. In short, he was interested in Western science, but not Western values.[24]

In September 1986, at the Sixth Plenum of the Twelfth Congress, with Deng's acquiescence, the conservative ideologues outmaneuvered the progressives by blocking the discussion of political reforms. Instead, they passed a much-revised (eight times) resolution on the "Spiritual Construction of Socialism," which highlighted a provision titled "Anti-Bourgeois Liberalization." A shattering blow was dealt to the cause of democratization. It was against this background that the student demonstrations erupted in December 1986.

Dismissal of Hu Yaobang

A major result of the student unrest was the ouster of General Secretary Hu, who was too liberal and outspoken for his own good. He had survived for five years (1981–86) in that post, primarily owing to the support of Deng, who had groomed him to be his successor and who once confidently remarked that, with Hu in charge of the party and Zhao at the helm of the government, even if heaven should come crashing down, he would have no fear. But now the conservatives in the party, the government, and the miiltary descended on Deng to demand the resignation of Hu on grounds of his ineptness in dealing with the students and in stopping the inroads of Western bourgeois liberalism. Peng Zhen, chairman of the Standing

Committee of the People's Congress, three other ideologues, and two powerful military leaders headed the move to oust Hu.[25] A shrewd politician, Deng knew the futility of fighting this powerful coalition; besides, his own confidence in Hu had faltered. After several secret meetings in the second half of December 1986, Deng painfully accepted the decision that Hu had to go. Deng sacrificed Hu to keep the support of the conservative leaders.

After the New Year, Hu was not seen in public; his fall was imminent. Meanwhile, intensive preparations were made for the convocation of a special, enlarged Politburo, which opened on January 16, 1987. At the end of the day a formal announcement was made that Hu had resigned after making a "self-criticism of his mistakes on major issues of political principles in violation of the party's principle of collective leadership."

A glimpse of the intraparty squabbling at the highest councils may be seen from the eight party documents distributed for internal circulation during the early months of 1987. The scrutiny of Hu fell under six headings, which revealed policy differences as well as personal vendettas:

1. Hu practiced factionalism by favoring the promotion of members of the Communist Youth Corps, of which he was the former head.
2. Hu spoke carelessly on diplomatic occasions: during a visit to Tokyo in 1983 he declared that if the United States intervened in the Taiwan question, China might consider canceling the mutual visits of Premier Zhao Ziyang and President Ronald Reagan.
3. Hu did not carry out party rectification effectively.
4. Hu advocated an inordinately fast pace of economic reform creating economic imbalances and loss of control of the situation.
5. Hu favored the rule of man over the rule of law in administering party work.
6. Hu did not observe organization discipline but revealed state secrets to foreigners and journalists.

The enlarged Politburo meeting summarized Hu's mistakes as follows:

1. He violated the collective leadership of the party.
2. He committed mistakes in major political principles.
3. He repeatedly and arbitrarily interfered with the work of government.
4. He repeatedly ignored the advice of Deng Xiaoping.
5. He made arbitrary decisions on important diplomatic issues.
6. He showed a tendency toward complete Westernization in his political style of work.

Behind these formal charges was the deep resentment of Hu's constant plea for the retirement of the party elders. Reportedly, he had planned to announce his plans to retire Central Committee members at age 60 and Politburo members at age 72 at the Thirteenth Party Congress scheduled for October 1987. To be sure, the principle of retiring the aged leaders was accepted by the party and Deng, but the actual implementation was left to the General Secretary, and it proved extremely sensitive. With no official retirement system, position meant power, political clout, and economic privileges. The Long March generation elders were particularly sensitive to their indispensability. They would do anything to avoid retirement, which was equated with worthlessness. Deng, too, may have been uncomfortable with Hu's suggestion that Deng retire first to set an example for the other elders. To be sure, Deng had repeatedly protested that he wanted to retire but others would not let him. Hu might have naively taken Deng's words literally and irritated him, leading Deng to question Hu's political astuteness. The student upheaval and Deng's displeasure provided the older leaders with a golden opportunity to get rid of Hu and to keep themselves in power.

The military had no use for Hu either, for he had no close relationship with the army and had assigned a low priority to benefits for the military in the Four Modernizations. Besides, Hu had advocated a cut in the armed forces totaling one million and was an outspoken critic of the Vietnam War. Since September 1986, the military had predicted and worked toward his removal.

The hard-line elders were determined to oust Hu before the convocation of the Thirteenth Congress so as to deny him a role in the selection of the delegates and in the preparation of the agenda. With the support of the military, their combined strength was formidable; and Deng, a political conservative-centrist at heart, bowed to their demands, perhaps in the interest of preserving party unity and orthodoxy.

When Hu made his self-criticism and offered to resign, 21 of the 40 participants spoke to criticize him, including some of his closest former allies. Hu wept but agreed "never to regret and reverse" the verdict. The case was closed with Hu's retaining his seat in the Politburo and the Central Committee. There was no official disgrace; in fact, Hu's popularity soared. He lived in relative seclusion thereafter until death overtook him on April 15, 1989, aged 73.

Premier Zhao was appointed Acting General Secretary, concurrently with his other posts. The reformist cause had been dealt a severe setback, and conservative forces were on the rise.

Anti-Bourgeois Liberalization

Peng Zhen and Deng Liqun now unleashed their "Anti-Bourgeois Liberalization" campaign with a vengeance. A Media and Publications Office was created under the State Council in January 1987 to monitor the news media and publication of books, magazines, and newspapers. Three leading critics of the party were summarily dismissed from the party: the astrophysicist Fang, the journalist Liu, and the writer Wang. However, no physical abuse was visited on any of them. Fang was transferred from the prestigious position as Vice-President of the Chinese University of Science and Technology to a far less visible post as a researcher in a Beijing observatory. He was allowed to continue his research and attend scholarly meetings in China—and occasionally abroad—but was deprived of a public forum to speak from. His fame may have protected him from greater penalty, as was the case with the other two critics. Several other cultural and intellectual figures received chastisements of varying severity, but no one was subjected to the harsh treatment of the Cultural Revolution period.[26]

In response, a thousand Chinese students and scholars studying in the United States jointly dispatched a letter of protest to the party and the State Council on January 19. The letter expressed concern over the dismissal of Hu, the expulsion of Fang and others from party membership, and the rising tide of leftism reminiscent of "the cruel excesses of the Cultural Revolution." The students reaffirmed their support of reform, democracy, and the rule of law; and they stated their opposition to regression.

Deng lent his support to the Anti-Bourgeois Liberalization campaign but did not allow it to be developed at the expense of stability and unity. The campaign was to be limited to the party, the government, the army, and urban enterprises. The countryside, the other political parties, and independent intellectuals were off limits. Also prohibited was the use of any expressions or terminology reminiscent of the Cultural Revolution.[27]

From January to May 1987, the rising tide of conservatism penetrated deep into ideological, cultural, literary, and journalistic circles with harsh rhetoric and vicious innuendo. The Anti-Bourgeois Liberalization campaign threatened to envelop the major cities, and the reformers looked disorganized and powerless. The hard-liners called for the revival of the Maoist three-way coalition among the old, the middle-aged, and the young. They promoted the old virtues of frugality, hard work, plain living, and devotion to the state as an antidote to Western influence. The Maoist slogan "Learn from Lei Feng," a fictitious model worker, was revived. Cautious people started to store away their Western clothes in favor of Mao jackets.

But the majority of people did not want to return to the old days. Once exposed to some freedom and creature comforts such as television and refrigerators, they could not bear the thought of going back to the Spartan life of Maoist times. Even the children and grandchildren of the hard-liners took exception to their elders' high-flown moralistic preaching, and there was a national desire to avoid the reappearance of another Cultural Revolution. By May the high tide of Anti-Bourgeois Liberalization was spent. The party elders painfully discovered that they were not moving in the main stream of society. Their pronouncements fell on deaf ears; most people simply counted on their passing.

The party was indeed in a dilemma. It had enjoyed a monopoly of power since 1949, and its right to rule had never been questioned before. Now the younger generation clamored for democratization and yearned for a freer life such as that found in other modern societies. Marxism and Maoism had lost appeal, and the party itself was experiencing a crisis of confidence. Not to grant economic reforms and greater political relaxation would further alienate the people and drive the party farther from the realities of the time. But permitting democracy could lead to social disharmony and ultimately to the demise of communism in China. The top leadership strove to find a middle course that would make it neither unfaithful to its ideology nor guilty of "orthodox Marxist sectarianism." It groped for a theory that would permit market mechanisms, importation of foreign capital and technology, and borrowing of capitalist management skills—all within a flexible framework that could be viewed as both Marxist and Chinese. Such a formula, if found, could justify an extension of both economic reform and open-door policy, strengthen the position of the reformers, and deflate the zeal of the conservatives.

Premier Zhao, an economic technocrat at heart, temporized with the hard-liners to avoid a split. Only once did he confront them at an enlarged Politburo meeting on May 13, 1987, in an attempt to curb the excesses of leftism.[28] Deng was conspicuously quiet throughout the spring, nursing his wounds over the loss of Hu. In the end he realized that what was at issue was not who should resign, but rather the future of economic reforms and of the open-door policy. If the conservative ascendency were not checked, modernization itself would stall. The luxury of silence was over; Deng was compelled to declare his position.

On four occasions in May and June, before foreign visitors, Deng vigorously affirmed the need to curb leftism and expand the scope of economic reforms and the open-door policy.[29] Newspapers and journals, which had been awaiting a signal, quickly echoed this line. This was a triumph for antileftism and a deflation of the Anti-Bourgeois Liberalization campaign. The reformers had regained a measure of coherence and started to plan for an offensive at the forthcoming enlarged Politburo meetings at the summer resort of Beidaiho in July. At Beidaiho, intense political jockeying took place among the various power brokers, and an agreement was reached on four principal issues: (1) a political report on the future course of development to be delivered at the Thirteenth Party Congress scheduled for October 1987; (2) retirement of the elders and selection of the future leadership; (3) an official statement on the nature of the present stage of socialist construction; and (4) political restructuring. The deliberations were kept secret until their final ratification by the Thirteenth Congress.

THE THIRTEENTH PARTY CONGRESS

The much-awaited Congress was held in the Great Hall of the People in Peking from October 25 to November 1, 1987, and attended by 1,936 delegates representing 46 million party members. For the first time, 200 foreign journalists, including some from Taiwan, were invited to view the opening and closing ceremonies. The Congress was significant in several ways. First and foremost, it reaffirmed the correctness of the policy of reforms and the Open Door that was adopted at the Third Plenum of the Eleventh Congress held in December 1978, and it made economic development the central task of the party. Secondly, it achieved a rejuvenation of the leadership by the voluntary retirement of the Long March generation of elders and secured their replacement with younger and better-educated technocrats. Thirdly, it adopted a new theoretical framework for the market-oriented reforms previously thought un-Marxist by the conservatives. Fourthly, it defined the scope of political restructuring so that administrative efficiency could be improved.

Acting General Secretary Zhao Ziyang opened the Congress with a glowing political report on the major accomplishments of the nine years since December 1978. The gross national product (GNP) and the average income of rural and urban residents had doubled, and the overwhelming majority of the one billion strong population was adequately fed and clothed. According to Zhao, building "socialism with Chinese characteristics" under Deng ranked as one of the "two major historic leaps" in the 60-year history of the Chinese revolution, the other being the success of Mao's New Democratic Revolution of 1949. By implication, Deng was placed on a par with Mao as one of the two leading contributors to the enrichment of Marxism-Leninism in China. Many now viewed the current modernization as a Second Revolution or a new Long March.[30]

Personnel Change

Deng personally orchestrated the retirement of more than 90 party elders who were critics of the market-oriented reforms, including Peng Zhen, 85, chairman of the Standing Committee of the National People's Congress, Chen Yun, 82, leading party economist and central planner; and Hu Qiaomu, 75, and Deng Liqun, 72, two orthodox ideologues and harsh critics of bourgeois liberalism, and Li Xiannian, 78, president of the People's Republic. Deng himself retired from all positions in the party but kept the chairmanship of the Military Commission through a special party constitutional amendment that allowed him to hold the post without being a Central Committee member. It was also arranged that General Secretary Zhao would become the first vice-chairman of the Military Commission; and General Yang Shangkun, the permanent vice-chairman. These arrangements could have been a hint that the military would accept Zhao as the potential successor to Deng.

The new 285-member Central Committee consisted of 175 regulars and 110 alternates. Some 150 aged leaders (43 percent) of the previous 348-man Central Committee failed to win reelection. Interestingly, Hua Guofeng, successor to Mao in 1976, kept his membership. Zhao Ziyang was confirmed as General Secretary by an overwhelming vote. The average age of the new ruling body was 55.2 years, down from the 59.1 of its predecessor. Eighty-seven of the full and alternate members were new, and 209 (73 percent) of all Central Committee members were college-educated.[31]

The Politburo, with 17 regulars and 1 alternate, was packed with younger supporters of reform. Nine of the 20 previous members retired, and former General Secretary Hu Yaobang retained his seat; so did his close associates, Vice-Premiers Wan Li and Tian Jiyuan. The average age was 63, 7 years younger than that of the previous body. In the new Standing Committee of the Politburo, the average age was 64, 13 years younger than that of its predecessor.

A balance of opinion was maintained in the all-powerful Standing Committee, with the election of the following five members: Zhao Ziyang, 68; Li Peng, 59, Hu Qili, 58; Yao Yilin, 70; and Qiao Shi, 63. It is generally accepted that Zhao and Hu were ardent supporters of market-oriented economic development and that Li and Yao were inclined toward the Soviet-style central planning, with Qiao Shi, a security specialist, in the middle. Actually, all of them claimed to be supporters of reform; they differed only in style, method, pace, and scope. Economic development had become such a national passion that few politicians dared to profess anything else.

Other important party appointments included Chen Yun as chairman of the 200-member Central Advisory Commission of Discipline Inspection and Hu Qili as the leader of a 4-member Secretariat.

With most of the conservative critics out of the way, the reformers gained a mandate to go full steam ahead. Yet they knew that the elders who retired did not relinquish their influence. Their willingness to retire probably was made with the understanding that their favorite choice, Li Peng, would be appointed to the Politburo Standing Committee as well as to the future premiership. Indeed, barely three weeks after the close of the Congress, Li was named Acting Premier, and later, at the National People's Congress in March 1988, was confirmed as premier.

Li Peng, the son of an early Communist martyr,[32] grew up in the household of the late premier Zhou Enlai. Li joined the

General Secretary Zhao Ziyang.

party at 17 and was sent to the Soviet Union in 1948 to study electrical engineering. Returning home 6 years later, he rose steadily as an expert in electric power and energy resources. Close to the party elders Chen Yun, Peng Zhen, and Deng Yingchao (Zhou's wife), Li enjoyed a broad spectrum of support among the conservative wing of the party, the bureaucrat-followers of Zhou in the government, and the Soviet-trained Chinese of the 1950s, who were well-placed in many different

Premier Li Peng.

walks of life. Sensitive of his educational background, Li made a point of disclaiming any preference for the Soviet economic system or central planning. Immediately after his election to the Politburo Standing Committee, he announced on November 2, 1987: "The allegation that I am in favor of a centrally planned economy is a complete misunderstanding. The economic system [of China] must be restructured." Upon his appointment as Acting Premier, he announced his support for the policy of economic reform and opening China to the outside world "while continuing to maintain the political stability and unity, and pursue, as always, the country's independent foreign policy."[33] In the political report delivered by General Secretary Zhao at the Congress, the statement "the state regulates the market and the market guides (economic) enterprises" could have been a contribution of Li's.[34]

The Primary Stage of Socialism

The constant charge of the conservative hard-liners and the lingering doubts among many others that market-oriented mechanisms were basically un-Marxist were irritating thorns in the side of the progressive movement. Yet market forces had to be recognized to make economic development work, and contact with the outside world was essential to modernization. The most urgent task for the reformers was to develop a theoretical framework to justify their work as being neither capitalistic nor un-Marxist, but as highly necessary and permissible within the limits of socialism. After groping in the dark for a long time, Chinese social scientists came up with the new concept that China was in the primary stage of socialism during which market forces, capitalistic techniques and management skills, and a mixed economy characterized by a multi-ownership system were all acceptable. Sanctioned by this theoretical support, Zhao stated confidently in his political report: "Reform is the only process through which China can be revitalized. It is a process which is irreversible and which accords with the will of the people and the general trend of events."

Zhao advanced the thesis that China did not go through the proper stage of capitalism because of her previously backward productive forces and underdeveloped commodity economy. To insist on China's going from capitalism to socialism was to be mechanistic and to commit the mistake of the political Right. But to believe that she could skip the primary stage of socialism and proceed straight to socialism was to be utopian and to commit the mistake of the political Left. "During this [primary] stage we shall accomplish industrialization and the commercialization, socialization and modernization of production, which many other countries have achieved under capitalist conditions," concluded Zhao.

Building socialism with Chinese characteristics, Zhao proclaimed, was an experiment that could not possibly have been foreseen by 19th-century European theorists.

> We are not in the situation envisaged by the founders of Marxism, in which socialism is built on the basis of highly developed capitalism, nor are we in exactly the same situation as other socialist countries. So we cannot blindly follow what the books say, nor can we mechanically immitate the examples of other countries [Russia?]. Rather, proceeding from China's actual conditions and integrating the basic principles of Marxism with those conditions, we must find a way to build socialism with Chinese characteristics through practice.

Zhao urged his fellow citizens to find ways to allow a multiownership system so as to avoid rigidity in economic structure, to expand the commodity economy, to raise labor productivity, and to achieve the Four Modernizations.

The theory was further developed along the following lines. The central task during this primary stage was to end poverty and backwardness. It was no longer class struggle, though that still existed as a contradiction. To ensure the policies of economic development and the Open Door, China had to have stability and unity through the application of the Four Cardinal Principles. The primary stage of socialism could last as long as 100 years from the 1950s, when the private means of production went through a socialist transformation, to the mid-21st century, when the socialist modernization would have been largely completed. This long process was divided into three phases: first, to double the GNP of 1980 and solve the problems of food and clothing for the people—a goal largely achieved; secondly, to double the GNP again by the year A.D. 2000 so as to provide a relatively comfortable standard of living; and thirdly, to reach a level of affluence enjoyed by most medium-developed countries by the middle of the next century. The expansion of science, technology, and education were the keys to this success.[35]

The gnawing questions that plagued the country were these: "Is the reform making China capitalistic, and is a certain new measure socialistic or capitalistic by nature?" Many Chinese and foreigners alike tended to associate "market mechanisms" with capitalist systems, and "central planning" with the Soviet or socialist system. The Chinese leadership was now reconciled to the idea that market mechanisms and central planning were both "neutral means and methods that do not determine the basic economic system of a society."[36] Hence, adoption of capitalist techniques and management skills, a mixed economy characterized by a multi-ownership system, and increased grass-roots participation in political affairs were all permissible during the primary stage. A current saying went thus: "Whatever promotes economic development is good; whatever hinders it is no good." Such ideas almost sound like American pragmatism.

Political Restructuring

Political restructuring did not signify that a Western style reform in which a democratic system complete with free elections, a free press, a three-way division of power, and alternating control of government by different parties would evolve. Rather, it simply meant improvement in administrative efficiency, simplification of unwieldy bureaucratic structures, and elimination of overstaffing. A key feature was the separation of the party from the day-to-day operation of the government and economic enterprises. Government administration of economic enterprises would be replaced by indirect control. Bureaucracy would be streamlined from top to bottom, and a meritocratic civil service system installed.

According to the party leadership, China had to maintain its unique style of government with the distinct character of a socialist democracy. People's congresses at different levels, democratic centralism, and "multiparty" cooperation would continue while grass-roots participation in government increased. With the development of an efficient legal system, people's rights would be protected from arbitrary official violations and extralegal procedures. In this way, a social democracy could be built.

An Assessment

The Thirteenth Congress was remarkable for several reasons. It firmly launched China onto the road of accelerated economic development and greater opening to the outside world. In no other Communist state had any ruling group voluntarily relinquished power in favor of a younger leadership. Even more remarkably, Chinese leaders had found that the traditional Communist system was unworkable unless it was adulterated with market mechnisms. The Soviet leader Mikhail Gorbachev seemed to have made the same discovery, but China was ahead of the Soviet Union in breaking away from the bondage of orthodox Marxism. China had forged an important new ideological tool—the development of a new theory to fit reality rather than bending "reality to theory."[37] Deng had turned economic reform into an irreversible commitment that enjoyed the vast support of the people. Meanwhile, Gorbachev was still "grinding slowly uphill in low gear," tackling nearly the entire Soviet bureaucracy. Knowledgeable sources placed greater odds on China's economic success than on Russia's.[38]

But, remarkable as it was, the Thirteenth Congress left many questions unanswered. First of all, its work represented no clear victory for the progressive reformers, but rather a compromise among disparate groups within the party. The conservative elders had retired but had not relinquished their influence and could still have used it to block more drastic liberalization.[39] Many sensitive issues such as price decontrol, inflation, leasing state enterprises to private operations, bankruptcy law, and transfer of the land untilization right (a euphemism for private ownership) could still prove explosive. In particular, the Wengzhou model of private ownership, a pet project of Zhao's, was certain to touch off controversy.

Secondly, Deng had arranged for Zhao to be the First Vice-Chairman of the Military Commission, but there was no assurance that Zhao could succeed him as the commander-in-chief or the paramount leader. In the past, all designated heirs had fallen failed to inherit the power: Liu Shaoji in 1966, Lin Biao in 1972, and Hua Guofeng in 1980. Instability has been inherent in the leadership succession in any Communist state. Common sense tempts one to ask, If Zhao was protected by Deng during his (Deng's) lifetime, what would happen to him after Deng was gone? It was necessary at this point that the rule of law replace the rule of man if stability was to be achieved.

Thirdly, accelerated economic development and greater opening to foreign influences would inevitably revive the old questions of "spiritual pollution," "bourgeois liberalization," and the perennial issue of "Chinese essence vs. foreign value." The Thirteenth Congress skirted these issues.

Fourthly, separation of party functions from the government and economic enterprises would affect the vested interests of millions. Its implementation could be excruciatingly slow and difficult.

Fifthly, the supremacy of the Four Cardinal Principles prohibited any rule other than the Communist and any freedom beyond what was permitted by the party. A modicum of dissent might be allowed to a select few—such as a famous astrophysicist, a journalist, a writer, or an artist—for purposes of window dressing and nothing more, but the extent of tolerance would be tightly controlled and strictly limited.

All in all, the Congress was a qualified success insofar as it represented a concensus among the disparate leaders to move the country forward economically. But the search for the higher goals of democracy, pluralism, and human rights would necessitate another Long March.

THE COASTAL DEVELOPMENT PLAN

In the period 1987–88 China evolved a new economic strategy for the coastal regions by which the development of these areas was to be accelerated and closely tied to international markets. The Coastal Development Plan had two basic components: (1) the importation of raw materials from abroad and (2) the exportation of processed finished goods to world markets to earn foreign exchange. The capital raised would be used to purchase high technology and modern equipment, which were meant to help finance China's heavy industry. These, in turn, would help the development of agriculture. The coastal economy would be made heavily export-oriented, with both ends of the production process—the supply of raw materials and the marketing of the processed goods—deeply involved in the world economy. The importation of foreign materials was seen as necessary at first, because China's inland provinces could not provide them; but as conditions improved, some of the raw materials could come from Western China. In the long run, the benefit would "trickle down" throughout the entire country.

The Coastal Development Plan followed logically from the adoption of the open-door policy in December 1978. From that point, the country continued to move in the direction of greater opening and more international contact, as evidenced by the creation of Four Special Economic Zones in 1979; the opening of 14 seaports; and the more recent opening of the Yangtze Delta, the Pearl River Delta, and the Southern Fujian Triangle, as well as the designation of Hainan island as the fifth economic zone, in 1985. There was a realistic acceptance of the fact that no two regions of China could develop at the same speed and that China should accelerate the development of the coastal areas now to maximize the benefits of the export trade.

The theoretical basis of this plan was advanced in June 1987 by a 34-year-old economic planner, who vigorously expounded the advantage of integrating China's coastal economy with international markets in a continuing cycle of importation of raw materials for processing and exportation of finished goods for foreign exchange to finance China's modernization.[40] The plan called for three stages of development. During the first stage of 5 to 7 years, the coastal economy would be made export-oriented, especially in the areas of textiles, foodstuffs, small electric appliances and light industrial products. Meanwhile, efforts would be made to improve communication with the inland provinces, but investment in heavy industry would have to wait until exports had earned sufficient foreign capital. In the second stage, again, of 5 to 7 years, inland products would begin to enter the international markets and greatly enlarge the foreign exchange earning capacity of the labor-intensive industries. In the third stage, between 1996 and 2000, there would be a substantial increase in the export of sophisticated, technology-intensive industrial products and a corresponding decrease in the export of labor-intensive goods. More surplus labor would flow into high-tech products, accelerating the speed and quality of economic growth. During the first stage, some 60 million farm laborers could be absorbed into the export-oriented activities; and during the second and third, 120 million. By the end of the century, China would be able to export $150 billion worth of goods yearly, which would require an annual export growth rate of 12 percent. This would not be excessively high compared with Japan's 17 percent, Brazil's 16 percent, and South Korea's 40 percent, during their peak years of economic development.

The Coastal Development Plan took into consideration the peculiar, dichotomized economic structure of China that had existed since the Liberation in 1949. Under Soviet influence, heavy industry received favored treatment at the expense of light industry, and agriculture was kept at a low level of technology, with vast amounts of farm labor tied to the land. In this dichotomy, contradictions were inevitable: greater industrialization would release more labor, but developing a higher technology would obviate the need for labor. Also, labor-intensive industries tended to enhance consumption, but development of these sophisticated industries required capital. Where to find it? Through the global market!

The coastal areas of China were ideally suited for labor-intensive, export-oriented industries because of the abundance of intelligent, diligent, and relatively well-trained, but inexpensive labor. These areas were also endowed with considerable scientific, technical information and telecommunication facilities, which offered a suitable environment for combined labor-intensive and knowledge-intensive activities. Indeed, rural industries were already booming in the eastern and southeastern coast: the Pearl (Zhujiang) River Delta near Canton, the Yangtze (Changjiang) River Delta, the Southern Fujian Triangle, and the Shandong and Liaodong Peninsulas— in short, the municipalities of Canton, Shanghai, and Tianjin; the provinces of Guangdong, Fujian, Zhejiang, Jiangsu, and Shandong; and the southern tip of Liaodong Peninsula (Lushun and Dalian). The rural industries were self-reliant and highly efficient, responsible for their own profits and losses. In 1987, they could boast of 85 million well-trained laborers producing Y450 billion worth of goods, outpacing the value of production of the agricultural sector. This vast, inexpensive labor force, if turned export-oriented, would place China in a highly favorable and competitive position for at least 20 years relative to the Four Little Dragons of Asia—South Korea, Taiwan, Hong Kong, and Sinpagore.[41] Furthermore, the currencies of Japan, South Korea, and Taiwan were rising in value whereas the American dollar and the Chinese yuan were depreciating, making Chinese products even more attractive in global markets. The China coast was ready to "process foreign raw materials," "to accept foreign orders according to specifications," and "to assemble foreign parts"; and the government was ready to "subsidize foreign traders with Chinese products" (*Sanlai yibu*).

The Coastal Development Plan appealed to the reform-minded General Secretary Zhao Ziyang and was deliberated on in the high councils of state. After the Thirteenth Congress, Zhao made two inspection trips to the coastal areas of Shanghai, Jiangsu, Zhejiang, and Fujian provinces in November 1987 and January 1988, and he was thoroughly convinced of the feasibility of the plan. His optimistic report on "The Strategic Problems of Coastal Economic Development" won the full support of Deng Xiaoping.[42] Deng endorsed the plan with the remark, dated January 23, 1988: "Completely approved. It is imperative that you go ahead boldly, speedily, and not miss this key opportunity!"[43] On February 6, 1988, the Politburo formally approved the plan, and coastal authorities were instructed to work for its success and to welcome foreign investment, joint ventures, and foreign management of Chinese enterprises in their respective jurisdictions.

The coastal development strategy must be viewed as an ingenious masterstroke of the reformers, who used it to link China with the world economy and, at the same time, to block any attempt by the conservatives to move the economy back to central planning and economic isolation. Yet the plan also made China heavily dependent on the international economy, subjected her to the mercy of volatile and fluctuating foreign markets, and forced China to forfeit control of her economic fate. It was essential that Chinese products be of high quality to compete with the exports from the other Pacific nations and to secure a foothold in the global markets. To win foreign orders and contracts and to set up networks of distribution in foreign countries, it would be necessary for China to train large numbers of sales and trade representatives who should be well versed in foreign languages, market conditions, and international business practices. Moreover, for the project to be successful, time was of the essence. If it had been put into practice 20 or 30 years before, China would have taken a proud place alongside Japan and the Four Little Dragons of the Pacific Rim, but now China would have to face much stiffer resistance from the West and Japan owing to protectionism and what seemed to be a looming threat of worldwide economic slowdown or recession in the early 1990s. In the final analysis, the adoption of the coastal development strategy confirmed the unwelcome truth that communism by itself could not transform China into a modern state; it needed capitalist help.

SOCIETY IN FLUX: RISING INFLATION
AND FALLING ETHICS

China's fast economic growth was accompanied by a high
inflation rate, officially put at 12.5 percent in 1985, 7 percent
in 1986, and 8 percent in 1987, but unofficially estimated at 20
to 30 percent a year. The ravages of inflation were felt by all
salaried people and affected their outlook, life-style, behavior,
and ultimately their social ethics. Without a doubt, of all the
reform measures, price decontrol and wage adjustment were
the most painful and least successful. The government was
determined to carry out pricing reforms because the old system of subsidies on food, cooking fuel, housing, and virtually
everything else ignored the law of value and drained the state
budget. It insisted that price decontrol was the key to the
success of the economic reforms and that momentary discom-
fort was to be preferred to future pains. But for the people,
decontrol led to price rises that always outpaced wage adjustments. In May and June of 1988, control on four foods—pork,
eggs, vegetables, and sugar—was lifted, and prices shot up
30–60 percent overnight in the big cities. The government
subsidy of Y10 to each worker, Y8 to each college student, and
Y7 to each middle school student, was hardly sufficient to offset inflation, even though the government argued that fast
economic growth in the past ten years should have mitigated
the pains of deregulation.[44]

Inflation heightened corruption in government, nepotism
among the children of high cadres, backdoor deals, and black-
marketeering. An adviser to the government admitted: "Now-
adays it is almost impossible to do anything without bribing
officials."[45] The profit motive transcended all other considera-
tions. Frequently, an article carried four prices: a state-set
price, a market price, a negotiated price, and a foreigner's
price. Airline and train tickets were not only hard to get, but
they carried different prices for different travelers. Universities
were asked to profit from sideline activities to subsidize education. Knowledgeable persons worried that China had become

a country of traders (*quan min jie shang*). A pun became current in society: *xiang qian kan*, which homonymously means "looking forward" or "looking to money." Practice of one-upmanship, fraud, and economic crimes was rampant; and gouging and overcharging were common in hotels, restaurants, and state offices.

The hardships common in the 1980s seemed to reduce people's feelings of self-worth and make them grumpy and sullen. Life became characterized by indifference, callousness, and rudeness. Psychologists suggest that such an attitude reflected utter frustration and hopelessness rather than enjoyment of being rude. Inflation added yet another burden to the weary souls of those already struggling with economic problems. Watching their life savings steadily eroded by rising prices, people dreaded the return of the hyperinflation of the period 1945–49 and desperately sought ways to beat it.

Between 1983 and 1988, most salaried city dwellers saw their purchasing power cut by 100 percent or more; and their standard of living drastically lowered. A dinner in a good restaurant cost five times more in 1988 than in 1983. A college graduate who made Y55 a month in 1956 could support a family of four, but in 1988 with a higher salary of Y133 he could not; his daily wages could buy him only two watermelons! In terms of gold, his 1987 income was only 49 percent of the 1979 value and 15.7 percent of the 1956 value.

In 1987 an average worker's family spent 35 to 45 percent of its income on food and another 25 to 35 percent on other necessities.[46] There was little left to meet all the inevitable exigencies of life. Frustration gave rise to anxiety, selfishness, resentment, and rudeness. Public ethics sank to the point of disintegration. Confusion in values and chaos in management were everywhere.

Decontrol provided the occasion for price increases, but two other fundamental causes of inflation should not be overlooked. One was the rise in the money supply at a rate of 20 percent annually between 1984 and 1988, resulting in a rapid increase in the issuance of paper money. The other was the large amounts of surplus cash in bank deposits (Y307.5 billion) and liquid cash—some Y420 billion by the end of 1987. Frequently, people rushed to the banks to withdraw money in order to buy needed goods before a new round of price increases. When too much money chased after too few goods, the proverbial inflation resulted.

Public discontent and protest against price rises led to many stormy sessions in the Politburo at the summer resort of Beidaiho in July 1988. General Secretary Zhao continued to espouse price reform as the heart of his economic restructuring, while Premier Li Peng and Vice-Premier Yao Yilin argued for a slowdown, if not suspension of decontrol, on grounds that wage increases had not kept pace with price increases. In the end, concern over public discontent prevailed. The government took measures to cool the economy by controlling credit, tightening the money supply, and curbing construction and capital outlay. In late August, it announced that there would be no further price decontrol for the rest of 1988 and 1989. People sighed with relief.

One group, however, seemed to thrive in these unsettled times. They were the emerging individual entrepreneurs and private businesspersons (*Getihu*), who mostly engaged in handicrafts, light manufacturing, home appliance repair and sales, and transport and consumer services. They achieved success through hard work, vision, judgment, risk-taking, and good management—much as anywhere else. Numbering 225,000 in June 1988 and employing 3.6 million people, these private enterprises were condoned by the state as legitimate on the grounds that they were conducive to the development of productive forces. Many of these individuals became millionaires. A farmer in Shenyang, Liaoning Province, organized a transport team and made Y1 million in 1987. Another entrepreneur invested Y1 million in a steel rolling mill, and maintained 100 workers on her payroll. A 31-year-old owner of a one-hour Kodak film processing shop in Fuzhou controlled assets of $539,000 and lived in a $108,000 air-conditioned house. A wood-carving "king" employed 3,000 workers and amassed $20 million. A motorcycle helmet maker in Beijing did so well that a foreign firm offered him a joint venture and paid him

$82,000 a year in salary.[47] On a lesser scale, many individual entrepreneurs of little education—owners of small appliance shops, tea farmers, owner-drivers of taxis—were making Y30,000 to Y100,000 a year, 10 to 30 times the salaries of professors and surgeons. Not surprisingly, some of the most money-hungry elements turned to crime and engaged in the robbing of ancient tombs in hopes of finding instant wealth.[48]

Had money-mania driven China to capitalism? Most Chinese theorists thought not because the total output of the private sector hardly amounted to 1 percent of the national industrial production value.[49] Nonetheless, the spirit of enterprise was gripping the nation, and it was not surprising that the Chinese translation of Lee Iacocca's autobiography, which extols the virtue of individual initiative, was a best-seller in 1987–88.[50]

In this climate, the primacy of ideology was extenuated, leading to a blurring of direction and a rise in self-doubt. Reverence for Marxism and Maoism yielded to more pragmatic assessments. Zhao Ziyang regarded Mao's last two decades as "twenty lost years," and Deng Xiaoping, in June 1988, advised the visiting President of Mozambique "not to practice socialism."[51] One Chinese theorist asked: "Who knows what Marxism is, anyways? Today, we live in a technological world beyond the imagination of Marx."[52] Another stated that Marx saw only the early stages of capitalism and Lenin experienced little "real-life socialism in his lifetime." Still others believed that capitalism and socialism should borrow from each other for mutual benefit, and China's turn to a "socialist commodity economy," which, in practice, meant adoption of some of the mechanisms of capitalism, was entirely justified during the primary stage of socialism.[53]

China in 1988 was in a state of flux. The Maoist order was largely gone, but a substitute was not yet born. With a 17 percent economic growth rate and 26 percent inflation, China was experiencing the growing pains of a developing nation. In those unsettled and unsettling times, economic euphoria, ideological confusion, falling morality, and widespread corruption formed a vortex of paradoxes, from which a new order was struggling to emerge.

NOTES

1. Anhui University and Hofei Institute of Technology.
2. Professor Fang Lizhi was elected with 3,503 votes; Professor Weng Yuankai, 2,406 votes; student leader Sa Ma 2,164 votes; the fourth is unknown.
3. *Shiyue Pinglun* (October Review), Hong Kong, 14:4–5:6–8, special issue (1987).
4. Mostly from Tongji and Jiaotong Universities and, to a lesser extent, from Fudan University.
5. *Los Angeles Times,* Jan. 6, 1987. The protester was proud of knowing the title of the famed American movie.
6. He Dongchang, a Central Committee member.
7. *Los Angeles Times,* Dec. 31, 1986.
8. Jiang Zemin.
9. *Los Angeles Times,* Dec. 22, 1986.
10. Professor Fei Xiaotong.
11. Among them was one Yang Wei, 32, holder of an M.A. in molecular biology from the University of Arizona, where he studied from 1983 to 1986. Arrested in January 1986 in Shanghai, he was not tried until December. He was sentenced to two years of imprisonment for "counterrevolutionary" activities including participation in a prodemocracy demonstration in Shanghai, and association with the Chinese Alliance for Democracy and its publication, *China Spring.* Headquartered in New York, the Alliance and its publication are highly critical of the lack of democracy in China.
12. *Christian Science Monitor,* Jan. 6, 1988.
13. *People's Daily,* Jan. 6, 1987. The word "liberalization" rather than "liberalism" is used to denote an unfolding process rather than a fact—a subtle difference.
14. Wei Jingsheng.
15. U.S. Dept. of State, Bureau of Public Affairs, Washington, D.C., "President Reagan, A Historic Opportunity for the U.S. and China," April 27, 1984.
16. *Los Angeles Times,* April 28, 1984.
17. *The Christian Science Monitor,* May 1, 1984.
18. *Sino Express,* New York, May 6, 1984.
19. Sha Yexin, quoted in *Los Angeles Times,* Jan. 7, 1987.

20. Gist of Fang's speeches delivered before Jiaotong University, Shanghai, Nov. 15, 1986; Tongji University, Nov. 18, 1986; Anhui Economic and Cultural Research Center, Sept. 27, 1986.

21. Party internal materials for use by district party secretaries and regiment commanders and above: critiques of Fang Lizhi and Liu Binyan, reprinted in *Jiushi Niandai* (The Decade of the Nineties), Hong Kong, June 1987, 37–40. Tr. by author, with minor editing.

22. Wang Ruowang's criticism of Deng's views appeared under the title, "Liangji fenhua zhi wojian—yu Deng Xiaoping tongzhi shangque" (My views on the polarity of the two extremes—A discussion with Comrade Deng Xiaoping), *Workers Daily*, Shenzhen Economic Zone, Nov. 15, 1986, reprinted in *The Decade of the Nineties*, Hong Kong, Feb. 1987, 58–59.

23. Shang Rongguang, "Bridging Ocean-Wide Chasm," *Beijing Review*, Jan. 18–24, 1988, 31. His name is Liu Zunqi, 76 years old.

24. Central Committee Documents, Nos. 2 and 4, 1987, reprinted in *Chaoliu Yuekan* (Tide Monthly), Hong Kong, April 15, 1987, 14–17.

25. Peng and three other powerful ideologues, Deng Liqun, Hu Qiaomu, and Bo Ibo, all Politburo members, were sometimes dubbed the new Gang of Four. The two military leaders were General Yang Dezhi, Army Chief-of-Staff, and General Yang Shangkun, Vice-Chairman, the Military Commission.

26. They included Su Shaozhi, philosopher and reformist theoretician and head of the Marxist Institute; Wang Ruoshui, a former deputy editor of the *People's Daily;* Wu Zuguang, a playwright; and a number of other writers. They were asked to resign from the party.

27. Central Committee Documents, Nos. 2 and 4, 1987.

28. Zhao criticized three leading conservative ideologues, Deng Liqun, Hu Qiaomu, and Bo Ibo.

29. The foreign visitors included the Canadian Prime Minister Brian Mulroney, the First Vice-Premier of Singapore, and Japanese and Yugoslavian delegations.

30. *Beijing Review*, Nov. 2–8, 1987, 10, 12, 18–19; *U.S. News and World Report*, Oct. 12, 1987, 41.

31. *Beijing Review*, Nov. 16–22, 1987, 6.

32. Li Shixun.

33. *Los Angeles Times*, Nov. 25, 1987.

34. *Beijing Review*, Nov. 2–8, 1987, 12.

35. Zhao Ziyang, "Advance along the Road of Socialism with Chinese Characteristics"—a report delivered at the Thirteenth National Congress of the Communist Party of China on October 25, 1987, *Beijing Review*, Nov. 9–15, 1987, 23–49.

36. David Holly, "New Leaders, Reforms to be Weighed at Chinese Party Congress," *Los Angeles Times*, Oct. 24, 1987.
37. Henry A. Kissinger, "China Now Changing Rules and Ruling Party," *Los Angeles Times*, Oct. 25, 1987.
38. Joseph C. Harsch, "A New Look," *The Christian Science Monitor*, Nov. 5, 1987, and "Fortunes Shift for Leaders of World's Three Powers," *Ibid.*, Nov. 6, 1987.
39. Adi Ignatius, "China's Party Meeting Unlikely to Settle Succession Issue," *The Wall Street Journal*, Oct. 23, 1987.
40. Wang Jian, "Xuanze Zhengque di changqi fazhan zhanlue—guanyu 'Guoji da xunhuan' jingji fazhan zhanlue di gouxiang" (Correctly select a long-term development strategy: the concept of a "Grand International Cycle" economic development plan), *Jing ji ribao* (Economic Daily), Beijing, Jan. 23, 1988, 3. Ideas in this seminal article provided most of the information of this section.
41. The average wage of a Chinese worker in 1987 was one-fifth of that of a comparable worker in Taiwan and South Korea, and one-eighth of those in Hong Kong and Singapore. *Da Kong Bao*, Hong Kong, Feb. 12, 1988, 1.
42. A summary of the report appears in English under the title, "Zhao on Coastal Areas' Development Strategy," *Beijing Review*, Feb. 8–14, 1988, 18–23.
43. *Da Kong Bao*, Hong Kong, March 21, 1988, 2.
44. *Beijing Review*, May 23–29, 1988, 10; June 20–26, 1988, 7–9.
45. *Newsweek*, Hong Kong, June 6, 1988, 25–26.
46. Feng Jing, "The Life of Ordinary Chinese People," *Beijing Review*, July 4–10, 1988, 21–26.
47. *The Christian Science Monitor*, June 9, 1988; Oct. 4, 1988. *Asiaweek*, Hong Kong, July 1, 1988, p. 19; *U.S. News and World Report*, Sept. 8, 1986.
48. *China Daily, Beijing*, June 28, 1988.
49. *Beijing Review*, July 18–24, 1988, 12–13.
50. *U.S. News and World Report*, Feb. 8, 1988, 30.
51. President Joaquim Chissano. *Asiaweek*, Hong Kong, July 1, 1988, 18.
52. *U.S. News and World Report*, Feb. 8, 1988, 30.
53. *Asiaweek*, July 1, 1988, 20–21.

FURTHER READING

Amnesty International, *China: Violations of Human Rights* (London, 1984).

Benton, Gregor (ed.), *Wild Lillies, Poisonous Weeds: Dissident Voices from People's China* (Dover, N.H., 1982).

Brzezinski, Zbigniew, *The Grand Failure: The Birth and Death of Communism in the Twentieth Century* (New York, 1989).

Ch'en, Hsi-yuan, "Ts'ung kuo-chi ta hsun-huan tao chia-k'uai yen-hai ching-chi fa-chan" (From the 'Grand International Cycle' to acceleration of coastal development), *Chung-Kung Yen-chiu* (Chiuen Communist Studies), Taipei, 22:7:88–94 (July 1988).

Cohen, Roberta, "People's Republic of China: The Human Rights Exception," *Human Rights Quarterly*, 9:447–549 (1987).

Chu, David S. K., *Sociology and Society in Contemporary China, 1979–1983* (Armonk, N.Y., 1984).

Duke, Michael S., *Blooming and Contending: Chinese Literature in the Post-Mao Era* (Bloomington, 1985).

Edwards, R. Randle, Louis Henkin, and Andrew J. Nathan, *Human Rights in Contemporary China* (New York, 1986).

Goldman, Merle, *China's Intellectuals: Advise and Dissent* (Cambridge, Mass., 1981).

————, Timothy Cheek, and Carol Lee Hamrin (eds.), *China's Intellectuals and the State: In Search of a New Relationship* (Cambridge, Mass., 1987).

Goodman, David S. G., *Beijing's Street Voices: The Poetry and Politics of China's Democracy Movement* (New York, 1981).

Hamrin, Carol Lee, *China and the Future: Decision Making, Economic Planning, and Foreign Policy* (Boulder, 1987).

————, and Timothy Cheek (eds.), *China's Establishment Intellectuals* (Armonk, N.Y., 1986).

Hayhoe, Ruth, and Marianne Bastid, *China's Education and the Industrial World: Studies in Cultural Transfer* (Armonk, N.Y., 1987).

Kallgren, Joyce K., and Denis Fred Simar (eds.), *Educational Exchanges: Essays on the Sino-American Experience* (Berkeley, 1987).

Kissinger, Henry A., "China Now Changing Rules and Ruling Party," *Los Angeles Times*, Oct. 25, 1987.

Kinkley, Jeffrey C. (ed.), *After Mao: Chinese Literature and Society, 1978–1981* (Cambridge, Mass., 1985).

Lampton, David M., Joyce A. Modancy, and Kristen M. Williams, *A Relationship Restored: Trends in U.S.-China Educational Exchanges, 1978–1984* (Washington, D.C., 1986).

Link, Perry (ed.), *Roses and Thorns: Second Blooming of the Hundred Flowers in Chinese Fiction, 1979–80* (Berkeley, 1984).

————, *Stubborn Weeds: Popular and Controversial Chinese Literature After the Cultural Revolution* (Bloomington, 1983).

Liu, Binyan, "Dierzhong zhongcheng," (*The second kind of loyalty*), *Cheng Ming* magazine, Hong Kong, 10:48–61 (Oct. 1985).

Louie, Kam, *Inheriting Tradition: Interpretation of the Classical Philosophers in Communist China, 1949–1966* (New York, 1986).

Mosher, Steven W., *Journey to the Forbidden City* (New York, 1985).

Nathan, Andrew J., *Chinese Democracy* (New York, 1985).

———, R. Randle Edwards, and Louis Henkin, *Human Rights in Contemporary China* (New York, 1986).

Orleans, Leo A., *Chinese Students in America: Policies, Issues, and Numbers* (Washington, D.C., 1988).

Rozman, Gilbert, *The Chinese Debate About Soviet Socialism, 1978–1985* (Princeton, 1987).

Sa, Kung-ch'iang, "P'ing Chung-Kung yen-hai ti-ch'ü ching-chi fa-chan hsin chan-lueh" (On Communist China's new coastal economic development strategy), *Chung-kuo ta-lu yen-chiu* (Studies on Mainland China), *Taipei*, 30:11 (May 1988).

Schram, Stuart R., "China After the 13th Congress," *The China Quarterly*, No. 114:177–197 (June 1988).

Seymour, James D., *China's Satellite Parties* (Armonk, N.Y., 1987).

——— (ed.), *The Fifth Modernization: China's Human Rights Movement, 1978–1979* (Stanford, 1980).

Shapiro, Judith, and Liang Heng, *Cold Winds, Warm Winds: Intellectual Life in China Today* (Middletown, Conn., 1986).

Siu, Helen F., and Zelda Stern (eds.), *Mao's Harvest: Voices from China's New Generation* (New York, 1983).

Sullivan, Lawrence R., "Assault on the Reforms: Conservative Criticism of Political and Economic Liberalization in China, 1985–86," *The China Quarterly*, 114:198–222 (June 1988).

Tung, Constantine, and Collin MacKerras (eds.), *Drama in the People's Republic of China* (Albany, N.Y., 1987).

Wang, Jian, "Xuanze zhengque di changqi fazhan zhanlue—guanyu 'Guoji da xunhuan' jingji fazhan zhanlue di gouxiang" (Correctly select a long-term development strategy: the concept of a "Grand International Cycle" economic development plan), *Jingji ribao* (Economic Daily), Beijing, Jan. 23, 1988.

Wortzel, Larry M., *Class in China: Stratification in a Classless Society* (New York, 1987).

Zhao, Ziyang, "Advance Along the Road of Socialism with Chinese Characteristics"—a report delivered to the Thirteenth National Congress of the Communist Party of China, Oct. 25, 1987, *Beijing Review*, Nov. 9–15, 1987, 9–15.

———, "Zhao on Coastal Areas' Development Strategy," *Beijing Review*, Feb. 8–14, 1988, 18–23.

8

Taiwan's "Economic Miracle" and the Prospect for Unification with Mainland China

Walking down the main streets of Taipei, one witnesses an unending flow of motorcycles, buses, and cars, with hotels, modern apartments, and high-rise office buildings on each side. Inside the offices is the controlled chaos of successful enterprise; the electronic chorus of elevators, air conditioners, typewriters, and computers is punctuated by the ringing of telephones and the raised voices of those making overseas calls. Farmers, a world away from Taipei's bustle, proudly show the fruits of their labor; nicely clothed and fed, with modest but comfortable homes, they appear content with their lives.

This is modern Taiwan, transformed from an agricultural society to an industrial power within a generation. The title "Little Japan" evokes a mixed reaction of open displeasure and secret pride. In East Asia, Taiwan is indeed second only to Japan in terms of industrialization, foreign trade, and quality of life. Taiwan's success is its most important weapon in the struggle for survival, security, and international ties. A close look at Taiwan's accomplishments will help explain its current position and future course.

By 1988, Taiwan had enjoyed peace, stability, and sustained

economic growth for 35 years. The rate of growth averaged 7.3 percent per annum in the 1950s, 9.1 percent in the 1960s, and nearly 10 percent in the 1970s. According to *Euromoney*,[1] during the decade of 1974–84, Taiwan had the second highest growth rate in the world, next only to Singapore. The speed of development accelerated even more during the 1980s. In 1980 Taiwan registered a GNP of $40.3 billion, a per capita GNP of $2,100, and a foreign exchange reserve of $7.4 billion. In 1984, the 10.52 percent growth generated a GNP of $57.5 billion, a per capita GNP of $3,046, foreign trade amounting to $52 billion,[2] and a foreign currency reserve of $16 billion. In 1988, all the figures surged ahead again: the GNP rose to $119 billion; the per capital GNP, to about $6,053; the foreign trade, $110 billion; and foreign currency reserves, $75 billion—the third largest in the world after Japan's $81.1 billion and West Germany's $78.8 billion. Amazingly, with only 20 million people, Taiwan held more than 10 percent of the world's reserves.[3] Most of Taiwan's gain came from trade surpluses with the United States—$10.1 billion in 1985, $13.6 billion in 1986, and $16 billion in 1987. In 35 years, Taiwan's GNP (in real terms) had grown more than 1,000 percent; and if the future growth rate were to average a modest 6.5 percent per annum for the next 12 years, the per capita income would reach an impressive $15,000 by the year 2000, and foreign trade would reach $290 billion, making it a developed nation and one of the 10 largest trading nations in the world.[4]

It is noteworthy that wealth had not been concentrated in a few hands but was shared by a majority of people, in fulfillment of the ancient ideal of an "equitable distribution of wealth" (*chün-fu* 均富). The income ratio of the highest and lowest 20 percent of wage earners in 1952 was 15 : 1; but in 1964 only 5.33 : 1; and by 1987, 4.69 : 1, less of a gap than in the United States.[5] Televisions, refrigerators, washing machines, and telephones had become common; and unemployment was 1.69 percent in 1988. The average lifespan for a man was 71, and for a woman, 76; and the daily intake of calories was 2,845 and of protein, 80 grams, both exceeding international standards. Inflation has been kept low, at only 1.1 per-

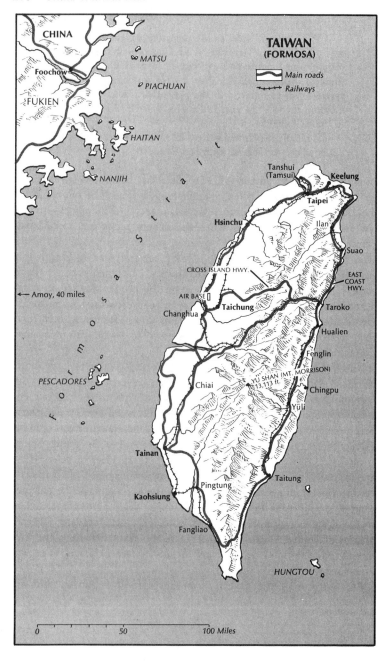

CHINA

MATSU

Foochow

PIACHUAN

FUKIEN

HAITAN

NANJIH

TAIWAN
(FORMOSA)

Main roads
Railways

Tanshui
(Tamsui)   Keelung

Taipei

Hsinchu   Ilan

Suao

CROSS ISLAND HWY.

EAST
COAST
HWY.

Amoy, 40 miles

AIR BASE

Taichung   Taroko

Changhua

Hualien

Fenglin

PESCADORES

YU SHAN (MT. MORRISON)
13,113 ft.

Chiai   Chingpu

Yuli

Tainan

Taitung

Pingtung

Kaohsiung

Fangliao

HUNGTOU

0   50   100 Miles

cent in 1988. Almost unique in the simultaneous attainment of rapid economic growth, price stability, and the equitable distribution of wealth, Taiwan can be said today to enjoy the highest standard of living in Chinese history.

CAUSES OF TAIWAN'S ECONOMIC SUCCESS

Economic Strategy

Taiwan's economic strategy has given priority to agriculture, light industry, and heavy industry in descending order. From 1949 to 1960, the thrust of policy was toward development of agriculture and light industry, beginning with a three-stage land reform program and followed by labor and technological innovations that accelerated farm production. Measures were also taken to expand the physical and social infrastructure, to stabilize prices, to reform the foreign exchange system, and to develop light, import-replacement industries.

Small and resource-poor, Taiwan had no choice but to depend on trade. Recognizing this, the economic planners emphasized industrialization and exports in the 1960s. Measures were adopted to increase the production of durable consumer goods (light industry); encourage labor-intensive, export-oriented assembly industries; and diversify agricultural products for export. Electronics, synthetic fiber, and plastic industries grew rapidly and moved into the world market. With labor costs low and quality control high, Taiwan's products competed successfully in foreign markets.

In the 1970s the emphasis was shifted to developing sophisticated and heavy industry as well as to expanding the infrastructure. In 1973 Ten Major Projects (seven of them infrastructure-related) were launched at a cost of $7 billion: (1) the North-South Freeway known as the Sun Yat-sen Memorial Express Way, (2) the international airport at Taoyuan outside Taipei named after Chiang Kai-shek, (3) electrification of the west coast railway trunk line, (4) the northern coastal railway, (5) the Taichung Harbor, (6) the Suao Harbor expansion,

(7) the nuclear power plant at Chin-shan near the northern tip of the island with two generating units, (8) the modern steel mill called the China Steel Corporation, (9) the giant China Ship Building Corporation, and (10) a petrochemical complex. The last three were located at or near Kaohsiung, which was transformed into a special municipality in 1979 on a par with Taipei.

With the completion of these ten projects in 1979, Taiwan took on the appearance of a "rich developing nation." The projects injected a large dosage of capital into the economy and relieved the recession of 1974–75. Moreover, a large number of economic planners, engineers, and technicians working on these projects gained valuable experience, and numerous workers received training in the process, giving all a new confidence in their ability to build a modern society with their own hands.

To utilize these new skills fully and to modernize the island further, the government immediately launched the Twelve New Projects with emphasis on technology- and capital-intensive industries. These included expanding steel mills; adding nuclear power plants; constructing new cross-island highways; completing Taichung Harbor and the round-the-island railway system; extending the freeway; improving regional irrigation and drainage; building major sea dikes; increasing farm mechanization; and constructing new towns, cultural centers, and housing. With the successful completion of these projects at a cost of $5.75 billion, Taiwan became one of the Newly Developed Countries.

In 1985 the government launched the Fourteen Key Projects to enlarge the economic base at an estimated cost of $20 billion. These projects consisted largely of infrastructural construction and improvement of existing structures. They included the third-phase expansion of the China Steel Corporation; the construction of new railways; an underground rapid transit system in metropolitan Taipei; modernization of telecommunication facilities; development of four national parks, additional flood control projects, dikes, and garbage disposal sites; exploitation of oil and water resources; and preservation of the natural ecology. Projected completion dates were scheduled for 1990–91.

Means of Modernization

Modernization required capital, qualified personnel, and scientific management. Although government and domestic private investment had constituted a major source of capital, foreign and overseas Chinese (ethnic Chinese of Singapore, Hong Kong, the United States, and so forth) investments had been heavy owing to Taiwan's favorable investment conditions. In 1960 the Statute for Encouragement of Investment offered a deferrable five-year income tax exemption for capital-intensive and high-technology industries. It set a maximum income tax liability of 25 percent after the tax holiday and offered other privileges such as exemptions from export taxes, customs duties, business taxes, and so on. In 1979 the statute was revised to offer tax credit further to attract foreign capital, and the substantial investments from abroad continued to grow.

The creation of three Export Processing Zones—two in Kaohsiung area and one near Taichung—in the 1960s also encouraged foreign investment by simplifying customs procedures and export regulations. By 1974 a total of $156,755,000 had been invested in 291 Export Zone projects, and exports totaled $511,322,000 with a favorable balance of over $200 million.

Introduction of new production techniques from abroad had also played an important role in rapid economic development. Under the Statute on Technical Cooperation a total of 837 cases of technical cooperation under private agreements was made between 1952 and 1974. Japan led the way with 615 cases, and the United States followed with 151 while Europe accounted for 57 cases, and other countries, 14.[6]

The qualified personnel that encouraged investment and modernization had been provided by Taiwan's excellent educational system. A nine-year free education was available to all. By the period 1977–78, 99.6 percent of the elementary school age group were attending primary schools; 50.9 percent of those between 15 and 17 years of age were attending senior high school; and 25.2 percent of those between 18 and 21 were attending the 101 colleges and universities. In addition, Taiwan had sent a large number of students to the United States for advanced studies.[7] Thus, there was no shortage of trained personnel on the island.

Abundant incentives and privileges as well as trained personnel and cheap labor prompted foreign and overseas Chinese investments to grow quickly from a few million dollars each year in the 1950s to $213 million in 1978. In 25 years (1952–78) those investments totaled $1.92 billion—31 percent ($595 million) from overseas Chinese, 30 percent ($586 million) from the United States, 17 percent ($321 million) from Japan, and 12 percent ($227 million) from Europe. Favorite investment targets were electronic and electrical products ($633 million) and chemicals ($291 million), followed by services, machinery and instruments, metal products, and textiles.

The United States' recognition of the People's Republic of China on January 1, 1979, had little impact on economic growth and foreign investments in Taiwan. The 1979 GNP registered a 20 percent increase; foreign trade, 31 percent; and foreign investments, 50 percent. More remarkably, informal trade with mainland China via Hong Kong and Japan reached $100 million in 1979 and $1.9 billion in 1987.[8] Taiwman's foreign trade in 1987 was the second largest in Asia and fourteenth in the world.

Rapid industrialization had caused inevitable environmental and social problems including traffic, pollution, industrial waste, inflation, juvenile delinquency, and the migration of the rural inhabitants to urban centers swelling the cities and causing a steady decline of the farm population.[9] The most serious social and economic problem appears to be the uncontrolled birthrate, which had resulted in an astounding population density of 520 people per square kilometer (9,213 per square kilometer in Taipei).[10] With an annual growth rate of 1.62 percent, the present population of 19.5 million will double in 44 years. Repeated government efforts to cut the rate to 1.25 percent per year had met with no success; new attempts were being made to raise the age of marriage, and various birth control methods were being promoted.

Social Change

Under the impact of rapid industrialization, profound changes took place in social structure and family relationships. The most significant of these changes was in the rapid rise of the middle class within the last 20 years, accounting for 50 percent of the population by 1985. They were a fluid heterogeneous group of small businesspersons, professionals, technical and managerial personnel, who had received a good education and possessed considerable wealth. Prominent among them were lawyers, engineers, architects, doctors, pharmacists, accountants, public functionaries, and business managers. Vocal and public-spirited, they participated in politics and spoke out forcefully on public issues. They enjoyed life through spending rather than saving as was the old Chinese tradition. Having reached a preferred status in life, they were fearful of radical social and political change. Everything considered, they had no use for communism.

Family relations also underwent significant and far-reaching changes. Parental authority declined sharply in matters relating to children's marriages and career selections. Children chose their own mates or met them through introductions by friends or matchmakers: parental consent was sought later but generaly only as a formality. Parents also lost the traditional power to oblige children to follow in the family line of work. Universal education and plentiful openings in industry made the young more independent and assertive than ever before. They made their way in society through hard work rather than family influence; 74 percent of those surveyed showed little interest in family inheritance as a means of gaining social recognition. Those who lived at home did not automatically surrender their paychecks to parents as in the past, and those who lived away sent token remittances. The values of the traditional society rapidly gave way to new ones created by rapid

Cousin Lee, a caricature of a typical Chinese on Taiwan, by Ranan R. Lurie.

industrialization; greater individual freedom and faster social mobility were the hallmarks of change.[11]

Rapid accumulation of wealth had its adverse effects on economic behavior and social ethics. Years of trade surpluses and the unusually high savings rate of 34 percent flooded society with idle cash looking for outlets. Speculation in stocks, bonds, commodities, and real estate became rampant, driving prices ever higher. In the process, numerous economic crimes and fraudulent schemes were perpetrated, injuring the moral fiber of society. Other signs of nouveau riche behavior included conspicuous spending, lavish entertainments, and a near obsession with sponsoring beauty contests.[12]

In a society where the old values were rapidly changing,

there was a need for identity and reassurance. An American political caricaturist, Ranan R. Lurie, was invited to draw a cartoon character of the typical Chinese on Taiwan. In December 1985, the celebrated "Cousin Lee"—a young man in a martial arts (kung-fu) costume with a strong chin, large ears, bushy eyebrows, and a shock of black hair and exuding determination, strength, and vitality—was born. The government authorities were pleased with what they saw as a positive image of Taiwan.

Chiang Ching-kuo deserves much credit for his leadership in economic development and in weathering the storm of American rapprochement with Beijing. An efficient administrator surrounded by economic, scientific, and managerial experts, he was keenly interested in economic affairs and the livelihood of the people. As premier in 1973 he initiated the Ten Major Modernization Projects, followed by Twelve more large ones. At Chiang Kai-shek's death in 1975, Vice-President C. K. Yen succeeded as president, and the younger Chiang was elected chairman of the Nationalist Party. Yen finished his term in May 1978, and Chiang Ching-kuo, 68, was elected president for a six-year term by a nearly unanimous vote in the National Assembly.

Chiang Ching-kuo maintained an extreme filial piety to his father, but the two were quite different in training, outlook, temperament, and life-style. The elder Chiang was more formal, stern, distant, and militarily oriented; the younger Chiang was more personable, approachable, and economically oriented. He visited farmers, soldiers, and hospital patients and mixed with intellectuals, artists, writers, and baseball players with equal ease. In this way he acted in the ancient tradition of "loving the people" (*ch'in min*). He was well liked by both Taiwanese and mainlanders on Taiwan, for he symbolized unity and economic development as well as improvement of the people's livelihood.

Chiang's administration was characterized by political innovation, economic development, social stability and welfare, and military preparedness. He believed that the age of individual heroism was past and urged all to contribute their utmost in

The late President Chiang Ching-kuo visiting with the people.

building a promising future. He was especially mindful of cultivating able young talent and of promoting native Taiwanese into the mainstream of government. His vice-president (Shieh Tung-ming), the governor of Taiwan, the mayor of Taipei, several cabinet ministers, and a large number of the members of the Legislative Yüan as well as of the representative assemblies were Taiwanese. Chiang's administration exhibited an increasing liberalism, but he steadfastly refused to yield the Nationalist claim to jurisdiction over all of China or to negotiate with Beijing (unless it gave up communism); nor would he tolerate the Taiwanese Independence Movement, negotiations with the Soviet Union, the propagation of communism on Taiwan, or attacks on the Nationalist party and the Three People's Principles.

The Legacy of Chiang Ching-kuo (1910–88)

President Chiang was elected to a second term in 1984, with Dr. Lee Teng-hui, a Taiwan-born agricultural economist, as vice-president. Though he continued to promote major infrastructural construction (i.e. Fourteen Key Projects) to strengthen the economic base of Taiwan, Chiang, who was 74 and feeling the effects of diabetes, became increasingly occupied with the larger and more fundamental issues of the future of the Kuomintang and Taiwan.

By the period 1986–87, international events and radical social changes at home convinced him that only through political liberalization and strengthening of the rule of law could Taiwan evolve into a true democracy characterized by economic prosperity, political maturity, and social stability. The new order he envisioned would blend attributes of Western democracy with the Chinese political and cultural heritage and create a distinct polity that would serve as an alternative to the way of life on Mainland China.

Chiang's thinking was doubtlessly influenced by major developments abroad and in Taiwan in the years immediately preceding. The tide of democracy had swept through several countries in Asia. In the Philippines, the people's power had overthrown the Marcos regime in 1986; and in South Korea, there had been continuous protest against the authoritarian regime of President Chun Doo-Hwan. Students on Mainland China had demonstrated during 1985–86 to demand greater freedom and democratization. Chiang wanted to spare Taiwan the pain of similar occurrences by taking the initiative and moving toward liberalization.

Rapidly changing social conditions at home drew his attention to the rising aspirations of the new middle class. Economically affluent and well educated, they were socially active and politically conscious. They viewed public participation as part of modern citizenship and did not hesitate to voice their opinions on such issues as human rights, economic crimes, a free press, political pluralism, and air pollution and traffic jams. The role of the Kuomintang came under increasing scrutiny.

Originally founded as a revolutionary party to overthrow the Ch'ing Dynasty, the foreign imperialists, and the warlords of China, it became the dominant force that led the government during the period of Political Tutelage (1928–48), with its director-general ruling supreme. His word was law, and rule by decree became common. But now times had changed; the rule of man would have to be replaced by the rule of law. The political structure would have to evolve toward a constitutional democracy. It was time for democracy on Taiwan to become institutionalized and independent of the human factor.

Within the KMT itself, internal democratization and reorganization seemed necessary in order to break the Old Guard's grip on the party. Democratic elections of party officials for fixed terms had to be held; and key features of the platform, approved by elected representatives at a national convention, much as in any democratic society. Public sentiment and liberal elements within the KMT favored a gradual transformation of the KMT from a revolutionary party to a regular party—ready and willing to renounce power and assume the position of the Opposition if and when it failed to win popular support.[13]

Taking these sentiments to heart, President Chiang was persuaded that the time had come for the people, the government, and the party to assume the greater responsibilities of democratic politics. He took the initiative of laying the groundwork for a constitutional democracy, characterized by the rule of law, peaceful change, social stability, and a renovated KMT. He knew that only he, the last supreme, charismatic leader, could effect these fundamental changes and set in motion a process that would not be unlike mountain-climbing—very hard and time-consuming, but exhilarating nonetheless. Herein lay the true contributions of Chiang Ching-Kuo. He voluntarily gave up his family control of the party and loosened the party monopoly of political power, thus paving the way for the growth of law and democracy.

To assist him in implementing his master plan, Chiang, in March 1986, appointed a 12-member commission from the KMT Central Committee to study and report on 6 fundamental issues: (1) the lifting of the Emergency Decree that activated martial law, (2) the legalization of the formation of new political parties, (3) the strengthening of local autonomy, (4) the implementation of a genuine parliamentary system, (5) reform within the KMT, and (6) falling ethics and rising crime. Out of these deliberations came the decisions to lift the 38-year-old martial law (July 15, 1987), to recognize the legitimacy of "loyal opposition" by granting permission to form new political parties, and to allow Taiwan residents to visit relatives on Mainland China (November 2, 1987).

Actually, political parties had existed "illegally" before this time; now, on September 28, 1986, six of them filed for formal status, the largest being the Democratic Progressive Party (DPP). In the December 1986 elections, the DPP won 11 seats in the National Assembly with 18.9 percent of the popular vote and 12 seats in the Legislative Yüan with 22.17 percent of the popular vote[14]—an impressive show for an opposition party.

Another major contribution of Chiang's was his persistent introduction of new blood into his party and government. Most of the new members were well educated and relatively young— holders of advanced academic degrees abroad, predominantly from famous American universities.[15] They contributed greatly to the more liberal atmosphere in Taiwan. Indeed, the third and fourth generation KMT leaders were quite a different breed from their predecessors. Many of them were Taiwan-born, indicating a trend to "return political power to the local people."

After the New Year in 1988, Chiang's health failed rapidly. Death came on January 13. The sense of loss was overwhelming, for he had been a beloved leader. Within hours, Vice-President Lee was sworn in as the new president in strict accordance with the constitutional procedures. The transition was smooth, peaceful, and swift; there was no succession crisis.

The Era of Lee Teng-hui

President Lee, 65 at the time of his accession to the presidency, was a scholarly statesman who held a doctorate in agricultural economics from Cornell University. A devout Christian with

President Lee Teng-hui, Republic of China on Taiwan, 1988.

broad vision and a sterling character, he was an experienced administrator, having been mayor of Taipei (1978–81), governor of Taiwan (1981–84), and vice-president from 1984 until 1988. He symbolized a new generation of leaders who came from the grass-roots segment of the populace, without the benefits of influential family connections, but who rose to the top through dedication, managerial skill, and political common sense. He viewed his mission as mainly carrying on the unfinished work of his predecessor and advancing the cause of constitutional democracy, bringing it to a higher plateau. Under his leadership, political liberalization and opening to the mainland received new impetus. Although the "Three-No's Policy"—no official contact, no negotiation, and no compromise—continued, he was receptive to ideas suggested by academics and businesspeople that Taiwan adopt a realistic and flexible stance. In point of fact, Taiwan maintained a thriving indirect trade with the mainland through Hong Kong, which reached $2.7 billion in 1988. Taiwan visitors to the mainland from November 1987 to November 1988 numbered 250,000, with each spending an average of $4,000 in gifts, travel, and other expenses; it was estimated that the total expenditures during the first year exceeded $1 billion—a boon to Beijing's coffer. Not a few suggestions had been made that Taiwan use its surplus capital, technical know-how, and developmental experience to help modernize the mainland. Some venturesome Taiwan businesspeople had, in fact, quietly set up manufacturing facilities in China through contacts in Hong Kong. Indeed, China's cheap labor and rich resources provided an ideal complement to resource-poor, capital-rich Taiwan.

At the Thirteenth Congress of the KMT in July 1988, when Lee was confirmed as chairman of the party, many Taiwanborn members rose to leadership positions. In the 31-member Central Standing Committee, for the first time a majority (16) were Taiwanese. In the cabinet reshuffle that followed, 8 of the 15 new appointees were Taiwanese. It is noteworthy that 13 of the 15 new appointees held advanced academic degrees from abroad, and the other 2 held professional degrees from Taiwan.[16] The cabinet was doubtless one of the best-educated in the world.

The Congress adopted several measures with respect to people-to-people contacts between Taiwan and the mainland:

1. Permission for indirect trade with, and investment in, Mainland China to enable the industrial sector of Taiwan to secure raw materials from, and relocate outdated labor-intensive production in China.
2. Permission for Taiwanese journalists to go to the mainland on assignment.
3. Permission for mainland scholars who eschewed communism and who fought for academic freedom, as well as intellectuals living abroad, to visit Taiwan.
4. Permission for mainland residents to visit sick relatives or attend funerals on Taiwan.
5. Permission of cultural and sports exchanges.
6. Establishment of a special government office to take charge of relations with the mainland and to make sure that Taiwan's security and social stability were not compromised.[17]

Though proud of its economic growth. Taiwan takes greater pride in its role of preserver of the Chinese cultural heritage. The Palace Museum holds more than 300,000 invaluable Chinese paintings, calligraphy, porcelain, jade and bronze pieces, and other art objects from the previous imperial collections. The new National Theater and the Concert Hall in the Chiang Kai-shek Memorial Park, completed in October 1987, greatly enrich the cultural life of Taiwan with their programs of Chinese operas and Western symphonic and chamber music. The people on Taiwan openly proclaim that though their island is small in size, it is economically dynamic and culturally great and that it has the potential of becoming "a great country of tomorrow." Taiwan is determined to create a model of modern development based on free enterprise and the Three People's Principles as an alternative to the system on the mainland and hopes that Beijing will ultimately recognize it as the way to modernization.

THE PROSPECT FOR REUNIFICATION

The reunification of China is the common desire of all Chinese, Nationalist and Communist. Taiwan had openly expressed concern for the livelihood of the people on the mainland, and not a few mainlanders harbored secret admiration for the economic success of Taiwan. Beijing no longer talked of liberating Taiwan but of its reunification with the motherland. Meanwhile, Taiwan no longer talked of reconquering the mainland but of unifying all China under the political philosophy of the Three People's Principles of Dr. Sun Yat-sen.

Beijing considers the reunification a top priority of the 1980s, of equal importance with socialist modernization and continued opposition to Soviet hegemony. To this end, it offered a reunification plan based on three principles: (1) the Nationalist government must give up all claims to being the legal government of all China, (2) Taiwan may retain its present economic and social system and its standard of living, and (3) Taiwan may retain a degree of autonomy including the maintenance of an army. To begin the reconciliation, on New Year's Day 1979, Beijing proposed postal, commercial, and air and shipping relations with Taiwan. Then, a day before National Day on October 1, 1981, Marshal Ye Jianying intensified the peace offensive with a nine-point proposal:[18]

1. In order to bring an end to the unfortunate separation of the Chinese nation as early as possible, we propose that talks be held between the Communist Party of China and the Kuomintang of China on a reciprocal basis so that the two parties will cooperate for the third time to accomplish the great cause of national reunification. The two sides may first send people to meet for an exhaustive exchange of views.

2. It is the urgent desire of the people of all nationalities on both sides of the Straits to communicate with each other, reunite with their relatives, develop trade, and increase mutual understanding.

   We propose that the two sides make arrangements to facilitate the exchange of mails, trade, air and shipping services, and visits by relatives and tourists as well as academic, cultural, and sports exchanges, and reach an agreement thereupon.

3. After the country is reunified, Taiwan can enjoy a high degree of autonomy as a special administrative region, and

it can retain its armed forces. The central government will not interfere in local affairs on Taiwan.

4. Taiwan's current socioeconomic system will remain unchanged; so will its way of life and its economic and cultural relations with foreign countries. There will be no encroachment on the proprietary right and lawful right of inheritance on private property, houses, land and enterprises, or on foreign investment.

5. People in authority and representative personages of various circles in Taiwan may take up posts of leadership in national political bodies and participate in running the state.

6. When Taiwan's local finances are in difficulty, the central government may subsidize it according to the circumstances.

7. For people of all nationalities and public figures of various circles in Taiwan who wish to come to and settle on the mainland, it is guaranteed that proper arrangements will be made for them, that there will be no discrimination against them, and that they will have the freedom of entry and exit.

8. Industrialists and businesspeople in Taiwan are welcome to invest and engage in various economic undertakings on the mainland; and their legal rights, interests and profits are guaranteed.

9. The reunification of the motherland is the responsibility of all Chinese. We sincerely welcome people of all nationalities, public figures of all circles, and all mass organizations in Taiwan to make proposals and suggestions regarding affairs of state through various channels and in various ways.

It is noteworthy that Ye called for talks between the two ruling parties rather than between governments, sidestepping the sensitive question of which legitimately governed all China. However, the proposal seemed as much directed at Taiwan as at others. The first five points would appeal to world, especially American, public opinion; and the sixth, suggesting that the mainland was in a position to assist Taiwan financially, seemed designed for home consumption to lift the party prestige before the one billion people of China. The peace offensive also coincided with a strong diplomatic move to pressure the United States not to sell sophisticated defensive weapons such as the F5E fighter to Taiwan—a sale that Beijing insisted would stiffen the resistance of Taiwan.

On October 9 and 10, 1981, a grand celebration was held at the Great Hall of the People to honor the 70th anniversary of the 1911 republican revolution, on which occasion party Chairman Hu Yaobang made a persuasive appeal to Taiwan. He took note of the failure of the two earlier collaborations between the two parties (1923–27, 1937–41) but suggested that past experience need not deter one from trying again: "We do not wish to settle old accounts here. Let bygones be bygones. Let the lessons of the past help us cooperate better in the future." Hu proposed removing barriers of long-standing animosity and building mutual trust anew through contact and talk. Capitalizing on traditional Chinese respect for the deceased, Hu announced that Dr. Sun's mausoleum and Chiang Kai-shek's ancestral tombs were in good repair and invited Taiwan leaders to come to see for themselves. Hu assured Taiwan leaders that they would be warmly welcomed whether they wished to talk or not. A third cooperation between the parties, said Hu, would let Dr. Sun rest in peace.

In conjunction with this speech, October 1981 saw a major campaign to honor Dr. Sun as the great revolutionary forerunner who made possible the later successful struggles of the Chinese people. By placing his portrait prominently in Tiananmen Square, by reprinting his *Complete Works*, by exhibiting his memorabilia and pictures of his life, and by holding an international academic conference in Wuhan to commemorate the 1911 revolution, the Communists hope to claim legitimacy as Sun's loyal followers, thereby establishing some common ground for initiating negotiations with the Nationalists.

Certainly it was Beijing's strategy to appear reasonable and magnanimous to the world, especially the United States. But the nine-point proposal in essence asked the Nationalists, in the larger interest of reunification, to forfeit their de facto independence and their claim to legitimacy as representatives of the Chinese people, to cease to be a separate entity in world politics, and to accept the lesser status of an autonomous special region of China on a par with other provinces.

President Chiang Ching-kuo adamantly refused to respond to the peace overture as a "smiling diplomacy" of the "United Front" variety designed to weaken the will of the people on Taiwan and to discredit his government in world opinion. Taiwan accused the Communists of "usurping" the legacy of Dr. Sun and warned that the peace offensive could be a prelude to the infiltration and even the military invasion of the island. Beijing's repeated refusal to renounce the use of force revealed its true intention, said Taiwan, and cooperation was possible only if Beijing gave up communism in favor of free enterprise and the Three People's Principles. Until then, there would be "no contact, no negotiations, and no compromise" with the Communist regime. Experience (1924–27, 1937–41) had shown that cooperation with it was futile. The situation was made the more impossible by Beijing's insistence on the Four Cardinal Principles—the socialist line, the proletarian dictatorship, the Communist leadership, and Marxism-Leninism and The Thought of Mao. These would rule out any meaningful participation by the Nationalists in any coalition government. Taiwan adamantly rejected Beijing's call for the "Three Links" (*San-t'ung*)—mail, trade, and air-and-shipping services—and the "Four Exchanges" (*Ssu-liu*)—mutual visits of relatives and tourist as well as academic, cultural, and sports groups. With a per capita GNP of $6,000 in Taiwan in 1988, and one of $300 on the mainland, the economic gap would prove as difficult to bridge as the political chasm.

After China's successful negotiations with Britain in 1984 for the return of Hong Kong in 1997, Deng Xiaoping proudly announced his formula of "One country, two systems," as the way to reunification. Just as China would allow Hong Kong to keep its social and economic systems for 50 years beyond 1997, so that there would be a capitalist Hong Kong within a socialist China, China would also permit Taiwan to keep its political, economic, and military systems after its unification with the mainland provided that Taiwan accept the status of a Special Administrative Region under the central government in Beijing.

Taiwan found such a formula repugnant and the idea of placing it and Hong Kong in the same category unrealistic. The two were, indeed, in very different positions vis-à-vis China. First of all, Britain had no intention of fighting over Hong Kong and therefore retained no bargaining power. Second, Hong Kong had no army of its own and depended on the mainland for its food and water supply. The people of Taiwan, in contrast, were politically active, self-sufficient in food supplies, and had no desire to give up their way of life. Taiwan maintained a highly trained, modern military force, ever ready and able to defend the island against any invader. Furthermore, Taiwan was "protected" by the United States–Taiwan Relations Act of 1979, under which the United States supplied defensive weapons to Taiwan, and any invasion of the island by the mainland could be construed as detrimental to the "security of the Western Pacific and of grave concern to the United States."

Above all, Taiwan's leaders equated the Three People's Principles with the Lincolnian ideals of "government of the people, by the people, and for the people." They wanted the people of China to see Taiwan as an alternative to Communism and accept the Three People's Principles as the basis for reunification. Hence, the idea of "One country, two systems" was totally unacceptable to Taiwan.

Friends of Taiwan and enlightened elements on the island had long urged a more flexible policy toward the mainland, describing the "Three No's Policy" as negative, self-limiting, and lacking in initiative. Finally, in 1987 and 1988, Taiwan approved a series of new measures to relax the bans on (1) visits by Taiwan residents to the mainland; (2) the formation of new political parties; (3) visits to Taiwan by mainlanders under controlled conditions; and (4) indirect trade with, and manufacturing on, the mainland via Hong Kong, as noted earlier. President Lee Teng-hui showed a new flexibility of spirit when he stated that Taiwan would adjust its mainland policy if Beijing renounced (1) the use of force against Taiwan, (2) the Four Cardinal Principles, and (3) attempts to isolate Taiwan in the international community or exclude it from world bodies. At the Thirteenth Congress of the Kuomintang in July 1988, there was a strong sentiment that Taiwan should extend its freedom, prosperity, and democratic way of life to the mainland. Thirty-four senior members, headed by Ch'en Li-fu, a man once condemned by the Communists as a war criminal, proposed to allocate $10 billion from Taiwan's $75 billion foreign currency reserves as a low-interest, long-term loan to China for economic development and the betterment of the people's livelihood. This loan was to be made available on condition that Beijing renounced communism and the use of force against Taiwan.[19]

Beijing's response was swift and effusive. Calling the proposal "admirable," "praiseworthy," "positive," and "constructive," Beijing issued a conciliatory and friendly statement on the virtues of economic cooperation between the two entities:

> We are willing to consult and cooperate with anyone who offers positive and reasonable proposals for the peaceful reunification of the country. . . . The economies of both sides have their advantages and disadvantages. This makes it possible for them to supplement each other and offers a good opportunity for cooperation. . . . Both sides should . . . pursue the goal of common prosperity.
>
> We welcome contact and consultation with Taiwan authorities on Taiwan's participation in the construction of ports, airports, railways; the exploitation of resources on the mainland; the development of an outward-looking economy and high-tech products; and the construction of coastal and special economic zones. We hope that both sides can cooperate in economic and cultural fields, and we are ready to conduct talks on these matters with the Taiwan authorities either on the mainland, in Taiwan, or any other place.
>
> If this proposal can be put into effect, it will exert a positive influence on the development of relations between both sides, and [perhaps lead to] the peaceful reunification of the country.[20]

It seems that apart from the attraction of a $10 billion low-interest loan, Beijing saw hopes of a breakthrough in its relationship with Taiwan. Undoubtedly, the pressure of Taiwan's economic success and political liberalization made Beijing want to exploit fully the possibilities of dialogue.

In August 1988, Beijing sent a message through a Chinese professor of political science at the New York University (James Hsiung) that it was willing to renounce the use of force against Taiwan and cancel the Four Cardinal Principles in its constitution if Taiwan would move toward reunification by joining the mainland to write a new constitution as the basis of a coalition government. Observers believed that Beijing might be willing to play down, or even quietly give up, the first three Cardinal Principles; but it certainly would not renounce the leadership of the Communist Party, for doing so would be tantamount to abdication of its power. Taiwan responded to Beijing's "peace offensive" with suspicion. It set up a nine-man task force to keep a close eye on mainland policy and to explore ways of exporting Taiwan's economic prosperity and political democracy to the mainland.

Though official contact between the two was slow to develop, unofficial contacts continued to grow. Three Taiwan scientists obtained approval to attend a conference of the International Council of Scientific Unions held in Beijing in September 1988; and mutual visits of doctors, athletes, and chess (Gō) players were under consideration. In April 1989, a group of Taiwanese gymnasts attended the Asian Junior Gymnastics Championships in Beijing for the first time in 40 years. More importantly,·in May 1989 Taiwan's finance minister, Shirley Kuo, led a delegation of 11 high officials to attend the annual meeting of the Asian Development Bank held in Beijing under the name "Taipei, China." Taiwanese journalists, filmmakers, and teachers were also permitted to visit the Mainland for business or pleasure.[21]

Thus, some stirrings were visible on both sides, but the mutual mistrust was too great for things to proceed at anything but a snail's pace. Realistically, conditions did not seem ripe for a genuine reconciliation. Perhaps within 10 to 20 years some kind of political federation could be attempted to pave the way for an ultimate unification. However, the process will, no doubt, prove as difficult as the unification of East and West Germany or of North and South Korea.

A hundred years ago leaders of the Self-strengthening Movement sought "wealth and power" as the key to China's survival in the modern world. During the May Fourth Movement (1919), survival dictated national independence and unity, science and democracy, liberty and the improvement of the people's livelihood. Later, the demand for freedom of thought and for the liberation of the creative spirit of individuals appeared.[22] Constitutional democracy was the dream. Any government that could fulfill these aspirations would have the support of all Chinese.

In its 4,000 years of recorded history, China has been divided and reunited countless times. If history is any guide and if politics is the art of expecting the unexpected, then one need not lose heart over the present difficulties. The genius of the Chinese people will find a way to make all China one again.

NOTES

1. A European financial journal.
2. Thirty billion dollars in exports against $22 billion in imports.
3. Figures of the International Monetary Fund as reported in *Los Angeles Times*, Jan. 4, and March 7, 1988.
4. *The Free China Journal*, Taipei, March 24, 1986.
5. *The Christian Science Monitor*, editorial, July 1980. In the United States, 9 to 1; in Mexico, 20 to 1. *The Free China Journal*, Taipei, August 11, 1988.
6. *A Review of Public Administration: The Republic of China*, compiled by the Administrative Research and Evaluation Commission, Executive Yüan, 1975 (Taipei, 1975), 79–80, 96.
7. In the period 1979–80, there were 17,560 students from Taiwan enrolled in United States colleges and universities, next only to Iran's 51,310. Other large foreign student groups included these: Nigeria, 16,360; Canada, 15,130; Japan, 12,260; and Hong Kong, 9,900. See *The Chronicle of Higher Education*, May 11, 1981, 14. In 1985, Taiwan sent 22,590 students

to study in U.S. colleges and universities, comprising the largest number of foreign students.

8. U.S. Department of State, "Review of Relations with Taiwan," Current Policy No. 190, June 11, 1980 (Washington, D.C.).

9. Farm population fell from 51.9 percent of the total in 1953 to 21.6 percent in 1986. *The Free China Journal*, May 12, 1986.

10. *The Free China Journal*, Dec. 9, 1984, June 22, 1987.

11. Lai Tse-han, "She-hui pien-ch'ien chung ti chia-t'ing chih-tu" (The family system in a changing society), *Overseas Scholars*, Jan. 31, 1985, 11–15.

12. In 1988 the "Miss Republic of China" contest was revived for the first time in 24 years, with the first prize of $350,000; the "Miss Wonderland" contest took place in May 1988, with a $20,000 first prize; and the 37th "Miss Universe" contest was held in Taiwan with a $250,000 first prize. The Taiwanese sponsors spent $4.2 million to stage the last pageant. *The Free China Journal*, April 11, May 9 and 16, 1988.

13. Views of Dr. Ma Ying-jeou, Deputy Secretary-General, KMT. *Free China Review*, editorial, March 1988; Alexander Ya-li Lu, "Democratic Values Win Another Round," *Ibid.*, October 1987, 8–9; Wei Tsai, "Transformations in the Body Politic," *Ibid.*, 14–15.

14. *The Free China Journal*, Taipei, Feb. 21, 1987; Peter Chang, "Party Politics Redefined," an interview with Dr. Ma Ying-jeoh, Deputy Secretary-General, KMT, *Free China Review*, Oct. 1987, 16–17.

15. To name a few: Lien Chan, Ph.D., University of Chicago; Frederick Chien, Ph.D., Yale University; Ma Ying-Jeou, S.J.D., Harvard Law School; Wei Yung, Ph.D., Stanford; James Soong, Ph.D., Georgetown; and Shaw Yu-ming, Ph.D., Chicago.

16. *The Free China Journal*, July 25, 1988. Ten of them held the doctorate—and one, an M.A.—from American universities; one each, a doctorate from a West German and Japanese university; and two others, with an M.A. and an LL.B. from Taiwanese universities.

17. *Los Angeles Times*, July 13, 1988; *The Free China Journal*, July 18, 1988.

18. *China Daily*, Peking, Oct. 1, 1981.

19. *The Free China Journal*, July 18, 1988.

20. *Renmin Ribao* (People's Daily) Sept. 7, 1988: *Beijing Review*, Sept. 19–25, 1988, 18–19. Minor editing by author.

21. *The Free China Journal*, Aug. 22, Sept. 1, 1988; April 10, 20, 24, 1989.

22. Shao Yü-ming, "Shih-lun Chung-Kung cheng-ch'uan tsai Chung-kuo chin-tai-shih shang ti kung-kuo" (An appraisal of the

achievements and failures of the Chinese Communist regime in modern Chinese history), *Hai-wai hsüeh-jen*, 99:8 (Oct. 1980).

FURTHER READING

A Review of Public Administration: The Republic of China, compiled by the Administrative Research and Evaluation Commission, Executive Yüan (Taipei, 1975).

Chan, F. Gilbert, *China's Reunification and the Taiwan Question* (New York, 1986).

Chiu, Hungdah and Shao-chuan Leng, *China: Seventy Years after the 1911 Hsin-hai Revolution* (Charlottesville, Va., 1984).

Chou, Yangsun, and Andrew J. Nathan, *Democratizing Transition in Taiwan* (Baltimore, 1987). Occasional Papers/Reprint Series in Contemporary Asian Studies, School of Law, University of Maryland.

Clough, Ralph, *Island China* (Cambridge, Mass., 1978).

Cohen, Myron, L., *House United, House Divided: The Chinese Family in Taiwan* (New York, 1976).

Cooper, John F., and George P. Chen, "Taiwan's Elections: Political Development and Democratization in the Republic of China" (Baltimore, 1984). Occasional Papers/Reprint Series in Contemporary Asian Studies, University of Maryland, School of Law.

Chu, Yungdeh Richard (ed.), *China in Perspectives: Prospects of China's Reunification* (Hong Kong, 1987).

Department of State, "Diplomatic Relations with the People's Republic of China and Future Relations with Taiwan" (Washington, D.C., Dec. 1978).

Department of State, "Review of Relations with Taiwan," Current Policy No. 190, June 11, 1980 (Washington, D.C.).

Economic Development: Taiwan, Republic of China, compiled by the Council for Economic Planning and Development (Taipei, May 1979).

Faurot, Jeannette I. (ed.), *Chinese Fiction from Taiwan* (Bloomington, 1980).

Gold, Thomas B., *State and Society in the Taiwan Miracle* (Armonk, N.Y., 1986).

Greggor, A. James, and Maria Hsia Chang, "The Taiwan Independence Movement: The Failure of Political Persuasion," *Political Communication and Persuasion*, 2:4:363–91 (1985).

Ho, Samuel P. S., *Economic Development of Taiwan, 1860–1970* (New Haven, 1978).

Hsu, Paul S. P., "The Uses of Taiwan in the Developing World," *Sino-American Relations*, VI:I:19–27 (Spring 1981).

Huang, Mab, *Intellectual Ferment for Political Reforms in Taiwan, 1971–1973* (Ann Arbor, 1976).

Jacobs, J. Bruce, "A Preliminary Model of Particularistic Ties in Chinese Political Alliances: *Kan-ch'ing and kuan-hsi* in a Rural Taiwanese Township," *The China Quarterly*, 78:237–73 (June 1979).

Knapp, Ronald G. (ed.), *China's Island Frontier: Studies in the Historical Geography of Taiwan* (Honolulu, 1981).

Lai, T. C., *Three Contemporary Chinese Painters: Chang Da-chien, Ting Yin-yung, Ch'eng Shih-fa* (Seattle, 1976).

Lau, Joseph S. M., and Timothy A. Ross (eds.), *Chinese Stories from Taiwan, 1960–1970* (New York, 1976).

Lee, Teng-hui, "Goals and Strategies for Taipei City," *Sino-American Relations*, VI:I:3–8 (Spring 1980).

Lerman, Arthur Jay, *Taiwan's Politics: The Provincial Assemblyman's World* (Washington, D.C., 1978).

Li, Victor H. (ed. with intro.), *The Future of Taiwan: A Difference of Opinion* (White Plains, N.Y., 1980).

Nickun, James E., and David C. Schak, "Living Standards and Economic Development in Shanghai and Taiwan," *The Chinese Quarterly*, 77:25–49 (March 1979).

Shao, Yü-ming, "Wo-men tsou na-t'iao lu" (Which way shall we go?), *Hai-wai hsüeh-jen* (Overseas scholars), 101:11–16 (Dec. 1980).

Silin, Robert H., *Leadership and Values: The Organization of Large-Scale Taiwanese Enterprises* (Cambridge, Mass., 1976).

9

Postscript: The Violent Crackdown at Tian-an-men Square, June 3-4, 1989

Nineteen eighty-nine, the Year of the Snake, opened with ominous signs of an impending explosion in China. The country faced rising inflation, falling ethics, widespread corruption, official profiteering, a widening gap in income between the privileged few and the great masses, and an increasing loss of faith in communism. To be sure, these phenomena existed in the preceding years (see chapter 7), but the underlying discontent was brought to the surface and threatened to come to a head. Frustration and unrest were rampant in many parts of the country.

The forces of democracy and liberalization ceaselessly clashed with those of repression and authoritarianism, both openly and secretly, but tension was always present. This clash took on added significance in light of two major trends in international politics: the rising tide of freedom and democracy, and the retreat of communism in Poland, Hungary, and the three Baltic states (Lithuania, Latvia, and Estonia). Even in the Soviet Union, *glasnost* and *perestroika* were changing the face of communism. Instability, unrest, and compromise seemed to characterize the Communist world, and some political scientists predicted the demise of communism as a shaping force of history.[1]

The year was also significant because of the many anniversaries of historical importance: the fortieth anniversary of the founding of the People's Republic of China (October 1, 1949), the seventieth anniversary of the May Fourth Movement (1919), and the bicentennial anniversary of the French Revolution (July 14, 1789), which championed liberty, equality and fraternity. On any of these occasions pro-democracy demonstrations could erupt, warned university students, whose quest for political liberalization had been cut short two years earlier. Feeling ill at ease, the government called for redoubled vigilance on the part of party members and the armed forces, urging them to guard against disturbances and to prevent a Polish-style Solidarity movement from happening in China.

THE GATHERING STORM

The year had barely begun when noted astrophysicist Fang Lizhi sent a letter to Deng Xiaoping on January 6 calling for the granting of a general amnesty either on the occasion of the seventieth anniversary of the May Fourth Movement or the fortieth anniversary of the founding of the People's Republic. Fang specifically asked for the release of Wei Jingsheng, an electrical worker sentenced in 1979 to fifteen years in prison for promoting democracy as a "Fifth Modernization" and warning that Deng could become another Mao. Fang's letter won the endorsement of fifty-one famous Chinese scholars abroad and thirty-nine leading intellectuals in China. Incensed, Deng and the government refused to respond.

The democratic cause suffered a setback during President George Bush's visit to China in late February 1989. Following President Ronald Reagan's precedent of hosting a group of Soviet dissidents at the American Embassy in Moscow the previous summer, Bush invited four leading Chinese liberals to a state dinner on Sunday, February 26. The guests included Fang Lizhi, his wife Li Shuxian, and three others,[2] all of whom were active supporters of General Secretary Zhao Ziyang's reforms and sharp critics of the conservative leadership. Most Chinese regarded the invitation as an American statement of support for democracy and liberalization in China. President Yang Shangkun and Premier Li Peng threatened to boycott the dinner if Fang and his wife attended. However, they did accept the compromise situation whereby President Bush would not move from table to table to exchange toasts with Fang and his wife. Yet even this proved too much of an affront. At the last minute the Chinese leaders changed their minds and sent police to keep Fang and his wife from attending the banquet. Bush was unaware of the incident, assuming all through dinner that they were among the guests.

This government action outraged Chinese students and intellectuals. They waited for an opportunity to vent their wrath and renew the pro-democracy demonstrations cut short two years earlier. The death of former General Secretary Hu Yaobang on April 15 provided just such an opportunity. Dismissed in January 1987 for his lenient attitude toward the students, Hu had become for many a symbol of openness and political liberalization. The students wished to honor his memory with an elaborate commemorative service, and they also planned to use the occasion to insist on the clearing of his name and to push forward demands for freedom of speech, assembly, and the press, as well as strong anti-corruption measures. Posters appeared at Beijing University, eulogizing Hu and lampooning the conservative leaders: "A good man has died, but many bad ones are still living," and "A man of sincerity has passed away, but hypocrites are still around."

The party refused to clear Hu's name; to do so would have been an admission of guilt by all those involved in his dismissal, including Deng and other hard-liners. Thousands of students marched in the streets and staged a sit-in at Tian-an-men Square, chanting "Long live democracy! Long live freedom! Down with corruption!" On April 22, three students ridiculed the government by kneeling at the steps of the Great Hall of the People, with one of them raising above his head a large scroll listing their demands and shouting: "This is how petitions were presented to emperors. What era is this? We still have to use this method, which means we have no freedom." The students boycotted their classes and continued the demonstrations in the Square for six weeks, drawing increasing support from fellow students in the provinces, as well as from local and provincial workers, intellectuals, journalists, professors, researchers, musicians, actors, ordinary citizens, and even some members of the party and the armed forces. By mid-May the ranks of the pro-democracy protest had grown to over a million. Smaller demonstrations also broke out in twenty-three other cities. It had become a tidal wave of protest that cut across classes, creating a stirring spectacle for television viewers both at home and abroad. The crowning insult to the leadership came on May 30, when students of the Central Art Institute erected on the Square a thirty-foot statue of the Goddess of Democracy, loosely modeled upon the Statue of Liberty. Positioned in the northern sector of the Square, opposite the entrance to the Imperial Palace, the statue stared defiantly at the giant portrait of Mao.

THE PARTY SPLIT

General Secretary Zhao Ziyang, like his predecessor Hu Yaobang, displayed surprising tolerance of the demonstrations and sympathy with the student's motives. As a promoter of reform and modernization, he had hoped to guide the party toward greater openness and a gradual transformation in the direction of political liberalization, though not necessarily a capitalistic democracy. He came into sharp conflict with Premier Li Peng and other veteran hard-liners such as Chen Yun, Peng Zhen, and President Yang Shangkun. Influenced by his advisors at the Chinese Academy of Social Sciences and his four "think tanks,"[3] Zhao may have wanted to draw on the rising student power to strengthen his position vis à vis the conservatives and to advance the cause of reform. On the other hand, the conservatives, who had won the first round of the contest two years earlier when they persuaded Deng to dismiss Hu for mis-

handling the student demonstrations, now schemed to implicate Zhao as a secret patron of the demonstrations and to oust
him from the post of general secretary. Thus, the student demonstrators had unwittingly become pawns in the seething political struggle within the party.

The hard-liners saw in student demonstrations a golden opportunity to crush the democracy movement and derail economic reform. A deftly precipitated clash with the students
and Zhao would enable them to kill two birds with one stone.
Chen Yun, the economist, and Yao Yilin, the vice premier, mas-
terminded a plot whereby Premier Li Peng was to be absolutely stern and unyielding with regard to student demands,
thereby goading students into greater belligerence. Meanwhile,
Zhao was to be attacked as a secret supporter of the demonstrators—a traitor within the party. The growing insolence of
the students and Zhao's sympathy for them would drive Deng
into a rage and cause him to react violently. He could then be
manipulated to smash the students and Zhao in one fell swoop,
just as he had been persuaded to oust Hu two years earlier.
Thus, the key to success was to enrage both the demonstrators
and Deng in order to escalate the confrontation to the point
where a military crackdown could be justified.[4]

On April 24, a Beijing municipal party secretary,[5] at the
behest of the conservative elders, submitted a "war report" to
the Central Committee. The report stated that, based on student wallposters, slogans, and secret reports compiled by state
security agencies, it appeared that the demonstrations had
been two years in the making, with the avowed purpose of
negating the socialist cause and overthrowing the Communist
leadership. The Politburo Standing Committee and President
Yang Shangkun agreed that the demonstrations were an "organized, planned, and premeditated anti-party, anti-socialist activity." On the following day Deng declared that the demonstrations constituted a "conspiracy" or "turmoil" (*tong luan*)
that must be suppressed. At his direction, two party writers[6]
formerly connected with the Cultural Revolution and the
1986 "Anti-Bourgeois Liberalization" campaign, wrote an editorial for the April 26 issue of *People's Daily* entitled "Clearly

Raise the Banner of Opposition to the Turmoil." The essence of the article was that the government was locked in a grand political struggle against a "turmoil" that had as its target the destruction of party leadership and the socialist system. Capitulation to student demands, it warned, would turn a promising country into a hopeless, turbulent one. The contents of the editorial were wired to Zhao, who was visiting North Korea, and received his endorsement in principle.

It was apparent that the hard-liners had won Deng over to their cause, just as they had two years earlier, and that the party would take a tougher stand against the demonstrators. Li Peng steadfastly refused to meet with student leaders, thereby losing a chance to defuse the issue and negotiate an early settlement. When he finally did consent to meet with them on May 18, he sternly lectured student leaders Wang Dan and Wuer Kaixi, leaving no room for a dialogue or a meeting of minds. Meanwhile, in Shanghai, the party boss, Jiang Zemin, dismissed Qin Bunli, the editor-in-chief of the *World Economic Herald,* for his pro-democracy stand.

When Zhao returned home on April 29, he was urged by his advisors[7] to refute the April 26 editorial and to fight for an affirmation of the student action as spontaneous, patriotic, and in conformity with the government's own anti-corruption policy. He tried to reverse the April 26 editorial, but to no avail. Then, on May 4, in a speech to the Asia Development Bank, which was meeting in Beijing, Zhao implied that there was division in the party, but that he was certain that the government would follow a "cool, reasoned, disciplined, and orderly way of resolving problems in a democratic and lawful manner." The hard-liners were incensed. They charged that Zhao had revealed leadership dissension in a statement that had not been cleared by the party in advance. Li Peng declared that Zhao's speech represented his personal view and that the party view could only be represented by Deng. Li increasingly succeeded in pitting Deng against Zhao.

A further controversy arose on May 16 when Zhao told visiting Soviet General Secretary Mikhail S. Gorbachev that since the Thirteenth Party Congress in November 1987, all important decisions had to be deferred to Deng for approval, imply-ing that Deng, not Zhao, was responsible for all key decisions as well as mistakes. Deng and the hard-liners were angry that Zhao had disclosed a "state secret" to a foreign guest.

During Gorbachev's three-day visit, the Chinese leadership was thoroughly humiliated by the million occupants of Tian-an-men Square. The official reception of the honored guest had to be shifted from the Square to the airport. Gorbachev's tour of the Forbidden City was canceled because of the large crowds assembled at its entrance, and plans for him and his wife, Raisa, to lay a wreath at the Hero's Monument in the center of the Square also had to be canceled. His press con-ference was transferred from the Great Hall of the People to the Diaoyutai State Guest House, where he was lodged. Ex-cept for a brief moment, his famous walkabouts had to be omitted for safety's sake. These last-minute changes created an impression that the Chinese leadership was weak, indecisive, and incapable of controlling the situation. Deng was all the more determined to teach the young people a stern lesson once the guest had departed. As patriarch of the extended Chinese family, Deng might have felt that the students were ungrateful for all the benefits his economic reforms had brought them, including the improved quality of higher education and stu-dent life. The price of insubordination would be unrelenting retribution.

The hard-liners insisted that the root cause of student unrest lay within the party itself. It was the mismanagement of the economy by Zhao and his predecessor, Hu, that led to high inflation, economic imbalance, and confusion. It was also their permissiveness toward the students and their halfhearted spon-sorship in 1983 of the "Anti-Spiritual Pollution" campaign (which lasted only twenty days) and the "Anti-Bourgeois Lib-eralization" campaign in 1986 that led to the current trouble. Further evidence pointed to Zhao's aiding and abetting the demonstrators through his open sympathy with their cause and leakage of vital information to them. Frequently the stu-dents learned of the Politburo's decisions before anyone else. The patronage by Zhao and his liberal advisors boosted their sagging morale and emboldened them to be more unyielding. Two of Zhao's advisors[8] were charged with having made a "most furious and vicious" May 17 Declaration, in which they bluntly stated: "Because the autocrat controls the unlimited power, the government has lost its own obligation and normal human feelings. . . . Despite the death of the Qing Dynasty seventy-six years ago, there is still an emperor in China, though without such a title, a senile and fatuous autocrat . . . Gerontocratic politics must end and the autocrat must resign." The inference was clear: Deng was that "decrepit autocrat."[9] Some demonstrators burned Deng's effigy, shouting "Deng Step Down," "Li Peng Step Down," and "Long Live Zhao Ziyang."

This development further convinced the hard-liners that Zhao and his advisors had conspired to unleash student power to split the party. By advocating a different course of action from Deng's toward the demonstrators, he was, in fact, setting up an alternative headquarters within the party with a second voice that confused both the party and the people. In addition to this grave sin, Zhao was also guilty, as charged, of attempting to reject the April 26 editorial, of making an unauthorized statement to the Asian Development Bank, of disclosing a secret to Gorbachev, and of permitting his two sons to engage in commercial speculation and profiteering. Deng, who had handpicked Zhao as his successor, now called him a "traitor." The split was complete; only punishment remained to be meted out.

A "war council" at the highest level, including only the seven or eight most senior party elders who had made great contributions to the party and the state, convened on or about May 17.[10] Their purpose was to decide what to do about the demonstrations and Zhao. They reduced the first issue to the choice of whether or not the party should retreat in the face of the student threat, which daily grew more serious as the ranks of the protestors increased and won a wide spectrum of popular support. To retreat meant acceptance of the students' demand for democracy and freedom; not to retreat meant forcible repression of the unrest.

The gerontocratic leaders were in a state of despair. The spectacle of a million demonstrators marching, singing, shouting, and waving huge banners day after day in the Square left them feeling impotent. Furthermore, demonstrations had erupted in twenty-three other cities, raising the spectre of an uncontrollable mass uprising. The elders concluded that in the final analysis the situation was tantamount to a war between communism and democracy. To give in would lead to the downfall of the leadership, the overthrow of the socialist order, and ultimately to a capitalist restoration of a beourgeois government, just as John Foster Dulles would have wished. They reasoned that the students' desire for change was insatiable; if one gave them an inch, they would take a mile. Where would it all end? They feared that the students would not quit until they had overthrown the Communist Party and the Four Cardinal Principles (the proletarian dictatorship, the socialist line, the leadership of the Communist party, and Marxism-Leninism and the Thought of Mao). The veteran economist, Chen Yun, aged eighty-five, delivered an emotional speech, perhaps with the intention of striking fear into the hearts of all concerned: "We seized power and established the People's Republic after decades of struggle and fighting, in which hundreds of thousands of our revolutionary heroes lost their lives. Are we to give it all up just to satisfy the students?" The council voted unanimously against retreat and for immediate dismissal of Zhao as general secretary of the party.[11]

Clearly, the elders wished to cling to their political power and economic privileges at all costs; to do so they had to defend the socialist order that made possible their special status. Killing the demonstrators was of no concern because they were "anti-party counter-revolutionaries" who deserved to be eliminated. Even the threat of loss of tourism, foreign investment, trade, credit, and loans paled when viewed from the larger perspective of the survival of the Communist leadership.

Deng declared that he did not fear foreign and domestic public opinion or bloodshed in any confrontation. He journeyed to Wuhan on May 19 to convene an enlarged meeting of the Military Commission, with the purpose of enlisting support for his policy of repression and possibly setting up "a second headquarters" in case the situation in Beijing deteriorated. Reportedly, preparations were also made for a secret flight abroad if all else failed. In Wuhan, Deng won support from the Navy, the Air Force, and virtually all the army regional commanders. Thus fortified, on May 20 he ordered Premier Li to announce the imposition of martial law in Beijing. Shortly thereafter, Deng also won the endorsement of his policy from nearly all the provinces and special municipalities. The stage was set for a military crackdown.

THE MIND-SET OF THE GERONTOCRACY

The psychology of the party elders played a key role in their decisions. As products of the Long March generation with a lifelong experience of sabotage, class struggle, civil war, foreign war, and endless mass campaigns of one sort or another, they had become highly sensitive to the question of safety, security, and, above all else, survival. Obsessed with power, they embraced the one-dimensional view that power was life, and life without power was not worth living. They believed that in any struggle one could not afford to be kind and humane. To survive, one had to be hard, brutal, and even heartless. He who struck first gained the advantage. Deng espoused this view unabashedly when he declared: "Whoever wins the battle for state power gets to occupy the throne. This is the way it was in the past, and the way it still is, in China as well as abroad."[12] Since their lives, positions, and privileges all depended on the survival of the socialist order, the party elders would go to any length to defend it.

Faced with widespread criticism of their advanced age, poor health, declining mental faculties, and alienation from mainstream society, the conservative leadership was all the more anxious to prove its capacity for vital decision-making and forceful action. Yet their sense of insecurity and fear of change always remained. In this confused and paradoxical state, they tended to overreact and to be impulsive and precipitous in their judgment.

The crackdown policy stemmed from a misreading, whether intentional or not, of the students' objectives. They asked to work with the government on anti-corruption measures and to discuss with its leaders the prospects for democracy, freedom of speech, of assembly, and of the press—the basic rights found in most civilized modern states. When the government refused to listen to their concerns, the frustrated students shouted for the dismissal of Li, Deng, and Yang, but they had neither the means nor the power to remove them or to overthrow the government. They lacked a platform of goals, a program of action, or an experienced, charismatic leader who could articulate their aspirations and unite the various splinter groups. Although the students in the Square and their supporters abroad declared that the government was so corrupt and irresponsible that it had lost its moral authority to rule, such a view lacked the force of a real threat. In opting to suppress the demonstrations by military force, the leadership lost a valuable opportunity to respond wisely and responsibly to the popular will and channel the tremendous potential of the people toward the constructive ends it had hoped to achieve.

After declaring martial law, the government leaders went into hiding and were not seen until after the crackdown. Zhao, however, made his last public appearance on May 19, when he visited the hungry strikers in the Square and apologized for his tardy arrival. Immediately afterward, he was ousted from his job. On June 24, Jiang Zemin was appointed as the new general secretary.

THE MASSACRE

From the declaration of martial law on May 20 to the bloody crackdown on June 4, a full two weeks intervened, long enough for Deng and Yang to develop an elaborate, well-planned military operation. President Yang, a professional soldier trained in the Soviet Union during the Stalinist era, was a powerful military figure, and second in command to Deng in the military hierarchy. Many of Yang's family members were placed in key army positions, so that they formed what the Chinese dubbed the "Yang family of generals." Yang himself was Executive Vice Chairman and Secretary General of the party's Military Commission; his brother, Yang Baibing, was Director of the Army's General Political Department; his son-in-law, Chi Haotian, was the Army's Chief-of-staff; and his nephew, Yang Jianhua, was commander of the 27th Army, which was to inflict most of the killing on June 3–4. Deng himself could handily draw from his own experience in military operations and political repression. In late 1948 he participated in the direction of the Huai-Hai (Xuzhou) Battle during the Chinese civil war and used tanks and artillery to annihilate the Nationalist opponents. In 1957, during the Anti-rightist Movement, he was party general secretary in charge of persecuting more than half a million intellectuals, winning high praise from Mao for his thoroughness.

Deng and Yang mobilized 600,000 troops from ten armies[13] across the country, as well as an armored division, a parachute division, and other special units. They were transferred to the outskirts of Beijing not to fight the students but to forestall any possible palace revolution or coup d'etat by Zhao and his military supporters. Of course, the sheer size of the military force could also coerce students into submission and pressure the Politburo and the People's National Congress into supporting the policy of repression.

During the two-week lull, the students who had "occupied" Tian-an-men Square for six weeks grew weary and exhausted. Many local students returned home or to their schools for rest and recuperation, but students from the provinces continued to pour in. Having traveled long distances, they were not willing to quit so soon. The local citizenry showed solidarity by offering them food, shelter, and other necessities. Many civilians helped students build barricades at key intersections to block the advancing troops. When the first contingent of troops arrived, they carried no weapons and were friendly, also accepting food and drink from the citizens. There was a general belief that the troops would not shoot their own people. Still, martial law had been declared and no one could be certain of the outcome. Few suspected that the friendliness of the first contingent of troops could have been a disarming ruse. Some professors quietly urged the students to disperse, since they had made their point, but the students would not leave. They set June 20, the date marking the opening of the emergency session of the National People's Congress, as the time of evacuation. With each passing day, fear of an impending military attack alternated with a sense of relief, that no violence had occurred. But in their hearts everybody knew that bloodshed was unavoidable.

On the evening of June 3 ominous signs of an impending crisis became apparent. A government television announcer gravely warned the citizens of Beijing to stay home and away from Tian-an-men Square because the People's Liberation Army would take any measures necessary to restore order. Students at Beijing University again took this warning as an empty threat. To show their solidarity, they headed straight for the Square.

Tian-an-men Square itself was filled with an impending sense of doom. At 4 p.m. on Saturday, June 3, an anonymous phone call was made to the student leaders' command post warning that the army was about to attack. The Student Association asked everyone to leave in order to avoid bloodshed, but 40,000 to 50,000 students and 100,000 other citizens vowed to stay and die, if necessary, in the cause of democracy and freedom. They still believed that the troops would not fire on their own unarmed people.

At 10 p.m. Premier Li ordered the troops to move at top speed to the Square, shoot all demonstrators without compunction, and clear the Square by dawn. Tanks, armored vehicles, and soldiers with automatic weapons struck from three directions in strict accordance with prearranged plans. One column attacked from the Revolutionary Military Museum located four miles from the Square, moving along the western section of the Avenue of Eternal Peace toward the Square, shooting and killing everyone in sight. Another column attacked from the eastern section of the Avenue, and a third descended from the north, all converging at the Square. Much of the killing occurred before the troops and tanks reached the Square itself.

Before midnight two armored vehicles sped into the Square with loudspeakers blaring a shrill warning of "notification." In the early hours of June 4, thirty-five heavy tanks charged into the main encampment, crushing those students who were still inside. At 4 a.m. the lights in the Square were turned off and loudspeakers again ordered the remaining demonstrators to clear out. Four hunger strikers, including the Taiwanese pop singer Hou Dejan, next secured from certain army officers safe passage for the remaining students, but before the latter could be notified the soldiers started to attack the Heroes' Monument area. At 4:40 a.m. a barrage of red flares burst overhead signaling another onslaught. Soldiers and military police stormed out of the Great Hall of the People, their automatic weapons firing dum dum bullets, using electric cattle prods, rubber truncheons, and other types of special weapons, while tanks and armored vehicles rode roughshod through the crowds of terror-stricken demonstrators. Eleven students—two from Beijing University and nine from Qinghua University—linked hands in a symbolic gesture to protect the Goddess of Democracy; they were mowed down together with the statue. By 6 a.m. those who could had already escaped, while the dead or maimed were scattered all over the blood-soaked killing field. The soldiers hurriedly bulldozed the bodies into large piles for burning on the spot or packed them in plastic bags for cremation outside the city at Babaoshan, where no registry was permitted to be divulged. The carnage was over in seven hours.[14]

An accurate accounting of the casualties is impossible. Western sources estimated that there were 3,000 dead and 10,000 or more wounded, though a later report by *The New York Times* revised the death toll to 400 to 800.[15] On June 16 Chinese government spokesman Yuan Mu told NBC anchorman Tom Brokaw that "in the whole process of clearing the square, there was no casualty [*sic*]. No one was shot down or crushed under the wheels of armored vehicles. The reports abroad that there was a bloodbath and that many people were crushed were incorrect." However, the government admitted that 23 students had been killed accidentally outside the square, while 5,000 soldiers were wounded and 150 of them had died.[16]

One cannot question the right of any government to defend itself, nor can one expect it to surrender supinely when threatened with the danger of extinction. The question here, however, was not survival or extinction but meeting with student leaders to discuss anti-corruption measures and political liberalization. Essentially, the issue was whether the government judged the challenge correctly and honestly and devised counter-measures appropriate to the occasion. The answer must be "no." In most civilized nations crowd control in massive public demonstrations involves the use of nonlethal implements—water cannons, tear gas, and even riot police armed with batons and shields—but not tanks and guns. In the last analysis, the threat to the Chinese leadership in May-June 1989 was largely fabricated, ultimately giving the government an excuse to kill the peaceful demonstrators as "anti-party counter-revolutionaries." If the octogenarians had been more patient and less impulsive, the demonstration would have exhausted itself in two or three weeks, since the students had already declared their intention to quit by June 20. All the bloodshed could easily have been avoided.

There is a tendency among many commentators to compare the violent events of 1989 with the Cultural Revolution, but there are fundamental differences between the two. First and foremost, the Cultural Revolution was directed from the top down by Mao, who used the students as Red Guards to crush his political enemies. The latter, like Mao, were veteran revolutionaries fully cognizant of the rules and dangers of intra-party struggles. It was a struggle between the hard-line rivals themselves. On the other hand, the demonstrations of 1989 were a spontaneous and patriotic movement started by young and idealistic students from the bottom up. The government used tanks and guns to crush peaceful protestors. The contest, if one can call it that, was brutal and utterly one-sided.

REWRITING HISTORY

Students of totalitarian systems realize that lies are routinely perpetrated during power struggles and liquidations of political enemies. The greater the violence, the greater the need for rewriting history through distortion. Stalin liquidated his Bolshevik associates on the pretext that they colluded with Leon Trotsky to oust him. Hitler's Minister of Propaganda, Joseph Goebbels, the inventor of the Big Lie theory, claimed that the bigger the lie, the greater the likelihood that people would believe it. In China's recent past, when Jiang Qing (Mao's wife) lost her bid to be Mao's successor, she was charged by the party, among other crimes, of being a secret agent of the Nationalist Party!

A catastrophe as ugly as the Tian-an-men massacre required the most blatant and implausible lies as a cover up. Shortly after the crackdown, Deng told a group of military leaders that it was necessary to "create public opinion on a grand scale and make the people understand what really happened."[17] The party propaganda machine then churned out stories claiming that a massacre never occurred, and that reports by foreign journalists were based on misinformation and misunderstanding of Chinese realities. What the heroic People's Liberation Army had suppressed were not student demonstrations but a "counter-revolutionary rebellion" fomented by a small group of ruffians, hooligans, bandits, and certain "good but naive" students, who received financial support from reactionary forces in the United States, Britain, Hong Kong, and Taiwan.[18] Some misguided party leaders[19] secretly lent them support and encouragement in the hope of using them to precipitate a coup d'etat to topple the government. These class enemies rightly deserved to be smashed, and if they escaped the initial crackdown they must be picked up "like rats" in follow-up sweeps. Each and every one one of them had to be brought to justice, with no show of mercy; only then could the manhunt be thorough enough to prevent any potential resurgence of protest.

The mass arrests began almost immediately after the bloody crackdown. An all-points bulletin was issued to ferret out 21 student leaders, and citizens were urged to inform on them. By July 17, some 4,600 arrests had been made, and 29 of the prisoners were given a quick trial and then shot in the back of the head. The scene was reminiscent of the "White Terror" perpetrated after the 1917 Bolshevik Revolution and during the Cultural Revolution (1966–76).

China in June 1989 was eerily Orwellian. Big Brother was everywhere. Tales abounded of a mother turning in her son and a sister informing on her brother. People walked through the streets but did not talk; they whispered among themselves and occasionally winked at passing foreigners. Laughter, vivacity, and openness disappeared from daily life. The government papers carried story after story about what had happened in Tian-an-Men Square but most urban dwellers did not buy the Big Lie, though a fair number of the rural population, who were cut off from urban life probably accepted the official version. Hong Kong and other foreign sources provided much information to people in the cities, and the Voice of America did its share of broadcasting information. In an age of long distance calls, fax machines, computer networks, and satellite transmission of televised images, it was impossible for the Chinese government to seal off the country completely. In the end the microchip that helped create the information revolution may have defeated the obsolescent totalitarian control of information.[20] Lu Xun, the famous writer, wrote the following in 1926: "Lies written in ink can never disguise facts written in blood. . . . This is not the conclusion of an incident, but a new beginning."[21]

The repercussions of the crackdown and the subsequent mass arrests have been staggering. The image of the Chinese government as an increasingly responsible member of the international community with a potent stabilizing influence on world affairs has been shattered beyond repair. Virtual universal condemnation followed the crackdown, along with economic and military sanctions, as well as a tacit ostracism of China from important diplomatic meetings. Relations with

Hong Kong and Taiwan have suffered severely. A million Hong Kong residents demonstrated to protest the Tian-an-men Square massacre and to register their distrust of Beijing's pledge that it would honor the capitalistic way of life in Hong Kong for fifty years beyond 1997. As for reunification with Taiwan, the idea is practically dead.

Foreign investments, credit, and loans have been cut back or put on hold, and many investors find it distasteful to do business with a regime that relied on brute force and bloodshed for survival. With the element of stability gone, China no longer appealed to foreigners as a good place for investments, and those who have invested in China hesitate to make new commitments. Tourism, which registered $2.2 billion in 1988, dropped dramatically, and luxury hotels built in the past few years are now mostly vacant despite vastly reduced rates. Economic slowdown and rampant inflation at an annual rate of 40 percent further erode the government's ability to pay its bills. Any continuation of last year's practice of paying the farmer with IOUs will surely provoke violent protests. The economic consequences of the crackdown are potentially catastrophic.

Because the momentum of reform and modernization has been dissipated, if not completely lost, and most of the reformers connected with Zhao Ziyang have either been arrested, dismissed, or have fled the country, the question remains as to who will carry on the work of economic reform. A recent international conference on superconductivity held in September 1989 in Beijing, highlights the setback in science and technology: no leading Western European or American scientists participated, with only the Russians in attendance. As of 1989, the prospect for quadrupling the GNP by A.D. 2000 seems remote. Most tragic of all, the spirit of the Chinese people has been gravely wounded and probably will not recover for at least a decade. Sadly, China has turned back the clock to the Anti-rightist and Cultural Revolution days. Deng will now be remembered not as the architect of China's modernization but as a brutal oppressor of freedom and democracy. Many believe that the "Mandate of Heaven," or the government's moral authority to rule, has slipped away. Indeed, the miraculous escape to Paris of the student leader Wuer Kaixi, and the intellectuals who advised Zhao, such as Yan Jiaqi, Chen Yizi, and Wan Runnan, and their formation of The Federation of Democracy in China in that city, has created an overseas opposition group and an alternative to the Beijing regime.[22] The new round of struggles has just begun.

NOTES

1. Zbigniew Brzezinski, *The Grand Failure: The Birth and Death of Communism in the Twentieth Century* (New York, 1989).
2. Su Shaozhi, a Marxist theoretician; Wu Zuguang, a playwright, and Yan Jiaqi, a political scientist.
3. Central Political Structure Reform Institute; China Economic Structure Reform Institute; State Council Agricultural Research and Development Institute; and China Trust International Relations Institute.
4. This information is based on interviews with Chen Yizi, former director of the China Economic Structure Reform Institute, and Su Shaozhi, former director of the Institute of Marxism-Leninism-and the Thought of Mao, Beijing, as reported in *Central Daily News*, Taipei, Sept. 10, 1989 and in *Ming Bao*, Hong Kong, Sept. 6, 1989.
5. Li Ximin.
6. Lu Ren and Xu Weicheng.
7. Bao Tong, director of the Central Political Structure Reform Institute, and Du Runsheng, director of the Rural Research Center.
8. Yan Jiaqi, a political scientist and former director of the Political Science Institute of the Chinese Academy of Social Sciences, and Bao Zunxin, a philosopher and an associate research fellow at the Historical Research Institute.
9. Beijing Mayor Chen Xitong's speech before the Eighth Session of the Seventh National People's Congress, held June 30, 1989, entitled, "Report on Checking the Turmoil and Quelling the Counter-Revolutionary Rebellion," *Beijing Review*, July 17–23, 1989, 12–13.
10. These eight were Deng Xiaoping, former president Li Xiannian, President Yang Shangkun, Vice-President Wang Zhen, economist Chen Yun, former chairman of the Standing Committee of the National People's Congress Peng Zhen, Deng

Yingtsao (Madame Zhou Enlai), and perhaps Bo Ipo, an economic affairs expert.

11. Speech by President Yang Shangkun before an Enlarged Emergency Meeting of the Military Commission, May 24, 1989.

12. Cited in Fox Butterfield, "Deng Is Said to Link Fear to Safety of Party," *The New York Times*, June 17, 1989, p. A4.

13. The 12th, 20th, 24th, 27th, 28th, 38th, 54th, 63rd, 64th, and 65th Armies.

14. See two moving eyewitness accounts of what happened at Tian-an-men Square June 3–4, 1989: one by a twenty-year-old student at Qinghua University (*The San Francisco Examiner*, June 11, 1989, and also *The New York Times*, June 12, 1989), the other by a twenty-three-year-old student leader, Chai Ling (*The Free China Journal*, Taipei, June 15, 1989).

15. *The New York Times*, June 12, 13, 21, p. A6; *The Chronicle of Higher Education*, June 14, 1989.

16. *Beijing Review*, June 12–25, 1989, 9, July 3–9, 1989, 15–16.

17. *The New York Times*, June 17, 1989, p. A4; see also Harrison E. Salisbury, "China's Peasants Get the Bad News," *The New York Times*, June 19, 1989, p. A15.

18. The Voice of America was particularly vilified for misreporting the China situation and for misinforming the Chinese public as to what happened. Two of its bureau chiefs in Beijing, Alan W. Pessin and Mark W. Hopkins were expelled from China.

19. Zhao Ziyang and his liberal advisors?

20. *The Christian Science Monitor*, June 14, 1989; *Los Angeles Times*, June 14, 1989.

21. Quoted in Daniel Williams, "China's Underground Presses Seized as Crackdown on Media Continues," *Los Angeles Times*, June 20, 1989, Part I, p. 10.

22. *The New York Times*, August 4, 1989.

Guide to Pinyin and Wade-Giles Systems

Pinyin	*Wade-Giles*
Ah Jia	Ah Chia
Baoshan	Pao-shan
Beijing	Peking
Bo Ibo	Po I-po
Chai Zemin	Ch'ai Tse-min
Chen Boda	Ch'en Po-ta
Chen Xilian	Ch'en Hsi-lien
Chen Yonggui	Ch'en Yung-kuei
Chen Yun	Ch'en Yün
Chengdu	Ch'eng-tu
Daqing	Ta-ch'ing
Dazhai	Ta-chai
Deng Liqun	Teng Li-ch'ün
Deng Xiaoping	Teng Hsiao-p'ing
Diaoyu tai	Tiao-yü-t'ai
Ding Sheng	Ting Sheng
Fang Lizhi	Fang Li-chih
Fei Xiaotong	Fei Hsiao-t'ung
gong nong bing	kung-nung-ping
Guangming Ribao	*Kuang-minh Jih-pao*
Guangzhou	Canton
Hai Rui	Hai Jui
He Long	Ho Lung
Hu Qiaomu	Hu Ch'iao-mu

Hu Qili	Hu ch'i-li
Hu Yaobang	Hu Yao-pang
Hua Guofeng	Hua Kuo-feng
Huang Hua	Huang Hua
Huang Huoqing	Huang Huo-ch'ing
Huang Kecheng	Huang K'e-ch'eng
Huang Zhen	Huang Chen
Ji Dengkui	Chi Teng-k'uei
jia tian xia	*chia-t'ien-hsia*
jia zhang zhi	*chia-chang-chih*
Jiang Hua	Chiang Hua
Jiang Qing	Chiang Ch'ing
Jiang Wen	Chiang Wen
Jidong	Chi-tung
Kang Sheng	K'ang Sheng
Li Dazhao	Li Ta-chao
Li Xiannian	Li Hsien-nien
Liang Xiao	Liang Hsiao
Liao Mosha	Liao Mo-sha
Lin Biao	Lin Piao
Liu Huaqing	Liu Hua-ch'ing
Liu Binyan	Liu Pin-yen
Liu Shaoqi	Liu Shao-ch'i
Lu Dingyi	Lu Ting-i
Mao Yuanxin	Mao Yüan-hsin
Mao Zedong	Mao Tse-tung
Nanjing	Nanking
Peng Chong	P'eng Ch'ung
Peng Dehuai	P'eng Te-huai
Peng Zhen	P'eng Chen
pingfan	*p'ing-fan*
Qiao Shi	Ch'iao Shih
Qinghua	Tsinghua
Qu Qiubai	Ch'ü Ch'iu-pai

Qun yan tang	Ch'ün-yen-t'ang
Shaanxi	Shensi
Shenyang	Shen-yang
Sichuan	Szechwan
Su Yu	Su Yü
Su Zhenhua	Su Chen-hua
Tangshan	T'ang-shan
Tao Zhu	T'ao Chu
Tian An Men	Tien-an-men
Tianjin	Tientsin
tianzai renhuo	*t'ien-tsai jen-huo*
tiyong	*t'i-yung*
Wang Dongxing	Wang Tung-hsing
Wang Hairong	Wang Hai-jung
Wang Hongwen	Wang Hung-wen
Wang Renzhong	Wang Jen-chung
Wang Ruowang	Wang Jo-wang
Wang Zhen	Wang Chen
Wei Guoqing	Wei Kuo-ch'ing
Wu De	Wu Te
Wu Zetian	Wu Tse-t'ien
xiafang	*hsia-fang*
Xie Fuzhi	Hsieh Fu-chih
Xu Shiyou	Hsü Shih-yu
Xu Xiangqian	Hsü Hsiang-ch'ien
Yang Dezhi	Yang Te-chih
Yang Jingren	Yang Ching-jen
Yang Shangkun	Yang Shang-k'un
Yao Wenyuan	Yao Wen-yüan
Yao Yilin	Yao I-lin
Ye Jianying	Yeh Chien-yin
yi qiong er bai	*i-ch'iung erh-pai*
Yi yan tang	*I-yen-t'ang*
Yu Huiyong	Yü Hui-yung
Yu Qiuli	Yü Ch'iu-li

Zhang Aiping	Chang Ai-p'ing
Zhang Chunqiao	Chang Ch'un-ch'iao
Zhang Jingfu	Chang Ching-fu
Zhao Cangbi	Chao Ts'ang-pi
Zhao Ziyang	Chao Tzu-yang
Zhongfa	Chung-fa
Zhongnanhai	Chung-nan-hai
Zhou Enlai	Chou En-lai
Zhu De	Chu Teh
zhufan	*chu-fan*
Zunyi	Tsunyi

On Questions of Party History

—Resolution on Certain Questions in the History of Our People Since the Founding of the People's Republic of China

(Adopted by the Sixth Plenary Session of the Eleventh Central Committee of the Communist Party of China on June 27, 1981)

THE DECADE OF THE "CULTURAL REVOLUTION"

19. The "cultural revolution," which lasted from May 1966 to October 1976, was responsible for the most severe setback and the heaviest losses suffered by the Party, the state and the people since the founding of the People's Republic. It was initiated and led by Comrade Mao Zedong. His principal theses were that many representatives of the bourgeoisie and counter-revolutionary revisionists had sneaked into the Party, the government, the army and cultural circles, and leadership in a fairly large majority of organizations and departments was no longer in the hands of Marxists and the people; that Party persons in power taking the capitalist road had formed a bourgeois headquarters inside the Central Committee which pursued a revisionist political and organizational line and had agents in all provinces, municipalities and autonomous regions, as well as in all central departments; that since the forms of struggle adopted in the past had not been able to solve this problem, the power usurped by the capitalist-roaders could be recaptured only by carrying out a great cultural revolution, by openly and fully mobilizing the broad masses from the

Extract from "On Questions of Party History," *Beijing Review, No. 27,* July 6, 1981.

bottom up to expose these sinister phenomena; and that the cultural revolution was in fact a great political revolution in which one class would overthrow another, a revolution that would have to be waged time and again. These theses appeared mainly in the May 16 Circular, which served as the programmatic document of the "cultural revolution," and in the political report of the Ninth National Congress of the Party in April 1969. They were incorporated into a general theory—of continued revolution under the dictatorship of the proletariat—which then took on a specific meaning. These erroneous "Left" theses, upon which Comrade Mao Zedong based himself in initiating the "cultural revolution," were obviously inconsistent with the system of Mao Zedong thought, which is the integration of the universal principles of Marxism-Leninism with the concrete practice of the Chinese revolution. These theses must be thoroughly distinguished from Mao Zedong Thought. As for Lin Biao, Jiang Qing and others, who were placed in important positions by Comrade Mao Zedong, the matter is of an entirely different nature. They rigged up two counter-revolutionary cliques in an attempt to seize supreme power and, taking advantage of Comrade Mao Zedong's errors, committed many crimes behind his back, bringing disaster to the country and the people. As their counter-revolutionary crimes have been fully exposed, this resolution will not go into them at any length.

20. The history of the "cultural revolution" has proved that Comrade Mao Zedong's principal theses for initiating this revolution conformed neither to Marxism-Leninism nor to Chinese reality. They represent an entirely erroneous appraisal of the prevailing class relations and political situation in the Party and state.

1. The "cultural revolution" was defined as a struggle against the revisionist line or the capitalist road. There were no grounds at all for this definition. It led to the confusing of right and wrong on a series of important theories and policies. Many things denounced as revisionist or capitalist during the "cultural revolution" were actually Marxist and socialist prin-

ciples, many of which had been set forth or supported by Comrade Mao Zedong himself. The "cultural revolution" negated many of the correct principles, policies and achievements of the seventeen years after the founding of the People's Republic. In fact, it negated much of the work of the Central Committee of the Party and the People's Government, including Comrade Mao Zedong's own contribution. It negated the arduous struggles the entire people had conducted in socialist construction.

2. The confusing of right and wrong inevitably led to confusing the people with the enemy. The "capitalist-roaders" overthrown in the "cultural revolution" were leading cadres of Party and government organizations at all levels, who formed the core force of the socialist cause. The so-called bourgeois headquarters inside the Party headed by Liu Shaoqi and Deng Xiaoping simply did not exist. Irrefutable facts have proved that labelling Comrade Liu Shaoqi a "renegade, hidden traitor and scab" was nothing but a frame-up by Lin Biao, Jiang Qing and their followers. The political conclusion concerning Comrade Liu Shaoqi drawn by the Twelfth Plenary Session of the Eighth Central Committee of the Party and the disciplinary measure it meted out to him were both utterly wrong. The criticism of the so-called reactionary academic authorities in the "cultural revolution" during which many capable and accomplished intellectuals were attacked and persecuted also badly muddled up the distinction between the people and the enemy.

3. Nominally, the "cultural revolution" was conducted by directly relying on the masses. In fact, it was divorced both from the Party organizations and from the masses. After the movement started, Party organizations at different levels were attacked and became partially or wholly paralyzed, the Party's leading cadres at various levels were subjected to criticism and struggle, inner-Party life came to a standstill, and many activitists and large numbers of the basic masses whom the Party has long relied on were rejected. At the beginning of the "cultural revolution," the vast majority of participants in the movement acted out of their faith in Comrade Mao Zedong

and the Party. Except for a handful of extremists, however, they did not approve of launching ruthless struggles against leading Party cadres at all levels. With the lapse of time, following their own circuitous paths, they eventually attained a heightened political consciousness and consequently began to adopt a sceptical or wait-and-see attitude towards the "cultural revolution," or even resisted and opposed it. Many people were assailed either more or less severely for this very reason. Such a state of affairs could not but provide openings to be exploited by opportunists, careerists and conspirators, not a few of whom were escalated to high or even key positions.

4. Practice has shown that the "cultural revolution" did not in fact constitute a revolution or social progress in any sense, nor could it possibly have done so. It was we and not the enemy at all who were thrown into disorder by the "cultural revolution." Therefore, from beginning to end, it did not turn "great disorder under heaven" into "great order under heaven," nor could it conceivably have done so. After the state power in the form of the people's democratic dictatorship was established in China, and especially after socialist transformation was basically completed and the exploiters were eliminated as classes, the socialist revolution represented a fundamental break with the past in both content and method, though its tasks remained to be completed. Of course, it was essential to take proper account of certain undesirable phenomena that undoubtedly existed in Party and state organisms and to remove them by correct measures in conformity with the Constitution, the laws and the Party Constitution. But on no account should the theories and methods of the "cultural revolution" have been applied. Under socialist conditions, revolution" have been applied. Under socialist conditions, there is no economic or political basis for carrying out a great political revolution in which "one class overthrows another." It decidedly could not come up with any constructive program, but could only bring grave disorder, damage and retrogression in its train. History has shown that the "cultural revolution," initiated by a leader laboring under a misapprehension and

capitalized on by counter-revolutionary cliques, led to domestic turmoil and brought catastrophe to the Party, the state and the whole people.

21. The "cultural revolution" can be divided into three stages.
1. From the initiation of the "cultural revolution" to the Ninth National Congress of the Party in April 1969. The convening of the enlarged Political Bureau meeting of the Central Committee of the Party in May 1966 and the Eleventh Plenary Session of the Eighth Central Committee in August of that year marked the launching of the "cultural revolution" on a full scale. These two meetings adopted the May 16 Circular and the Decision of the Central Committee of the Communist Party of China Concerning the Great Proletarian Cultural Revolution respectively. They launched an erroneous struggle against the so-called anti-Party clique of Peng Zhen, Luo Ruiqing, Lu Dingyi and Yang Shangkun and the so-called headquarters of Liu Shaoqi and Deng Xiaoping. They wrongly re-organized the central leading organs, set up the "Cultural Revolution Group Under the Central Committee of the Chinese Communist Party" and gave it a major part of the power of the Central Committee. In fact, Comrade Mao Zedong's personal leadership characterized by "Left" errors took the place of the collective leadership of the Central Committee, and the cult of Comrade Mao Zedong was frenziedly pushed to an extreme. Lin Biao, Jiang Qing, Kang Sheng, Zhang Chunqiao and others, acting chiefly in the name of the "Cultural Revolution Group," exploited the situation to incite people to "overthrow everything and wage full-scale civil war." Around February 1967, at various meetings, Tan Zhenlin, Chen Yi, Ye Jianying, Li Fuchun, Li Xiannian, Xu Xiangqian, Nie Rongzhen and other Political Bureau Members and leading comrades of the Military Commission of the Central Committee sharply criticized the mistakes of the "cultural revolution." This was labeled the "February adverse current," and they were attacked and repressed. Comrades Zhu De and Chen Yun were also wrongly criticized. Almost all leading Party and government departments in the different spheres

and localities were stripped of their power or re-organized. The chaos was such that it was necessary to send in the People's Liberation Army to support the Left, the workers and the peasants and to institute military control and military training. It played a positive role in stabilizing the situation, but it also produced some negative consequences. The Ninth Congress of the Party legitimatized the erroneous theories and practices of the "cultural revolution," and so reinforced the position of Lin Biao, Jiang Qing, Kang Sheng and others in the Central Committee of the Party. The guidelines of the Ninth Congress were wrong, ideologically, politically and organizationally.

2. From the Ninth National Congress of the Party to its Tenth National Congress in August 1973. In 1970–71 the counter-revolutionary Lin Biao clique plotted to capture supreme power and attempted an armed counter-revolutionary coup d'etat. Such was the outcome of the "cultural revolution" which overturned a series of fundamental Party principles. Objectively, it announced the failure of the theories and practices of the "cultural revolution." Comrades Mao Zedong and Zhou Enlai ingeniously thwarted the plotted coup. Supported by Comrade Mao Zedong, Comrade Zhou Enlai took charge of the day-to-day work of the Central Committee and things began to improve in all fields. During the criticism and repudiation of Lin Biao in 1972, he correctly proposed criticism of the ultra-Left trend of thought. In fact, this was an extension of the correct proposals put forward around February 1967 by many leading comrades of the Central Committee who had called for the correction of the errors of the "cultural revolution." Comrade Mao Zedong, however, erroneously held that the task was still to oppose the "ultra-Right." The Tenth Congress of the Party perpetuated the "Left" errors of the Ninth Congress and made Wang Hongwen a vice-chairman of the Party. Jiang Qing, Zhang Chunqiao, Yao Wenyuan and Wang Hongwen formed a gang of four inside the Political Bureau of the Central Committee, thus strengthening the influence of the counter-revolutionary Jiang Qing clique.

3. From the Tenth Congress of the Party to October 1976.

Early in 1974 Jiang Qing, Wang Hongwen and others launched a campaign to "criticize Lin Biao and Confucius." Jiang Qing and the others directed the spearhead at Comrade Zhou Enlai, which was different in nature from the campaign conducted in some localities and organizations where individuals involved in and incidents connected with the conspiracies of the counterrevolutionary Lin Biao clique were investigated. Comrade Mao Zedong approved the launching of the movement to "criticize Lin Biao and Confucius." When he found that Jiang Qing and the others were turning it to their advantage in order to seize power, he severely criticized them. He declared that they had formed a gang of four and pointed out that Jiang Qing harbored the wild ambition of making herself chairman of the Central Committee and "forming a cabinet" by political manipulation. In 1975, when Comrade Zhou Enlai was seriously ill, Comrade Deng Xiaoping, with the support of Comrade Mao Zedong, took charge of the day-to-day work of the Central Committee. He convened an enlarged meeting of the Military Commission of the Central Committee and several other important meetings with a view to solving problems in industry, agriculture, transport and science and technology, and began to straighten out work in many fields so that the situation took an obvious turn for the better. However, Comrade Mao Zedong could not bear to accept systematic correction of the errors of the "cultural revolution" by Comrade Deng Xiaoping and triggered the movement to "criticize Deng and counter the Right deviationist trend to reverse correct verdicts," once again plunging the nation into turmoil. In January of that year, Comrade Zhou Enlai passed away. Comrade Zhou Enlai was utterly devoted to the Party and the people and stuck to his post till his dying day. He found himself in an extremely difficult situation throughout the "cultural revolution." He always kept the general interest in mind, bore the heavy burden of office without complaint, racking his brains and untiringly endeavoring to keep the normal work of the Party and the state going, to minimize the damage caused by the "cultural revolution" and to protect many Party and non-Party cadres. He waged all forms of struggle to counter sabotage by the counter-revolutionary Lin Biao and Jiang Qing cliques. His death left the whole Party and people in the most profound grief. In April of the same year, a powerful movement of protest signalled by the Tian An Men Incident swept the whole country, a movement to mourn for the late Premier Zhou Enlai and oppose the gang of four. In essence, the movement was a demonstration of support for the Party's correct leadership as represented by Comrade Deng Xiaoping. It laid the ground for massive popular support for the subsequent overthrow of the counter-revolutionary Jiang Qing clique. The Political Bureau of the Central Committee and Comrade Mao Zedong wrongly assessed the nature of the Tian An Men Incident and dismissed Comrade Deng Xiaoping from all his posts inside and outside the Party. As soon as Comrade Mao Zedong passed away in September 1976, the counter-revolutionary Jiang Qing clique stepped up its plot to seize supreme Party and state leadership. Early in October of the same year, the Political Bureau of the Central Committee, executing the will of the Party and the people, resolutely smashed the clique and brought the catastrophic "cultural revolution" to an end. This was a great victory won by the entire Party, army and people after prolonged struggle. Hua Guofeng, Ye Jianying, Li Xiannian and other comrades played a vital part in the struggle to crush the clique.

22. Chief responsibility for the grave "Left" error of the "cultural revolution," an error comprehensive in magnitude and protracted in duration, does indeed lie with Comrade Mao Zedong. But after all it was the error of a great proletarian revolutionary. Comrade Mao Zedong paid constant attention to overcoming shortcomings in the life of the Party and state. In later years, however, far from making a correct analysis of many problems, he confused right and wrong and the people with the enemy during the "cultural revolution." While making serious mistakes, he repeatedly urged the whole Party to study the works of Marx, Engels and Lenin conscientiously and imagined that his theory and practice were Marxist and that

they were essential for the consolidation of the dictatorship of the proletariat. Herein lies his tragedy. While persisting in the comprehensive error of the "cultural revolution," he checked and rectified some of its specific mistakes, protected some leading Party cadres and non-Party public figures and enabled some leading cadres to return to important leading posts. He led the struggle to smash the counter-revolutionary Lin Biao clique. He made major criticisms and exposures of Jiang Qing, Zhang Chunqiao and others, frustrating their sinister ambition to seize supreme leadership. All this was crucial to the subsequent and relatively painless overthrow of the gang of four by our Party. In his later years, he still remained alert to safeguarding the security of our country, stood up to the pressure of the social-imperialists, pursued a correct foreign policy, firmly supported the just struggles of all peoples, outlined the correct strategy of the three worlds and advanced the important principle that China would never seek hegemony. During the "cultural revolution" our Party was not destroyed, but maintained its unity. The State Council and the People's Liberation Army were still able to do much of their essential work. The Fourth National People's Congress which was attended by deputies from all nationalities and all walks of life was convened and it determined the composition of the State Council with Comrades Zhou Enlai and Deng Xiaoping as the core of its leadership. The foundation of China's socialist system remained intact and it was possible to continue socialist economic construction. Our country remained united and exerted a significant influence on international affairs. All these important facts are inseparable from the great role played by Comrade Mao Zedong. For these reasons, and particularly for his vital contributions to the cause of the revolution over the years, the Chinese people have always regarded Comrade Mao Zedong as their respected and beloved great leader and teacher.

24. In addition to the above-mentioned immediate cause of Comrade Mao Zedong's mistake in leadership, there are com-

plex social and historical causes underlying the "cultural revoultion" which dragged on for as long as a decade. The main causes are as follows:

1. The history of the socialist movement is not long and that of the socialist countries even shorter. Some of the laws governing the development of socialist society are relatively clear, but many more remain to be explored. Our Party had long existed in circumstances of war and fierce class struggle. It was not fully prepared, either ideologically or in terms of scientific study, for the swift advent of the newborn socialist society and for socialist construction on a national scale. The scientific works of Marx, Engels, Lenin and Stalin are our guide to action, but can in no way provide ready-made answers to the problems we may encounter in our socialist cause. Even after the basic completion of socialist transformation, given the guiding ideology, we were liable, owing to the historical circumstances in which our Party grew, to continue to regard issues unrelated to class struggle as its manifestations when observing and handling new contradictions and problems which cropped up in the political, economic, cultural and other spheres in the course of the development of socialist society. And when confronted with actual class struggle under the new conditions, we habitually fell back on the familiar methods and experiences of the large-scale, turbulent mass struggle of the past, which should no longer have been mechanically followed. As a result, we substantially broadened the scope of class struggle. Moreover, this subjective thinking and practice divorced from reality seemed to have a "theoretical basis" in the writings of Marx, Engels, Lenin and Stalin because certain ideas and arguments set forth in them were misunderstood or dogmatically interpreted. For instance, it was thought that equal right, which reflects the exchange of equal amounts of labor and is applicable to the distribution of the means of consumption in socialist society, or "bourgeois right" as it was designated by Marx, should be restricted and criticized, and so the principle of "to each according to his work" and that of material interest should be restricted and criticized; that small production would continue to engender capitalism

and the bourgeoisie daily and hourly on a large scale even after the basic completion of socialist transformation, and so a series of "Left" economic policies and policies on class struggle in urban and rural areas were formulated; and that all ideological differences inside the Party were reflections of class struggle in society, and so frequent and acute inner-Party struggles were conducted. All this led us to regard the error in magnifying class struggle as an act in defence of the purity of Marxism. Furthermore, Soviet leaders started a polemic between China and the Soviet Union, and turned the arguments between the two Parties on matters of principle into a conflict between the two nations, bringing enormous pressure to bear upon China politically, economically and militarily. So we were forced to wage a just struggle against the big-nation chauvinism of the Soviet Union. In these circumstances, a campaign to prevent and combat revisionism inside the country was launched, which spread the error of broadening the scope of class struggle in the Party, so that normal differences among comrades inside the Party came to be regarded as manifestation of the revisionist line or of the struggle between the two lines. This resulted in growing tension in inner-Party relations. Thus it became difficult for the Party to resist certain "Left" views put forward by Comrade Mao Zedong and others, and the development of these views led to the outbreak of the protracted "cultural revolution."

2. Comrade Mao Zedong's prestige reached a peak and he began to get arrogant at the very time when the Party was confronted with the new task of shifting the focus of its work to socialist construction, a task for which the utmost caution was required. He gradually divorced himself from practice and from the masses, acted more and more arbitrarily and subjectively, and increasingly put himself above the Central Committee of the Party. The result was a steady weakening and even undermining of the principle of collective leadership and democratic centralism in the political life of the Party and the country. This state of affairs took shape only gradually and the Central Committee of the Party should be held partly responsible. From the Marxist viewpoint, this complex phenome-

non was the product of given historical conditions. Blaming this on only one person or on only a handful of people will not provide a deep lesson for the whole Party or enable it to find practical ways to change the situation. In the communist movement, leaders play quite an important role. This has been borne out by history time and again and leaves no room for doubt. However, certain grievous deviations, which occurred in the history of the international communist movement owing to the failure to handle the relationship between the Party and its leader correctly, had an adverse effect on our Party, too. Feudalism in China has had a very long history. Our Party fought in the firmest and most thoroughgoing way against it, and particularly against the feudal system of land ownership and the landlords and local tyrants, and fostered a fine tradition of democracy in the anti-feudal struggle. But it remains difficult to eliminate the evil ideological and political influence of centuries of feudal autocracy. And for various historical reasons, we failed to institutionalize and legalize inner-Party democracy and democracy in the political and social life of the country, or we drew up the relevant laws but they lacked due authority. This meant that conditions were present for the overconcentration of Party power in individuals and for the development of arbitrary individual rule and the personality cult in the Party. Thus, it was hard for the Party and state to prevent the initiation of the "cultural revolution" or check its development.

Index